The International Library of Sociology

THE POLITICS OF INFLUENCE

Founded by KARL MANNHEIM

THE POLITICS OF INFLUENCE

British ex-servicemen, Cabinet decisions
and cultural change (1917-57)

by

GRAHAM WOOTTON

First published in 1963 by
Routledge

Reprinted in 1998 by
Routledge
2 Park Square, Milton Park, Abingdon, Oxon, OX14 4RN
or
270 Madison Avenue, New York, NY 10016

First issued in paperback 2010

British Library Cataloguing in Publication Data
A CIP catalogue record for this book
is available from the British Library

The Politics of Influence
ISBN 978-0-415-17554-8 (hbk)
ISBN 978-0-415-60540-3 (pbk)
Political Sociology: 18 Volumes
ISBN 978-0-415-17820-4
The International Library of Sociology: 274 Volumes
ISBN 978-0-415-17838-9

Publisher's Note
The publisher has gone to great lengths to ensure the quality of this reprint
but points out that some imperfections in the original may be apparent

TO
SAMUEL H. BEER
AND TO
MARY

PREFACE

It is no longer controversial to say that the standard expositions of the British system of government focused too much attention on the formal institutions and too little on the forces that make those institutions work. What the commentators chose to do they often did well in many a polished essay, but in general the picture they painted was blurred and unevenly balanced. It was as if intelligent men had based their accounts of how football is played not on direct observation but on a close study of the Laws of the Game and the referee's handbook, supplemented by Press cuttings and the memories of a few ageing players.

Among the grossly neglected topics was the influence of non-party (or pressure) groups in the formulation of public policy. Although identifiable groups of this kind had been active since the eighteenth century at least, no considerable description of them appeared until 1908, when A. L. Lowell, professor of government at Harvard University and later its President, published his celebrated account of our political system. As with the study of party organization, we had to wait for an 'outsider' to reveal us to ourselves.

Lowell pioneered but hardly anyone chose to follow. Brief references may be traced, as in the works of James Kerr Pollock, Ramsay Muir and others, but no further considerable account of the activities of non-party groups in contemporary British politics appeared for another thirty years, until, on the eve of the last war, Sir Ivor Jennings illustrated their influence on Parliamentary legislation. But the book was hardly off the press before the winds of war swept across Europe and the world, uprooting Sir Ivor and covering over the path he had so recently rediscovered.

In the post-1945 rediscovery of pressure groups in Britain it was another professor of government at Harvard, Samuel H. Beer, who led the way with an article published in January 1955 and who has since done more than any other single person to keep the path open and illuminated. Professor W. J. M. Mackenzie of Manchester University followed hard on his heels, and since then several British and American writers have fallen into step. During the course of 1958 the first two general books on the subject of pressure groups in Britain made their astonishingly belated appearance.

Other works have followed, and so a start has been made in the long overdue task of correcting the traditional image of our political system. But for further progress two prerequisites at least will have to be fulfilled. One is that the great non-party associations shall be studied in detail, either individually or as a group of associations occupying common ground, and to a substantial degree from the 'inside' (for which one need not be an 'insider'). Considerable experience has convinced me that accounts based on the associations' pronouncements, published reports, official journals and other 'open' literature, while better than nothing, will never serve the larger purpose. For the study of pressure groups, although interesting, is, like psephology, not enough. It must serve the larger purpose, which is not, as it might sometimes seem, to banish the formal institutions (or official groups) from the standard books but rather to reveal the reciprocal interaction between these and the electorate, the political parties and the pressure groups in the decision-making process. In short, the ultimate aim must be to see our political procedures in the round.

The other prerequisite is that the conduct of such groups shall be analysed against the background of the historical circumstances and of the 'political culture' (those values, beliefs and emotions that bear upon political conduct). To relate pressure-group activities to the culture is of crucial importance. On the one hand, the rediscovery of pressure groups, so valuable as a corrective to received opinion, will itself hopelessly mislead if, as an American scholar, George E. Vincent, observed nearly sixty years ago, it causes us 'wholly to lose sight of the larger unity which actually underlies these apparently endless group-struggles'. It is to this larger unity that the study of the culture leads us. But the study of the culture is important for another reason. Over two generations ago, C. H. Herford (in his *The Age of Wordsworth*) drily remarked that in England 'excessive preoccupation with ideas has always been a less pressing danger than a too concrete concern with facts'. In British political studies this still seems so today. Some students of British pressure groups, at least, seem to have overlooked Alfred Marshall's warning that the 'most reckless and treacherous of all theorists is he who professes to let facts and figures speak for themselves'. Fact-collecting can never serve the larger purpose. We need the facts in detail but we also need a framework within which the facts make sense. One such framework may be fashioned from the concept of a culture, which, when related to particular historical circumstances and the distribution of official and unofficial power, may help to explain not only the objectives of pressure groups and the strategy adopted for achieving them, but (what the larger purpose also requires) the very emergence and character of the groups themselves.

Accordingly, I have tried in this study to provide an analysis in depth of the influence exerted by certain British ex-servicemen's associations on the Government, the Ministries and Parliament for the purpose of securing various decisions. Over a period of forty years, I examine the aims and methods of these associations against the background of the culture and circumstances, and offer an analysis of the conditions governing their general strategy as well as three case studies designed to show how certain decisions were in fact reached. Confining myself to one association, I try to assess the influence exerted, and then to isolate the factors that account for the degree of success generally achieved. I also touch upon the character and government of these associations, and attempt to explain why and how, although at first bitterly divided along Left-Right lines, they eventually avoided the extremism that is characteristic of the ex-servicemen's movement in some other countries.

This analysis, when synthesized with the results of many other inquiries, may eventually make possible a thorough revision of the standard accounts of the working of our political system, and in the meantime it helps to establish and suggest some modifications of received opinion. But I also believe that (in so far as such a sharp distinction can be made) this inquiry throws some light on how our social system works. Since the character and role of these associations cannot be understood without a knowledge of the situation in which they arose, I delve into some aspects of the social and cultural history of the First World War. In so doing I come to the conclusion that pressure groups may have a substantial role not only in the formulation and execution of policy (a view already gaining ground rapidly and perhaps even, at last, accepted), but also in the process of cultural change (a view which is very much less common). Certainly these associations helped to close the 'rift in the culture' that occurred in the First World War and so to carry the community forward to a new consensus. Thus, whereas in the 1950's I saw pressure groups only in narrow political terms, I now see them also as agents of cultural change in the broad sense. To some future student attempting a 'final' synthesis it may even appear that the political role of pressure groups is, after all, less important than their sociological one.

In acknowledging debts I must first single out Professor Samuel Beer. At an early stage in the work I had the advantage of a discussion with him; later I adapted for my purpose the political-culture 'model' developed by his Harvard 'school'. After the work had been completed I benefited greatly not only from his detailed criticisms but also from his encouragement. In this role he was joined by Professor Harry Eckstein, formerly of Harvard but now of Princeton, who also generously put his time at my disposal. Both of them helped me to quarry, as I hope, a presentable book from a formidable rock of material. They cannot, of course, be saddled with responsibility for whatever inadequacies remain.

I wish also to thank Professors K. B. Smellie and S. E. Finer for some criticisms and suggestions; Dr. Robert McKenzie and Mr. Richard Pear, from whose seminar I learned a good deal, not least when it met as a 'dinner-seminar' given, and largely conducted, by Lord Beaverbrook in his London home; Lord Beaverbrook himself for his hospitality then, and later for information about the Ashton-under-Lyne election in 1918; the late Countess Mountbatten of Burma for sight of her father's, Wilfrid Ashley's, papers preserved at Palmerston's old home, Broadlands, and her archivist, Mrs. G. Blois; the Council, staff and other members of the British Legion, especially Sir Frederick Lister, Lt. Col. G. R. Crosfield, Lord Fraser of Lonsdale, Mr. J. R. Griffin and Mr. A. G. Webb; for facilities or information on particular points I also thank Mr. D. E. Coffer, Sir Brunel Cohen, Major J. T. Spinks and Messrs. G. Fleet, R. L. Pennells, F. W. Pickering, J. Rivers, C. Lowe, 'Sandy' Haynes, G. Powell, T. J. Frowen, K. C. G. Chambers, Jim Prince and L. Pellowe; the Council and staff of the British Limbless Ex-Service Men's Association, especially Messrs. G. Chandley, C. W. Dunham and Mervyn B. Jones; Major Robert Barker, Mr. James Howell, Mr. J. Whitehead, and Captain Nelson M. Price, formerly leaders of the National (or Blackburn) Association; Major W. O. Prichard and Mr. S. T. Wilce Taylor, former General Secretaries of the Comrades of the Great War; and collectively the Officers' Association, the R.A.F. Association, the Soldiers' and Sailors' Families Association, the Forces Help Society and the Royal Patriotic Fund Corporation. I also wish to record the help of some officials of the Ministry of Pensions and National Insurance who enabled me to understand what it 'feels like' to be the recipient of pressure-group representations. To my wife, Mary, I owe a debt that increases every year; I thank her not only for her preparation of the typescript in its many versions but also for her patience and encouragement.

I have to acknowledge, finally, that this book is a revised version of a thesis for which the University of London awarded me the degree of doctor of philosophy. In that research Dr. A. M. Bohm smoothed my path and the Secretary and Committee of the University's Central Research Fund generously lubricated it. Another University—Oxford—through its Delegacy for Extra-Mural Studies also helped my progress by giving me a 'summer term' for study.

G.W.

Warborough,
Oxford.

CONTENTS

ABBREVIATIONS

GENERAL

Association	National Association of Discharged Sailors and Soldiers
BLESMA	British Limbless Ex-Service Men's Association
B.M.A.	British Medical Association
C.A.C.	Central Advisory Committee on War Pensions
Comrades	Comrades of the Great War
E.C.	Executive Council
Federation	National Federation of Discharged and Demobilized Sailors and Soldiers
F.B.I.	Federation of British Industries
G.P.C.	General Purposes Committee
H.C. Deb.	5th Series of Parliamentary Debates, House of Commons
Hist. B.L.	*Official History of the British Legion*, 1956
L.E.S.M.A.	See BLESMA
L.L.X.	Labour League of Ex-Servicemen
N.A.D.S.S.	See 'Association'
N.E.C.	National Executive Council
N.F.D.D.S.S.	National Federation of Discharged and Demobilized Sailors and Soldiers
N.F.U.	National Farmers' Union
N.U.M.	National Union of Manufacturers
N.U.T.	National Union of Teachers
N.U.X.	National Union of Ex-Service Men
O.A.	Officers' Association
P.L.P.	Parliamentary Labour Party
R.A.F.A.	Royal Air Forces Association
RESAT	Resolutions Action Taken (British Legion)
S.J.C.	Standing Joint Committee for Ex-Service Questions
S.S.A.F.A.	Soldiers', Sailors' and Airmen's Families Association
S.S.F.A.	Soldiers' and Sailors' Families Association
T.U.C.	Trades Union Congress
Verb. Rep.	Conference Verbatim Report, British Legion

JOURNALS

A.J.S.	*American Journal of Sociology*
A.P.S.R.	*American Political Science Review*
B.J.S.	*British Journal of Sociology*
C.O.R.	*Charity Organization Review*
Ed. Rev.	*Edinburgh Review*
J.P.	*Journal of Politics*
Journal	*British Legion Journal*
Parl. Aff.	*Parliamentary Affairs*
P.Q.	*Political Quarterly*
P.S.Q.	*Political Science Quarterly*
P.S.	*Political Studies*
West P.Q.	*Western Political Quarterly*

Introduction

I

THE UNIVERSE OF GROUPS

EXCEPT for a few hermits and 'knights of the road', we are always to be found in groups of one sort or another: we are brought up and usually live in families, attend school and church, play football in teams, work in factory, office or Government Department, become members of a trade union or college, join a political party or the Women's Institute, are elected to Parliament, even go to gaol. As Bertrand de Jouvenal has reminded us, man in an isolated state is not a fact of nature but a product of intellectual abstraction:

'Le fait naturel, aux deux sens de primitif and de nécessaire, c'est le groupe. Sans le groupe, point d'homme'.[1]

The 'whole structure of modern society is associational'.[2]

Within that structure it is necessary for the purpose in hand to identify two broad categories: official groups and unofficial groups, distinguished by their decision-making powers and sanctions. Decisions, of course, are being constantly taken by parents, teachers, managing directors, union leaders, shop stewards, referees and others in innumerable unofficial (or private) contexts, but all such decisions lack the (theoretically) unlimited range of decisions taken by members of official groups and especially the sanction that comes from the '*monopoly of the legitimate use of physical force* within a given territory'.[3] No one supposes that force is 'the normal or the only means' employed by the State, yet it remains 'a means specific' to the State.

'Official groups', then, as is implied by the juxtaposition of that term with those words of Max Weber's, here signify 'the State', but, of course, in observing the flow of political influence one never comes across any such entity but only groups—this Cabinet, that Ministry— each with its own idiosyncrasies and traditions. Accordingly, it is not simply convenient but essential to avoid in general 'that troublesome abstraction "State"' by thinking of it 'as its official

---

[1] 'Du Groupe' in 5 *Revue Française de Science Politique* 1955, 49–62.

[2] W. Y. Elliott quoted by Earl Latham, 46 A.P.S.R. 1952, 376, n.1.

[3] *From Max Weber: Essays in Sociology*, ed. H. H. Gerth and C. Wright Mills, 1957, p. 78.

decision-makers—those whose authoritative acts are, to all intents and purposes, the acts of the State'.[1] If, then, for the purpose of this inquiry, one restricts the conception of the State to the central government, ignoring components of it (the public corporations, the Courts, the local authorities) that might well be appropriate on other occasions, it follows that in these pages the term 'official group' (or the 'official decision-makers', or, simply, 'the decision-makers') embraces, as the context requires, the Cabinet,[2] Parliament and the Ministries.

Of the unofficial groups, many have no direct interest for an inquiry such as this. The 'social units' (such as families and leisure-time groups) are normally outside our field of vision; the 'economic units' as such (*e.g.* industrial companies) may be neglected, although their combination in other forms (*e.g.* as trade associations) is obviously another matter. Of the remainder many are engrossed in purely domestic activities, *e.g.* the Honourable Association of Oyster Openers,[3] although a tax on the purchase of oysters, or on the opening of oysters, would doubtless bring it into the fray. This leaves the 'petitioning' side of the political process in the hands of two kinds of groups. A few specialize in providing temporary decision-makers, as well as policy-guidance, for those official groups that are elective: these, of course, are the political parties. Very many more, still uncounted in this country, seek not, as it were, transmogrification but rather favourable decisions from the existing official groups. These, of course, are the non-party or pressure groups; the influence that some such groups exert is the subject of this inquiry.

In making their demands, groups generally do not participate in a Hobbesian war of all against all. It may well be true, as Gustave Ratzenhofer taught in the 1890's, that 'each interest forms a struggle-group in which leadership and authority are developed under the reacting influence of the led',[4] yet as an American sociologist, George E. Vincent, was quick to observe, 'it would be a serious error wholly to lose sight of the larger unity which actually underlies these apparently endless group-struggles'.[5] These groups are made up of interacting individuals, forming and re-forming for the manifold

---

[1] Richard C. Snyder, H. W. Bruck and Burton Sapin, *Decision-making as an Approach to the Study of International Politics*, 1954, pp. 36–7.

[2] Constitutionally, one should no doubt speak of 'the Government', but this group, although it accepts responsibility for decisions does not in fact meet for the purpose of taking them, and can hardly be said to *take* them except in some artificial retrospective sense. It is the Cabinet Conclusion that counts.

[3] Dorothy Emmet, *Function, Purpose and Powers*, 1958, p. 122.

[4] Quoted by George E. Vincent, 10 A.J.S. 1904, 150.

[5] ibid., 151.

purposes of communal life. These individuals are not moral neuters—they are bearers of certain values, holders of certain beliefs and harbourers of certain emotions, which altogether make up what has been called a 'political culture'.[1] The interplay between groups pursuing their own ends takes place within this political culture, which helps to shape not only the aims themselves but also the means of pursuing them.

A political culture, then, may be resolved into values, beliefs and emotional attitudes, within each of which one may distinguish elements that emphasize methods (authority) and others that emphasize ends (purpose). The values that individuals have about authority embrace general notions of *how* government ought to be conducted: the standards prescribe methods and procedures for arriving at decisions rather than the content of decisions (*e.g.*, that elections ought to be held at regular intervals). Provided that the decisions have been made in the right way they become authoritative because the procedures are held to have moral force.

If the concept of authority embraces methods, the concept of purpose is obviously concerned with ends. Here the essential consideration is that there are notions of the public interest with which it is believed public policy *ought* to conform. 'Ought' is important, for like the conception of authority, the conception of purpose also has moral force. Therefore the policy deemed to be consonant with the public interest will be supported for that reason also (as well, no doubt, as on grounds of self-interest and custom). Should Governments violate such values over a long period, the stability of the régime itself would be endangered.

Of course, values are not immutable. That the standard of authoritativeness gradually changes was dramatically illustrated in 1832, when 'blood would certainly have been shed'[2] if the Reform Bill had not been passed. For the 'old constitution had lost that minimum of popular support without which a governing class must try to sit on bayonets ... there had to be a drastic redistribution of political power'. In the language of this inquiry, the values prescribing how political decisions *ought* to be reached had so far altered (though, obviously, not universally) as to bring the country almost face to face with violence. The eighteenth century standard of authoritativeness was no longer acceptable.

This experience was a special case of the general change that the

---

[1] This term seems to have been invented by Gabriel Almond (Heinz Eulau, Samuel J. Eldersveld and Morris Janowitz, ed., *Political Behaviour*, 1956, p. 36) but has reached me chiefly through Samuel H. Beer, Adam B. Ulam and others, *Patterns of Government*, 1958, passim.

[2] K. B. Smellie, *A Hundred Years of English Government*, 2nd ed. 1950, p. 30.

conception of authority undergoes over the years. Similarly, the conception of the objects of government also changes over time, *e.g.*, the community moves from laissez-faire to collectivism, and in so doing reaches a new consensus.

Closely related to values are belief systems. For instance, underlying the value that political decisions *ought* to be preceded by full discussion is the belief that people generally are *in fact* capable of taking part effectively in such discussion. One might say that values imply beliefs about what people are like, sociologically speaking.

The third element in a political culture consists in emotional attitudes. Here the fundamental concept is of emotion as a stabilizing factor, of a community united by something more than narrow self-interest or the terror of the law. One thinks of the 'expressive symbols' such as flags, national anthems, national monuments, and of the great ceremonies (Coronation, State Opening of Parliament, 4th July, 14th July, May Day in Soviet Russia, Independence Day in Ghana) when the emotional commitment to a 'loyalty area' is demonstrated and reinforced.

These values and beliefs, and to some extent the emotions, are shared by official as well as unofficial groups and affect not only the formulation of demands and the means by which these are projected and pressed home, but also the character of the decisions by which such demands are reconciled. Much of the content of these decisions is provided by pressure groups as part of the purposes for which they try to exercise influence. Those purposes arise, fundamentally, in two ways. K. B. Smellie once characterized (American Federal) Government as 'the allocating of an economic surplus'.[1] The phrase may be adapted to the purposes in hand by saying that the production of goods and services in this country gives rise to an economic surplus, and that it is the business of many pressure groups to influence its allocation in a certain way. This may or may not be 'in their own favour' as such, *e.g.*, the British Legion, when demanding a basic pension of 90s. a week, may not have had many disability pensioners in its ranks, but the typical case would be the self-interested (though not necessarily selfish) one. Such a purpose may be called the economic objective, but it is not devoid of a sense of justice either at the given time or as between one generation and another.

Groups also pursue non-economic objectives, as when they try to persuade official groups to introduce, modify or abandon some rule or policy in our external relations (Soviet Russia), Colonial relations (Nyasaland), general defence measures (*e.g.*, unilateral disarmament), or in some domestic matter (homosexuality, the treatment of animals, prison administration, and the like). On the whole, however, most of

[1] K. Smellie, *The American Federal System*, 1928, p. 47.

the major pressure groups seem to pursue objectives that fall within the first category, which accordingly *tends* to make pressure politics the continuation of economic bargaining by other means. Hence it is important to bear in mind that, in the short run, groups advance claims and influence decisions in given economic circumstances. Since, however, the economic objectives do not exhaust the sum total of the objectives pursued, the general 'situation' in which groups find themselves must also be considered.

Serving, then, as a funnel for economic and non-economic claims, pressure groups set out to extract favourable decisions from the appropriate official group. Which official group is appropriate will vary over time, and, at any given time, according to the nature of the claim advanced and its implications for other groups (the 'public interest').

The variation over time is a familiar story: the Sovereign and the great officers of state; Parliament; Cabinet; Cabinet and Civil Service; these indicate well-recognized stages in the changing distribution of official power. Strictly speaking, such developments are continuous, *e.g.*, today the balance may be changing as between the Cabinet and Cabinet Committees on the one hand and between the Cabinet and great Departments of State on the other. But at any given moment the 'system' will appear to be 'stationary', and it will become known in a general way how power is distributed among official groups. So it will become possible for pressure groups to draw a rough map of official power, although it does not follow that their cartography will always be accurate.

Pressure groups also require a rough map of their own 'country', the realm of unofficial power. As a pressure group moves up-stage towards an official group, it must to some extent be aware that, back-stage and 'out in front', there are many other players. A number of these players will have already made explicit requests, or be about to make some, and so they walk on as competitors. To be competitors they do not have to enter from opposite sides: they may stand on the same side and yet find themselves in opposition, as when, in 1947, the Legion's claim for a 90s. basic pension (then 45s.) cut across the policy of BLESMA, whose Executive Council accordingly declared that it would not be 'stampeded into adopting the slogan "Double the Basic Rate" '.[1] But generally, of course, the groups occupy entirely different spheres, such as farming, school-teaching and medicine, so that the competition is likely to be on a grand scale. Even demands not yet (or never) formally lodged will have some relevance because the official groups are partly elective, and, wishing to continue as decision-makers, are obliged to estimate the needs of all unofficial groups.

[1] Annual Report for 1947, p. 5.

Such knowledge of the distribution of unofficial power is needed not only in formulating demands but also in enlisting the aid of other groups in support of them. For other groups are not always rivals, and may be persuaded to lend a hand. Thus in 1955 the Manchester City Council pleaded with the Government on BLESMA's behalf.[1] Groups may even be potential allies on a certain issue or range of issues: in 1957, eighteen ex-service associations, agreeing on (war) pensions policy, worked together in an attempt to prove that unity is strength.[2]

The main social values in a community, then, are achieved through groups, which are of two kinds, official and unofficial, distinguished by their decision-making range and sanctions. In this inquiry, our immediate concern is with some of those unofficial groups, conveniently called pressure groups, that seek to influence official groups, also called the decision-makers. The claims advanced by pressure groups usually relate to the community's economic surplus, so the economic situation is fundamental, but claims may also arise out of other circumstances. In pursuing their aims, pressure groups face a given power situation: the hierarchy of decision-makers and the universe of unofficial groups to which they themselves belong. Both the aims pursued and the means adopted, as well as the way in which the aims are perceived by the decision-makers, are shaped by the prevailing political culture.

[1] *Blesmag*, Jan. 1956, 10.

[2] See my article in 29 P.Q. 1958, 36.

PART ONE

The Formative Years (1917-21)

THE POLITICAL CULTURE: CHAPTERS II–V
THE CIRCUMSTANCES: CHAPTERS VI–VII

II

THE OBJECTS AND MODES OF GOVERNMENT

NEITHER the nature nor the aims of ex-servicemen's associations can be fully understood except in terms of the prevailing political culture. Particular circumstances served as a catalyst, but values and beliefs in the formative years are essential guides to understanding, especially if one hopes to discover why an extremist ex-servicemen's movement did not develop in this country.[1]

OBJECTS OF GOVERNMENT

Values and Beliefs

That the political culture prevailing at the outbreak of the First World War prescribed a limited role for official groups is a commonplace. This narrow conception of the role of government was reflected in various attitudes and practices governing the treatment of the families of serving soldiers and of the ex-service community in general. To assist the wives of soldiers in distress, for instance, was deemed to be no business of the Government. In the seventeenth century most Spanish veterans in the Low Countries had their wives with them, 'conjugal relations' not being at that time 'generally interrupted by military service'.[2] But the British Army agreed with the naval officer who said that 'in the Navy they knew of no such useless appendage or encumbrance as a sailor's wife',[3] and permitted only an extremely small number to marry 'on the strength', which conferred a right to accommodation in barracks or lodgings and certain allowances.

Such a policy had practical foundations: large numbers of wives could not be carried to Gibraltar, Aden, Malta or India. But cultural values had a role, as became clear when a regiment suddenly moved

---

[1] René Rémond, 5 *Revue Française de Science Politique*, 1955, 270–90.

[2] John U. Nef, *War and Human Progress*, 1950, p. 96.

[3] Quoted in James Gildea, *Historical Record of the Soldiers' and Sailors' Families Association*, 1885–1916, 1916, p. 254.

11

overseas. The distress of even on-the-strength wives was often serious and at times desperate, some being 'reduced to absolute starvation'.[1] The 'off-the-strength' wife (who had no official status) was left behind to 'enter the workhouse or encounter some worse evil'. Yet few seem to have thought it was the business of the Government as such to take action: the responsibility was not so much evaded as unrecognized.

Nor did Governments recognize an obligation to the parents of professional soldiers, who had no more official existence than off-the-strength wives. A recruit to the colours might leave behind him a considerable trail of distress leading back to his own home; to give aid and comfort to his parents (as such) was not considered to be a function of government.

Even a married soldier killed (or otherwise dying) was, until the South African War, deemed to have no widow, still less a mother. At least, the provision of pensions for widows and children did not become the Government's business until bacteria and bullets in the South African veld conspired to make it unavoidable. Even then, 'off-the-strength' wives were excluded and the suggestion of a far-sighted colonel that other dependent relatives such as mothers should also be considered fell on deaf ears.[2]

Whereas, after the South African War, a dead soldier might leave a widow who would be State-supported, a married soldier discharged through injury or ill-health was still treated as though he had no wife. The Chelsea Commissioners paid regard 'only to the degree of disablement affecting earning capacity . . . the length of service and character of the soldier himself, and any peculiar circumstances attending his conduct when wounded. His family circumstances, children or dependants, have never entered into the matter of the pension to which the incidents of his military service have entitled him'.[3] Thus there was a fiction of 'military man' as convenient for Chancellors of the Exchequer and taxpayers as the fiction of 'economic man' had been to early economists.

Nor was it considered the business of government to keep up (or arrange to have kept up) a discharged man's medical treatment. The responsibility of the naval and military authorities for the provision of treatment ceased on discharge, and even in 1915, as soon as it was evident that a man would not be able to return to active service, he was discharged 'without much regard to the question whether his

---

[1] ibid., p. 21.

[2] Lt.-Col. Thomas Tully, Cd. 248 (1900) (Mins. of ev.), Q. 1173., Committee of Enquiry into Charitable Funds (Cd. 196).

[3] H.C. 196 (1915), Select Committee on Naval and Military Services (Pensions and Grants), p. 253.

health or his physical condition could be improved by further treatment'.[1]

Still less was it thought to be the function of government as such to find work for ex-servicemen. This, of course, reflected a general attitude: a country that did not invent employment exchanges until 1909 was not likely to exert itself very much about finding work specifically for ex-soldiers. It is true that the problem was investigated often enough: between the 1870's and 1906 at least five major official committees brooded upon it, but essentially its solution was left to voluntary agencies.

In short, the prevailing values prescribed the voluntary principle in the ex-service field as (though decreasingly) in public affairs generally.

These values were buttressed by certain beliefs. The voluntary principle was a form of individualism and so carried within it all those beliefs about the inherent limitations of official groups that found expression in such phrases as 'State interference', 'red tape' and other verbal obstacles to creeping collectivism. But there were also beliefs specific to this inquiry. Pressure politics, it was earlier suggested, tends to be about the allocation of an economic surplus, and foremost among the beliefs sustaining the relevant values was the view that politicians could not be trusted to administer pensions with due regard to the length of the public purse. Other beliefs of the kind were that the voluntary principle was flexible and so able to meet hard cases, and that it embodied a 'cheerful human element'. Such views were still being expressed as late as 1917.[2]

MODES OF GOVERNMENT

Values and Beliefs

Values about the proper objects of government have their counterpart in values governing the means by which those objects may be pursued. From this point of view the outstanding feature of British decision-making in 1914 was the limited number of people who took part in it. In the relevant sense, democracy had been on the march (but not at light-infantry pace) since 1832, yet despite the extensions of the franchise in 1867 and 1884, the electorate remained small: as late as

---

[1] Cd. 7915 (1915), Departmental Committee on Provision of Employment for Soldiers and Sailors Disabled in the War, Report, para. 7. (The Murray Committee.)

[2] See below, p. 36.

the December election in 1910, it was still well below eight millions,[1] out of a total population of about 42 millions.[2]

Nor did the second and third Reform Acts 'suddenly transform the House of Commons'.[3] Members with aristocratic connexions declined but slowly, and were in any case replaced chiefly by 'hard-faced' men of business. The common man was still uncommon in the House until as late as 1906, and it was not until just after the 1914–18 War that Labour became, both in seats and votes, the second party in the land. As the Cabinets had been tinged with the colour of the Parliaments, the section of the community from which the elected decision-makers had been drawn was narrow indeed. The English statesmen of the period, living their 'leisurely and methodical existence, each working week folded between pleasant and often sumptuous country-house week-ends', tended to constitute a 'ruling class'.[4]

The belief that politicians could not be trusted to administer (war) pensions properly was related, as we know, to values about the functions of government; it also had implications for the modes of government. For there can be little doubt that the politicians who 'could not be trusted' were primarily the rising democratic politicians. The voluntary system had of course a class foundation: for instance, as the *Edinburgh Review* noted, S.S.F.A.'s work 'was undertaken by persons of the leisured class, for they were the only people who had the necessary time to devote to it'.[5] To preserve the voluntary system meant preserving a certain quantum of decision-making in the hands of particular unofficial groups. But this was precisely the issue raised by the growth of democracy, except that democracy meant an invasion of the field of *official* groups and, accordingly, of decision-making of a more fundamental kind, unlimited in scope and based on the monopoly of the legitimate use of physical force throughout the community. In both realms the basic issue tended to be the allocation of an economic surplus. Under the voluntary system, the allocation was unofficial, decentralized and based on only a part of the economic surplus; under *étatisme* (tending to be more and more democratic), the surplus that could be made available by official power was expected to be greater, and the distribution of it, naturally, would be both official and at least centrally-determined.

Logically, therefore, the voluntary system was related to the slow

[1] D. E. Butler, *The Electoral System in Great Britain*, 1953, p. 172.

[2] In 1911. *Annual Abstract of Statistics* No. 84, 1948, p. 7, Table 6.

[3] K. B. Smellie, *A Hundred Years of English Government*, 2nd ed. 1950, p. 123.

[4] James Pope-Hennessy, *Lord Crewe: The Likeness of a Liberal*, 1955, pp. 66–67, 79–80, writing particularly of the period 1908–16.

[5] Jan. 1917, 152.

growth of democracy: opposition to it came in large part from the rising democratic forces, *e.g.*, answering criticisms of the 'case work' aspect of voluntaryism, someone remarked that politicians 'trembled whenever some tub-thumper raised the class-war slogans of "inquisitorial" and "undemocratic" . . . '[1] On the other hand, the more democracy gained ground, the less would the voluntary principle be likely to survive. Thus differences in beliefs also tended to induce a division within the political culture. In so far as soldiers and ex-servicemen were part of the rising democratic forces, they constituted one 'side' of that division. Feeling that they, as distinct from the dodgers, profiteers and civilians generally, had 'done their bit', they put a high value on their own services, which tended to emphasize their separateness from the rest of the community. From this belief alone it was an easy step to launching their own associations. Intuitively they knew that this was a way of participating in the democratic process.

[1] 'X' in 38 C.O.R. 1915, 305.

III

THE VOLUNTARY PRINCIPLE

THE accepted values and beliefs about the objects of government, then, found expression as the voluntary principle, to which politician and private citizen had become emotionally attached. The broad pattern of this voluntary system (so far as it concerns this inquiry) had become clear and, in essentials, stabilized during the course of the South African War. In the spring of 1900 Lord Justice Henn Collins's Committee drew its outline by identifying three classes of central funds: those dealing with (a) the wives and dependants of living soldiers and sailors; (b) the widows and dependants of soldiers and sailors dying in the service; and (c) the sick and wounded soldiers and sailors at the front or invalided home, or discharged disabled. In the first category, the S.S.F.A. was 'by far the most important'; the Patriotic Fund was 'the most important' example of the second. Societies in the third category included Lloyd's Patriotic Fund; the Society for the Aid of the Sick and Wounded in War (to which the British Red Cross was affiliated); the *Daily Mail* Fund and the newly-formed Soldiers and Sailors Help Society.[1]

When war broke out in 1914 the broad pattern of voluntary action was much as it had been in 1900. S.S.F.A. and the Royal Patriotic Fund (reorganized as a Corporation) were still outstanding in their several spheres, but in the third category some societies had waxed and waned. The Red Cross was 'one of the great successes of the war'.[2] Lloyd's Patriotic Fund was still there to be drawn upon—a wry comment on the affairs of men, since it had been raised in 1803 on behalf of Englishmen who had battled against Frenchmen and would now be used on behalf of their descendants desperately fighting in defence of French territory. But the 'upstart' Soldiers Help Society, under Lord Roberts's beneficent patronage, had now drawn ahead, and was to be the mainstay of the discharged men themselves.

Such was the broad pattern; but there was another aspect of voluntaryism—the private enterprise employment 'exchanges'. Already in 1906 there were no fewer than eighteen of these. Eight

---

[1] Cd. 196 (1900), Committee of Inquiry into Charitable Funds, Report, p. 5.

[2] *The Times*, 28th Dec. 1916 (leader).

were largely commercial in character and so fall outside 'voluntaryism' in our sense of the term, as did the Corps of Commissionaires (1859), to which men paid subscriptions and which a Committee described as 'practically a large employer of labour'.[1] Of the remainder, six were of the regimental association type founded largely in the eighties and nineties and ranging from the Brigade of Guards Employment Society (1891) and the Royal Engineer Labour Bureau (1894) to the Naval Employment Agency (1896) and the Royal Army Temperance Association, which presumably rewarded sobriety with jobs.[2] The other three were the Army and Navy Pensioners' and Time-expired Men's Employment Society (1855); the Soldiers Help Society, whose emergence has been already noted, and the National Association for the Employment of Reserve and Discharged Soldiers (1885), which, receiving a substantial government grant, was also the most successful.[3] Presumably all or most of these bodies were still in operation when war broke out, so constituting yet another facet of the many-sided structure of voluntaryism. It was on this structure that the Asquith Government leaned in the hope of reducing to manageable size some of its complicated and multitudinous domestic problems.

But where was the money to come from? The existing voluntary bodies might provide the channels along which benevolence could flow, but where lay the source of the stream? The natural answer today would be: 'the Government of course', but that only emphasizes how deep a gulf divides us from 1914. It was a reflection of the prevailing values that almost immediately after war broke out the Prince of Wales should ask for funds to relieve distress and Queen Alexandra launch an appeal on behalf of S.S.F.A. The two appeals were soon fused, and the objective crystallized as the relief of 'all hardship, whether arising directly from war casualties or through unemployment caused by the inevitable dislocation of trade'.[4] To us this way of dealing with an anticipated grave national problem appears as Government neglect; indeed there were those (*e.g.*, the young G. D. H. Cole) who made that charge at the time.[5] But the collection of nearly £5 million within eight months shows that, although right in principle, Cole was ahead of his time, and that the

---

[1] Cd. 2991 (1906), Committee on the Civil Employment of Ex-Soldiers and Sailors, Report, p. 8 and para. 12. (The Ward Committee).

[2] ibid., pp. 7–8.

[3] ibid., para. 13. This government subvention indicated some government concern, but the existence of eighteen private employment agencies is a measure of it.

[4] Cd. 7756 (1915), Report on the Administration of the National Relief Fund, p. 2 (2). Commonly called 'The Prince of Wales' Fund'.

[5] *Labour in War Time*, 1915, pp. 95–6.

great age of voluntaryism was not yet dead. It took a prolonged citizens' war to bring it to an end.

For a citizens' war we were wholly unprepared, and nowhere is that unpreparedness more evident than in the misfortune that befell those families who were left high and dry after mobilization and the first great rush to the colours in the hot days of August, 1914.[1] The distinction between marriages 'on' and 'off' the strength could no longer be sustained. On 10th August the Prime Minister announced its abolition; in addition, monthly payments had to be replaced by weekly ones. Such was the speed of recruitment that the Army Pay Offices were overwhelmed. At the outbreak of war these had had only 1,500 soldiers' wives on their books; within a fortnight the number had risen to 250,000, paid weekly. As a result of this 'enormous accession of work', the War Office organization was swamped.[2] Nor could the Navy escape the burden of separation allowances, which became payable to sailors' wives for the first time in our history.[3]

In this emergency it was S.S.F.A. that bore the brunt of the 'enormous accession of work'. Acting locally for the National Relief Fund, it filled the gap by making advance payments (underwritten by the War Office)[4] against separation allowances. But this was not all. The commitments of a citizen-army had to be taken into account; when a balance was struck, it was plain that financial help over and above separation allowances could not be avoided. Hence S.S.F.A. (and Local Representative Committees) also made supplementary grants, especially towards the rent: 'without some assistance towards the payment of rent, thousands of soldiers' homes would have been broken up . . . .'[5]

If S.S.F.A. came to the rescue of serving soldiers' wives, the Royal Patriotic Fund Corporation gave 'immediate financial assistance to the families of those who fell in action'.[6] Also using money received from the National Relief Fund, the Corporation paid out, up to the end of 1915, some £200,000 in allowances varying from 7s. to 9s. a

[1] 225 Ed. Rev. 1917, 239.

[2] Cd. 7756 (1915), para. 10.

[3] ibid., para. 12; H.C. 196, p. 165.

[4] H.C. 196, Mins. of ev., Q. 34.

[5] Cd. 8169 (1915), Report of the National Relief Fund, p. 3 (3). As a general rule such help was limited to cases where the rent exceeded 4s. a week (7s. 6d. in London). This meant that it applied almost entirely to the towns: H.C. 196, Mins. of ev., Q. 1930.

[6] *Royal Patriotic Fund Corporation 1854–1954: A Short History*, n.d., p. 9.

week according to age, 'the station in life of the beneficiaries' and other factors.[1]

The new war disabled began to be discharged from the Army during the second week of September 1914.[2] They were looked after by the Soldiers Help Society, which, after July 1915, took charge of their families as well.[3] Throughout 1915 the 'most important' part of the Society's work was the granting of assistance to men discharged with partial disability pensions.[4] For the National Relief Committee, like the Murray Committee,[5] found that 'considerable numbers of men were being discharged with such pensions long before they had recovered sufficiently to be able to resume civil employment'. So the Relief Fund made sufficient money available to the Society to enable it 'to bring the family income up to a figure approximately the scale of total disability pensions'.[6]

In the first two years of the war the Soldiers Help Society played an outstanding role. Devine exaggerated when he wrote that, until July 1916, 'whatever was done for disabled soldiers and sailors after discharge, aside from their pension and insurance, was done by' that body, 'supplemented by one or two existing organizations which served as employment agencies and advisers'.[7] Such a view fails to take into account the fantastically luxuriant growth of voluntaryism at the time: an Act of 1916 required war charities to register, and by the end of October the following year, some 6,000 had done so.[8] By then some had been discontinued, but most of them still survived. The vast majority of these, of course, were local funds, but their existence on such a scale suggests that Devine's claim was rather too emphatic. There were also two London societies of appreciable importance. The Friends of the Poor sent visitors to the London hospitals to inquire about a man's 'capabilities for work in the future under changed conditions', and, when he was fit, tried to get suitable work for him. In a six months' period in 1916, this body claimed to have looked after the interests of 200 discharged men and to have trained or found work for perhaps a hundred more.[9] Even earlier, in 1915, Sylvia Pankhurst had founded the National League of Rights

---

[1] Cd. 8333 (1916), Report of the Royal Patriotic Fund Corporation, p. 61, App. XXXII; p. 23 and App. III.

[2] Edward T. Devine, *Disabled Soldiers and Sailors*, etc., 1919, p. 93.

[3] Cd. 8169, Report of the National Relief Fund, p. 4 (6).

[4] ibid.

[5] See above p. 13, n. 1 and text.

[6] Cd. 8169, p. 4 (6).

[7] Devine, op. cit., p. 134.

[8] E. C. Price, 42 (N.S.) C.O.R. 1917, 236–7.

[9] *The Times*, 2nd Nov. 1916.

for Soldiers' and Sailors' Wives and Relatives.[1] Its object was 'to protect the interests of soldiers and sailors both discharged and in the Services', although, on the other hand, it must be admitted that the emphasis seems to have been on pensions.[2]

Nevertheless Devine's earlier—and more careful—formulation that the Soldiers Help Society was the 'main reliance of the men discharged from the service' is undoubtedly true.[3] Already, since 1904, the Society had operated workshops for disabled soldiers; in March 1915, it continued the experiment by opening a toy-making factory in London. By the end of the year it was employing a hundred men.[4] Apart from so insulating disabled soldiers from the labour market, the Society (up to March 1916) found work for over six thousand discharged men.[5]

Thus one may conclude that many of the initial problems resulting from the 'citizen' character of the 1914–18 War were left to private charity. Although there was an eruption of war charities, the most important societies were legacies of the Victorian era. But if the discharged men had been born Victorians, their ideas and values were Georgian. The 'great object' of the Soldiers Help Society, Lord Cheylesmore had said in 1906, was 'not to pauperize the soldier'.[6] The soldier he had in mind was a veteran of the regular army ('Crimeans and old Mutiny men'); citizen ex-soldiers of the First War not only had no intention of being pauperized but also came out in opposition to the whole system of private charity, which they would have resented even if it had been more efficient. The contemporary writer who thought as late as the end of 1916 that the 'objection to what is sometimes contemptuously termed "charity" is valid only when charity is spasmodic and inefficient'[7] was ignorant of the new world already about him.

Nevertheless the efficiency of 'charity' (or voluntaryism) is not irrelevant to our investigations. It would probably be found that one of the changes in belief that (presumably) led to a change in values during the course of the war was precisely a changing estimate of the

[1] H.C. 247 (1919), Select Committee on Pensions, Mins. of ev., Q. 5273; *Labour Year Book*, 1919, pp. 231–2.

[2] *Labour Year Book*, 1919, ibid. 104 H.C. Deb., c. 32.

[3] op. cit., p. 132.

[4] ibid., p. 133.

[5] Cd. 8286 (1916) Report of the National Relief Fund, p. 4 (6).

[6] Cd. 2992 (1906) Committee on the Civil Employment of Ex-Soldiers and Sailors, Mins. of ev., Q. 168.

[7] L. V. Shairp, 225 Ed. Rev. 1917, 123. As this issue was published in January, the article may be ascribed to the end of 1916.

effectiveness of voluntary action in the circumstances of the time. The question therefore arises: how effective was voluntaryism?

To answer this question a special inquiry would be necessary: here only some broad considerations can be suggested. War charities generally had a 'social cost': some petty dishonesty and even fraud; the diversion of women and girls from 'worthier modes of national service'; and the expenditure of an 'enormous amount of money' in 'competitive advertisement', which a social worker denounced as 'quite unjustifiable on grounds of good economy, and inconsistent with any whole-hearted fellowship in charity'.[1]

But what of the older societies on which the main burden fell? A fundamental difficulty was that the S.S.F.A. network did not cover the whole of the country: very important centres of population were outside its effective range. In Birmingham, for instance, S.S.F.A., as Austen Chamberlain said, 'was practically non-existent': hence an *ad hoc* Citizens' Relief Committee under the Lord Mayor had had to be formed.[2] S.S.F.A. was also largely unrepresented in the mining valleys of South Wales, apparently because 'the South Wales miner' made 'too good money [*sic*] to be much attracted by one shilling a day'; hence, as Lloyd George put it in his characteristic way, 'the military caste was not represented at all in those mining areas'.[3] Yet, according to a War Office view, S.S.F.A., 'was allowed to take up the position of covering the whole area of the kingdom, which it was not really in a position to do effectually. We have got past that difficulty now, but the great part of the breakdown in the payments of these [separation] allowances during September and October was due to that cause.'[4] If so, the responsibility must rest with the decision-makers who 'allowed' and not with the unofficial group that '*was allowed*', but the inadequate coverage and great distress are not in doubt.

Nor, as pointed out by an anonymous writer who may well have had 'inside' knowledge, was S.S.F.A.'s organization geared for rapid expansion,[5] and so it is likely that the sudden burden swamped some of the branches. The Deputy-Mayor of Great Yarmouth may have indicated a not uncommon experience in recalling that:

'When war broke out in 1914, the Soldiers' and Sailors' Families Association had a great deal of work thrown upon them, so much so that the machinery was quite unable to carry it out, and the whole thing was

---

[1] E. C. Price, op. cit., pp. 237–40. For another aspect of 'philanthropy' see Rowland Kenney, 19 *The English Review* 1914, 112–18.
[2] H.C. 196, Mins. of ev., Q. 38, p. 186.
[3] ibid., Q. 38; 143; 39.
[4] ibid., Q. 146.
[5] 225 Ed. Rev. 1917, 140.

shifted into the Town Hall for anyone to take up who felt brave enough to do it. The Town Clerk courageously shouldered the burden, and by admirable organization and tactful management straightened everything out and put it on a very satisfactory footing.'[1]

Other branches may have been better organized but yet unwilling to incur so 'heavy a cash responsibility' as that entailed in advancing substantial sums for separation allowances on account.[2]

Of course, whatever a detailed study might reveal, it is perfectly clear that had there been no S.S.F.A. the situation would have been chaotic. The 'great statesman' who told W. Hayes Fisher. M.P., that without S.S.F.A. at the time of mobilization the distress would have been so great that 'there might have been a revolution'[3] was surely either misrepresented or exaggerating, but there is no doubt that it did discharge a very important role in our system of public administration. Yet the 'muddle and mess and delay in the payment of separation allowances' was 'one of the most tragic features of the campaign so far as it has affected civil life'.[4] Not even the combined efforts of *ad hoc* local committees and S.S.F.A. could avert hardship or prevent some people from accepting the cold charity of the Poor Law. From Scotland as well as England and Wales, reports reaching the Local Government Board 'indicated that the number of women compelled to have recourse to the Poor Law was so considerable that any delay threatened to produce grave consequences'.[5]

It was a harbinger of much that was to come that the Government took special steps to transfer funds to the Board of Guardians concerned in 'order to ensure that the families who had been assisted from this source should not be regarded as having received Poor Law Relief'; even the names and other entries were to be removed from the Guardians' records.[6] The workhouse was all very well for old regulars: a citizen-soldiery and their families had to be treated with more respect. In due course a revulsion against 'charity' was to be one of the main driving-forces behind the ex-servicemen's movement.

S.S.F.A.'s effective range was inadequate; the Royal Patriotic Fund Corporation hardly existed outside London. It had 'no regular branches of its own', only honorary agents, chiefly in the garrison towns and naval ports.[7] Elsewhere, even before 1914, it had had to

---

[1] *Yarmouth Mercury*, 16th Nov. 1918.

[2] H.C. 196, Q. 35.

[3] Gildea, op. cit., p. 178.

[4] Rowland Kenney, op. cit., p. 113.

[5] Cd. 8449 (1917), Report of the National Relief Fund, p. 4 (5).

[6] Cd. 7603 (1914), Prevention and Relief of Distress due to the War, Memorandum, p. 9; and Cd. 8129 (1915), Report of the Scottish Advisory Committee on the Administration of the National Relief Fund, p. 5.

[7] H.C. 196, p. 248.

fall back on S.S.F.A., and the outbreak of a citizens' war naturally made that body 'very much' its agent.[1] As the Permanent Under-Secretary at the War Office said tactfully in November 1914: 'considering the scale of the present war', the Corporation had the 'quality' but not the 'quantity'.[2]

Nor were its financial resources adequate. It had hardly any funds *of its own* for assisting the *new* war widows. The Chairman of its Executive Committee, W. Hayes Fisher, M.P., roundly declared in January 1915: 'We have no funds for that purpose; all our funds are allocated'.[3] As he himself revealed, his statement was not strictly accurate, because the Corporation had already received some £3,000 in unsolicited gifts, but of course he was right to dismiss that as 'scarcely worth talking about'.[4] What hobbled the Corporation was its inability to repeat its very successful 'Transvaal War' appeal: Hayes Fisher had immediately gone with the Duke of Connaught to see the Lord Mayor of London about another appeal but they had drawn a blank because the Government wanted them to wait until the Prince of Wales's Appeal Fund had been launched.[5] Thus the Corporation had neither the money nor the machinery to cope with the tasks set by a nation-in-arms.

Organizationally, the Soldiers and Sailors Help Society was far better equipped than the Royal Patriotic Fund to deal with the problems that fell within its scope. From the very beginning it had been able to deploy a small army of 'friends' throughout the country,[6] and years later felt able to claim even in the face of demobilization that '*every* man on discharge' was referred to its 'friend' located 'in his own Borough or Parish',[7] which implied a nation-wide coverage. But however superior its organization for meeting the new needs, the Society was for its 'new money' no less dependent upon the National Relief Fund than the two older bodies. From 6th August 1914 to the end of 1915, it disbursed some £60,000 on relief to discharged men and their families out of about £71,000 supplied from the National Relief Fund.[8] And whereas the Patriotic Fund and especially S.S.F.A. had been put to the test immediately, the Society's trial, for an obvious reason, was delayed. Throughout

---

[1] ibid., Q. 2290.

[2] Q. 21 and 153. This was Sir Charles Harris.

[3] Q. 2245.

[4] Q. 2252 and 2247.

[5] Q. 2247.

[6] Lt.-Gen. H. L. Geary, the Organizing Secretary, in Cd. 248 (1900), Q. 1327.

[7] *The Times*, 13th Dec. 1918. My italics.

[8] Cd. 8286 (1916), p. 43, App. III. The relief total included advances, of which some £4,900 was later recovered. From 1st July 1915, the Society assisted the family as well as the man. ibid., p. 4 (5).

1915 the numbers assisted in this way and by other methods remained comparatively small.[1]

These were the principal societies relevant to this discussion.[2] Generally speaking, although there were obvious deficiencies, they do not seem to have acquitted themselves ill under the first shock of war; certainly the situation would have been serious if they had not existed. But some people's beliefs about the effectiveness o voluntary-ism must have been coloured by the initial distress, which, perversely, might have been attributed to the societies as such, or at least taken as indications of their inadequacy or inappropriateness in the new circumstances. And judged by a severer standard, apart from specific defects, voluntaryism could doubtless have given a better account of itself if its efforts had been better co-ordinated. On the one hand, there seems to have been little groundwork of co-operation between ex-service charities and their 'civil' counterparts. Indeed a writer connected with the British Institute of Social Service could describe S.S.F.A. and the Help Society as 'two organizations, whose existence to most social workers was quite unknown' at the outbreak of war.[3] If that were generally true, such ignorance must have had a 'social cost'.

Within the ex-service field itself, effective co-ordination was (and remains to this day) one of the great unsolved problems.[4] In their different ways, the Herschell Committee in 1895, the Select Committee of the following year, the Prince of Wales's unofficial initiative in March 1900, and the Henn Collins Committee that reported two months later, had all grappled with it; the last-named was even well in advance of its time in implying that legislation might be necessary in order to ensure co-operation.[5] But the position when war broke out in 1914 was essentially the same as it had been a decade or more earlier. One result was that until July 1915, S.S.F.A. dealt with the families of discharged men, while the Soldiers Help Society assisted the men themselves; only then was the Society able to begin treating

---

[1] Cd. 8286, p. 4 (6).

[2] The Red Cross was important in a different field.

[3] Frederic G. D'Aeth, 10 *Progress* 1915, 141.

[4] This was true also of matters outside the scope of this discussion, *e.g.*, the outbreak of war 'found voluntary effort on behalf of the Army entirely un-organized', and apart from the Regimental Associations, 'no societies existed for the purpose of providing comforts and gifts for combatant troops at home or abroad'. Hence in September 1915 a special department was established at the War Office to co-ordinate such voluntary work. Cmd. 173 (1919), Report on the National Scheme of Co-ordination of Voluntary Effort resulting from the formation of the Department of the Director General of Voluntary Organizations, p. 3.

[5] Cd. 196, p. 13.

the discharged man and his family as a single unit. On the face of it, such an extreme example of the division of labour would seem to leave voluntaryism as a whole open to the charge of inefficiency in about the first eleven months of the war.

Whatever judgement on the efficiency of voluntary action in about the first year of war would be justified by a thorough examination of the evidence, the writing was obviously on the wall. By October 1915 we had already created an army of about 2,400,000 men,[1] and soon the planners were to be demanding another million and a half for the 1916 campaign.[2] This was a war of Titans (or at least of whole nations masquerading as Titans), and its significance for voluntary action was made plain by the Prince of Wales in February 1916 in a speech concerning the Royal Patriotic Fund Corporation but susceptible of extension to voluntary bodies in general:

'To realize the magnitude of the present problem and the difficulty of coping with it by any voluntary effort, compare, for a moment, the figures showing the relative havoc in human limb and human life caused by this war, up to the present time, with the figures of the South African War. The total number of all ranks killed in the South African War was 21,942. The total number of all ranks killed in the present war is 128,138. The total casualties in all ranks in the South African War was 44,876. The total casualties in all ranks in the present war is 549,467.'[3]

What it meant for the Help Society may be gleaned from its experience in the period just before and after the time when the Prince spoke. From the beginning of the war to the middle of 1916 it gave money grants in more than 102,000 cases, of which 28,000 related to the second half of 1915 and over 49,000 to the first half of the following year.[4] In the three months April–June 1916 the National Relief Fund had to give the Help Society £40,000, compared with £50,000 in the previous *six* months (September 1915–March 1916).[5] The soldiers were coming home—and there were many others on the way.

[1] Cmd. 1193 (1920), British Army Reports, Section II, Part I, p. 16.

[2] H. M. D. Parker, *Manpower*, 1957, p. 3.

[3] Gildea, p. 196. H.R.H. was not well briefed, *e.g.*, the total of all ranks 'killed' was 7,792: the figure he quoted was for all deaths in South Africa. See *The Times History of the War in South Africa*, Vol. VII, App. III, pp. 24 and 25. But of course the broad contrast stands.

[4] Cd. 8449 (1917), Report of the National Relief Fund, p. 5 (7); Cd. 8286 p. 4 (6).

[5] Cd. 8449, ibid.

IV

A CHANGING CULTURE

CULTURES are always in flux but there are periods when the speed of the change is especially marked. One such period is that which embraces a major war. In Britain, under the impact of a particular kind of war, the values governing the 'proper' objects of government began to change: thus, particular kinds of people previously ignored (or largely so) were brought within the ambit of government for the first time. A part of that adjustment has already come to our notice: the new eligibility of all soldiers' and sailors' wives for official maintenance.[1] Even those known, as the Archbishop of Canterbury put it, by that 'rather strange phrase "unmarried wives"' benefited.[2] Official circulars at the outbreak of war contained such 'blunt phrases' as 'No distinction must be made between the married and the unmarried',[3] which in one context shocked a social worker into thinking that such an injunction might 'become famous in history'.[4] Certainly it was an innovation but in a citizens' war account has to be taken of all the people whatever their morals.[5] The offending sentence was deleted but the practice of helping the unrighteous as well as the righteous continued.[6]

The parents of professional soldiers had had no more official existence than unmarried or 'off-the-strength' wives. In peacetime they could conveniently be ignored but in a citizens' war they became obvious candidates for financial consideration: mothers (and even sisters) took on a new importance and had to be provided for. Such provision was 'entirely new'. 'The War Office had no machinery whatever at that time for dealing with the dependants of soldiers'. The Select Committee on pensions and grants later universalized the principle by stating that the 'term "Dependants" should include any

---

[1] See p. 18.   [2] H.C. 196, Mins. of ev., Q. 2718.
[3] ibid.   [4] 38 C.O.R. 1915, 303.
[5] That the Episcopate should have been moved to protest to the P.M. is understandable (Q. 2718) but Countess Ferrers, of S.S.F.A., found that while there was 'very much to deplore, it has also not infrequently shown much to edify'. (38 C.O.R. 1915, 10). Another experienced social worker noted as 'the most remarkable feature' the 'undoubted faithfulness of the "wives"' and thought that 'generally their homes and children are above reproach...' (225 Ed. Rev. 1917, 146).
[6] Q. 2718.

person who is found as a fact to have been dependent on the sailor or soldier'.[1]

That decision had obvious implications for the relatives of men who were killed or who died of wounds. The South African War had been sufficient of a people-war for widows' pensions to be conceded, but, as already noted,[2] other degrees of dependency were still not recognized. In 1914 the Departments tried to maintain that restriction, but since they had conceded separation allowances simply on the basis of proved dependence, they left themselves open to the charge of inconsistency. For they proposed, in effect, to grant a separation allowance to, say, a widowed mother who had been supported by her son, but not to give her a pension when that son was killed. 'What is the meaning of that?' Bonar Law asked at once during the Select Committee proceedings.[3] Harris, the War Office spokesman, tried to disarm criticism by pointing out that even separation allowances were 'entirely new', but he also revealed that the possibility of pensions for such dependants was being studied at the War Office.[4] The Select Committee probably only anticipated the result of that study by recommending pensions for these dependants on the basis of the benefit received from the dead soldier (or sailor) during his lifetime (though the amount was not to exceed a widow's pension).[5]

As with separation allowances and with pensions for relatives of men killed, the problem of a discharged man's dependants assumed considerable proportions. The professional soldier was in this context (as in so many others) deemed to be a man without family commitments: so, as we have seen, the Chelsea Commissioners paid attention 'only to the degree of disablement' and other Service factors.[6] In a people-war the fiction had to be abandoned. In September 1914 the Army Council asked the Chelsea Commissioners, when assessing the claims of totally incapacitated private soldiers who had wives and children, to consider taking 'into account not only the needs of the man himself but of his dependants also'.[7] The Commissioners, however, were unwilling to differentiate between married and single soldiers, and held to the view that 'the pension granted is for the soldier himself, no matter what his domestic arrangements may be ...'[8] They also thought that the necessary investigation of family circumstances would prescribe an impracticable procedure. The 'discretionary sixpence' they had asked for would 'enable the invalid

[1] H.C. 196, Mins. of ev., Q. 5, and 1st Special Report, para. 7.
[2] See p. 12. [3] H.C. 196, Q. 5.
[4] ibid.
[5] ibid., 1st Special Report, para. 13.
[6] See above, p. 12. [7] H.C. 196, p. 252.
[8] ibid., Doc. C.

to maintain a small family in a fairly adequate manner', while relief for larger families 'should be provided from some fund other than the Army Pension Fund'.[1] It was for the Commissioners a natural response but as unavailing as Canute's. The Army Council showed that they were better judges of the tide. Early in November the Government recognized the principle that disabled men had wives and other dependants for whom some State provision was obligatory; the Chelsea Commissioners reluctantly acquiesced.[2]

The disabled had other problems than pensions: many of them still needed medical treatment, and all wanted work. As the Murray Committee revealed, many had been summarily removed from the Services before their health had been restored. The values implied in such a practice could not survive a citizens' war. The Murray Committee recommended that the State should take a 'liberal view of its duties in this respect'.[3] The discharged man should not only be restored to health (where possible) but also trained in a new trade if he so desired, and found employment where necessary.[4]

In making such recommendations the Committee were applying a principle they themselves had enunciated at the outset of their report, when they expressed their opinion that:

'the care of the sailors and soldiers who have been disabled in the war, is an obligation which should fall primarily upon the State; and that this liability cannot be considered as having been extinguished by the award of a pension from public funds. We regard it as the duty of the State to see that the disabled man shall be, as far as possible, restored to health, and that assistance shall be forthcoming to enable him to earn his living in the occupation best suited to his circumstances and physical condition.'[5]

That principle epitomized the change in values that was then taking place; a new conception of the proper objects of government was emerging from the new circumstances. But progress towards that new consensus was slow indeed. The very Committee that had placed so fundamental a responsibility upon the official groups also declared:

'We ought, however, to add that, in expressing this view, we are far from wishing to exclude or discourage the very valuable assistance which may be rendered voluntarily by persons and associations who take an interest in the welfare of our sailors and soldiers.

While the primary responsibility for the care of those who have suffered in the service of the country rests with the State, the best results of the action of the latter can only be achieved with the co-operation and assistance of the other agencies to which we have referred.'[6]

[1] ibid.

[2] ibid., p. 253.

[3] Cd. 7915 (1915), para. 8.

[4] ibid., p. 5, passim.

[5] para. 2.

[6] para. 3.

Here one may be uncovering an 'inarticulate major premise' that throws light on the curious vacillations and tortuous administrative developments of these early war years. The conception of the role of government was changing, but the older values were still retained and cherished. As late as June 1915 Sir George Murray, speaking to a conference in London about the central principle[1] of his Committee's Report, was far from confident that the Government would adopt his Committee's view.[2]

The Government did in fact adopt the basic principle of the Murray Report but showed itself reluctant to accept the financial implications. Here it is necessary to recall that in 1914 the administration of army pensions was shared between the Commissioners of Chelsea Hospital, the War Office and the Royal Patriotic Fund Corporation. The exceptionally powerful Select Committee appointed in November 1914 to consider naval and military pensions proposed not to reform that structure but to add to it.[3] Dealing with widows and other dependants, they formulated the principle that such pensions could not 'be settled by fixed rules, but must, to a large extent, be dealt with on the merits of each individual case'. They accordingly proposed that, after a certain time had expired from the notification of death, 'some body, either an existing organization re-organized and strengthened, or a new body to be specially created for the purpose, should have discretion to frame schemes for pensions or grants to dependants'.[4] They also invited voluntary bodies such as the National Relief Fund to supplement, where appropriate, the Government allowances and pensions on a scale to be drawn up by the new body.[5]

That first report had been agreed on 1st February.[6] By the time the Committee had concluded their deliberations some two and a half months later, 'the body' they had mentioned had crystallized into the Royal Patriotic Fund Corporation, which, once again, was to be re-organized. They proposed the appointment of a Statutory Committee of the Corporation, whose functions would be to decide questions of fact about pensions payable out of public funds to dependants other than widows and children; to supplement 'out of voluntary funds of a national character' the State pensions and separation allowances; and to act in a judicial capacity in certain disputed claims.[7] This central body was to work through local committees in counties, boroughs and urban districts.[8]

[1] See text to n. 5, p. 28.   [2] 38 C.O.R. 1915, 62.
[3] H.C. 196, 1st Special Report, para. 13.
[4] ibid.
[5] ibid., para. 19.   [6] ibid., pp. x–xiii.
[7] H.C. 196, 2nd Special Report, para. 4.
[8] ibid., para. 2.

Although the Patriotic Fund had had a statutory basis since 1903, when it was re-organized to meet the very severe criticism of its performance in the war that had just ended,[1] it still represented a kind of voluntary action, but in general the Select Committee's recommendations tended to undermine the voluntary principle, as S.S.F.A.'s bitter complaints and active lobbying served not so much to confirm as to emphasize.[2] S.S.F.A., like the National Relief Fund, was to be represented on the Statutory Committee but only as a small minority; throughout the country, too, it would lose control to a more or less 'municipalized' administration. By the same token the National Relief Fund would in effect yield 'responsibility for the relief of naval and military distress'.[3] Even allowing for the peculiar status of the Patriotic Fund, it seemed that the days of voluntaryism were numbered.

This trend was apparently reinforced in the Bill itself by the embodiment of some of the recommendations of the Murray Committee, requiring the new central body to 'make provision for the care of disabled officers and men after they have left the service, including provision for their health, training and employment'.[4] Obviously, this clause would seriously weaken the position of the Soldiers Help Society.

Yet the Government still hoped to draw upon the financial resources of voluntary enterprise. In the House, McKenna made it plain that the Select Committee had expected the trustees of the National Relief Fund to pay the piper; with that expectation in mind the Committee had proposed two seats for representatives of the Fund.[5] At the time the trustees certainly had ample resources at their disposal. The appeal had been made primarily for the relief of civil distress but very little had in fact been spent on it compared with the relief of military and naval distress, and so little even in that way compared with the money in hand that the trustees were able to play banker to the Treasury, loaning one million pounds in an unspecified form, and two millions in Treasury Bills, until the end of 1915.[6]

Whether the trustees would be willing to finance the Statutory Committee, however, was another matter, and the Government seems

[1] The Henn Collins Committee called for a radical change in its administrative methods and for 'complete and cordial co-operation' with local funds, or 'public confidence, which has been rudely shaken, will never be restored'. (Cd. 196, p. 12.)

[2] Gildea, pp. 179–190.

[3] Cd. 8286, p. 3 (3).

[4] Devine, p. 120.

[5] Devine, pp. 110–11; Cd. 8750 (1917), Report on the War Pensions, etc., Statutory Committee, p. 7.

[6] Cd. 8169, pp. 10–11, App. I.

to have been actuated by little more than pious aspiration. At any rate, the Statutory Committee itself did not have 'a brass farthing',[1] only functions to discharge. The Chancellor had 'sold the skin before he had shot the bear'.[2] The climax of this farce came, appropriately, just before the Bill was given its third reading, when McKenna came to the House to announce that the trustees would not hand over the money. As a penalty, the Fund's representation on the Statutory Committee was taken away; so too was S.S.F.A.'s.[3] The Bill then passed the House of Commons, the possibility of raising the funds by voluntaryism having been completely removed even before the measure had been read there three times.

That the issue was 'voluntaryism' was made clear during the debates in the House of Lords, where the peers insisted on a series of amendments that, in general, would have made the contemplated functions the responsibility of government, and would accordingly have converted the proposed body into a government authority.[4] But to this the Government remained solidly opposed, and it in its turn insisted on restoring the *status quo ante*.[5] Thus, at last, in November 1915, a year all but a week after the appointment of the Select Committee, the Naval and Military War Pensions, etc, Act reached the Statute Book. The Statutory Committee retained its voluntary appearance, its local committees were to have substantial representation of people experienced in the work of S.S.F.A. and Soldiers Help—but it still had no money.

It was an inauspicious beginning, and in fact the Statutory Committee did not work (as distinct from prepare to work). Holding their first meeting in January 1916, the members naturally had to consider immediately their financial position; not surprisingly, they failed to discover the funds that were deemed to be 'at their disposal'. The inevitable happened: Parliament was compelled to provide. A new Act was passed making a million pounds available, though the fantasy was kept up by the bland assertion that the grant was made as a supplement to the 'funds at the disposal of the Statutory Committee'.[6]

That grant at least kept the ship afloat. But there were organizational as well as financial difficulties. It took a long time to establish the local administration, and so the Statutory Committee had to go cap in hand to S.S.F.A. and Soldiers Help to ask them to carry on

[1] Quoted in Devine, p. 122.

[2] W. A. Bailward in 38 C.O.R. 1915, 269.

[3] Devine, 124; 38 C.O.R. 1915, 270.

[4] Devine, 124–6.

[5] ibid.

[6] Cd. 8750, p. 7.

with the work, which in turn meant asking the National Relief Fund to continue its financing of those two Societies. Luckily these three bodies were willing to remedy, as far as possible, what the politicians had bungled; and so voluntaryism even in the older sense continued until the end of June 1916.[1]

Thus when the soldiers began to come back from the Somme, they found that the community was already moving towards a new consensus (or, in this context, agreement about the objects of government) but with a slow and uncertain step. The Statutory Committee device stands as a landmark in the change of values, indicating the line between the old and the new. The very muddle was a revelation. For apart from the foolish expectations about its finances, 'the whole plan' (as *The Times* remarked) 'was based on a wrong principle'. 'The Government wanted to combine the voluntary and the official element, and they took the Royal Patriotic Fund Corporation as representing the voluntary side. They made it the nucleus of the Statutory Committee, and so put the voluntary element at the centre. But the real voluntary element actively at work in the present war was at the circumference—in the local branches of the great soldiers' and sailors' associations, which absorbed all the persons most interested in the work and administered the funds subscribed for it, both locally and centrally. They were turned out by the Government's scheme and replaced by official local committees'.[2]

The contrast between voluntaryism at the centre and at the circumference was by no means as sharp as the leader-writer suggested. The Statutory Committee was a committee of the Patriotic Fund, itself a creature of statute; on the other hand, many of the new local committees had a leavening of former voluntary workers.[3] But essentially the criticism was sound: the Government had made a fundamental miscalculation. Since in general they were intelligent men, their failure must be partly ascribed to the survival of an older set of values about the objects of government. That such values were still widespread in 1914–15 was shown by the response to the National Relief Fund. But even in 1914 and much earlier a different set of values had revealed themselves. These had been articulated by Lord Wantage in 1900 during the Henn Collins Committee hearings. Discussing the sick and wounded in war, the Earl of Northbrook posed the question: 'Where does the duty of the Government end and the liberality of the public begin?'[4] To which Lord Wantage replied that it was the 'duty of the Government to provide'; at least 'in the

---

[1] ibid.   [2] 28th Nov. 1916.

[3] Cd. 8750, p. 23; Gildea, pp. 211, 202, 216 and 218; 225 Ed. Rev. 1917, 156.

[4] Cd. 248, Mins. of ev., Q. 1104.

main'—he recognized that the Government could not do it fully.[1]

That was straw in the wind; by 1914, such views were the property of the Left as well as of the Right. G. D. H. Cole, for instance, strongly criticized 'the whole idea of relieving distress out of a national voluntary fund', not only as leading inevitably to parsimony but also because it 'hindered the provision of any effective relief' by seeming 'to relieve the Government of any further responsibility'.[2] Relief should have been officially provided, thus recognizing the 'right of the citizen to be maintained by the community in a crisis not of his making', and saving 'him from the charity-mongering excesses of unemployed members of the upper and middle classes'.[3]

Cole's criticism was directed at one form of voluntaryism but is susceptible of application to voluntaryism in general. As the war went on, the inevitable limitations of voluntary action persuaded many to adopt his conclusions if not his philosophy. Social workers and others observed among some M.P.s 'an undercurrent of hostility to anything in the nature of voluntary organization'.[4] And the Statutory Committee itself had to take note of 'the trend of public opinion in the direction of making the whole cost for supplementary pensions and other grants a direct charge on the National Exchequer . . .'.[5] The values were changing.

Beliefs about the objects of government were also undergoing a sea change, as may be seen from the subsequent history of the Statutory Committee. In October 1916 the Government announced its proposal to establish a Pensions Board under one of the existing Ministries.[6] The intention was to transfer to the Board most of the Statutory Committee's work of administering supplementary pensions,[7] but not the care and training of wounded soldiers.[8] The House of Commons would have none of it. 'Unofficial members of all parties imposed their will so effectively on the Government', the Parliamentary Correspondent of *The Times* reported, that the 'Bill was virtually withdrawn after a short debate, to be remodelled in accordance with the wishes of the House'.[9] But he added this significant comment:

'Ministers have bowed to *force majeure*, and the chief concern of the public now will be to secure that their amendments in the scheme shall not

[1] ibid., Q. 1107 and 1105.

[2] *Labour in War Time*, 1915, p. 95.

[3] ibid., 96.

[4] W. A. Bailward, 38 C.O.R. 1915, 271.

[5] Cd. 8750, p. 8.

[6] Devine, op. cit., p. 161.   [7] ibid.

[8] *The Times*, 28th Nov. 1916.   [9] ibid.

bring the question of pensions into the arena of party politics to be used as a power in the electioneering game. Any tendencies of this sort will be vigorously resisted.'[1]

That this danger was seriously considered in some influential quarters is confirmed by a *Times* second leader published that very day:

'One of the future dangers to be carefully avoided is that war pensions may become the sport of party politics, and the establishment of a full-blown Ministry undoubtedly increases that danger. We shall have the parties bidding against each other for popular support by *promises* of enlarged pensions.'[2]

Such anxieties had been expressed before. In 1915, W. A. Bailward had pointed to dangers he foresaw in the administration of pensions and grants: 'the pension fund in the United States has become a political engine of evil omen, and, as Lord Bryce has put it, "a source of infinite waste".'[3]

The reference to the United States is significant. If it cannot be shown that *The Times* leader-writer had the Grand Army of the Republic in mind, that may nevertheless be presumed because there was scarcely any other relevant experience to go on; at least, it was the outstanding example of the connexion between politics and (war) pensions. Members of the circle to which Geoffrey Dawson, as editor of *The Times*, belonged, were undoubtedly aware of it. One evening 'when the War was yet middle-aged', Wilfrid Ashley, M.P., grandson of the seventh Earl of Shaftesbury, was discussing the American Civil War and its aftermath with an American newspaper editor, and heard from him that 'one of the outstanding features in his memory was the number of maimed men in the country town where he lived, the noisy thump as they stumped on the wooden sidewalk when passing his father's house'. Ashley also learned (if he did not already know) about the Grand Army, and 'of its widespread influence, for good and evil, which the organization exercised in the life of the United States for at least twenty years after the conclusion of peace'.[4] It is very likely[5] that the 'evil' was a function of that relationship between pensions and politics of which *The Times* leader-writer had written.

Three days later *The Times* carried a letter, signed 'Observer', that took the leading article as its text. That he too had American experience in mind was revealed when he referred to the 'danger of war pensions becoming a political party cry, and hence, as in the

---

[1] ibid.   [2] ibid.

[3] 38 C.O.R. 1915, 273.

[4] *Comrades' Journal*, Feb. 1919, 4.

[5] Mary Dearing, *Veterans in Politics*, 1952, passim.

flagrant case of America, a national danger and disgrace'. He supported his view by a recent experience of his own. He had been present at the formation of a new local committee 'in a remote part of the country'. 'The astute Radical agent' packed the meeting and got his nominees elected in place of the 'non-political ladies' who had served before. So 'the association for a large district was turned from a benevolent association of persons well acquainted with the facts and above influence, into a party organization presumably to be used in party interests'.[1]

What alternative did these anxious commentators have in mind? *The Times* had already shown its hand. In the second leader already cited, the suggestion had been made that 'later on, when the scheme has taken permanent shape and the administration has established a smooth-working routine, the whole thing might well be transferred to a permanent non-political board'.[2] 'Observer' also took this line but showed a greater sense of urgency; after revealing the machinations of the 'Radical agent', he went on to argue for a non-political Board while things were in the melting pot. 'If once the thing becomes political, it will remain so'.[3] On the same day *The Times* revealed that it, too, was coming round to some such compromise. 'Many members', it was reported, were not 'fully satisfied' that everything had been done 'to prevent the danger of pensions becoming an electioneering issue. A single and all-powerful Minister is, after all, but a politician, and it is suggested that he should work through a Board of Commissioners. Such a Board, it is contended, would secure beyond doubt effective control over Government officials and good executive management and provide a check on anything like political corruption'.[4] Here was a belief that helped to maintain voluntaryism.

'Observer's' letter reveals the other aspect of the belief that politicians could not be trusted to administer pensions with propriety. There were many who feared not only electioneering in the broad sense but also improper influence locally. In 1915 W. A. Bailward asserted that local pensions committees were sometimes subjected to political pressure, and that there had been extravagance in spending funds to which the committee members had not contributed.[5] Earlier in the year Eleanor Rathbone had expressed the view that 'the administration of large sums of money by local authority [*i.e.*, a local committee] dependent upon the popular vote opened up the possibilities of corruption and favouritism'.[6] Later, the *Edinburgh Review* was to take up the same position: 'One of the worst effects of

[1] *The Times*, 1st Dec. 1916.
[3] 1st Dec. 1916.
[5] op. cit., pp. 274 and 275.

[2] 28th Nov. 1916.
[4] 1st Dec. 1916.
[6] 39 C.O.R. May 1916, 225.

D

the change [the setting up of the Statutory Committee and the local war pensions committees] has been to introduce the unhealthy atmosphere of local politics into the relief work'. Some of the working-class members were not only 'too class-conscious' but also too 'open-handed' with public funds. Under a State system there was a danger of political pressure to get benefits for 'political friends and supporters'.[1]

These remarks cannot of course be assumed to be completely representative of current beliefs; all the commentators spoke from the standpoint of voluntaryism. Nor do the beliefs have to be valid; they need only have been held by some influential groups in order to be cited as having given some support to the prevailing values about the objects of government.

The prevailing values about the functions of government also drew some support from two other beliefs about the virtues of voluntaryism and the disadvantages of *étatisme*. One of these took the form of an out-of-hand condemnation of government red tape. For General Elles, of the Surrey S.S.F.A., an expedient such as the Statutory Committee had 'the brand of officialdom on it', by which he meant 'red tape'.[2] The Government, another S.S.F.A. worker asserted, had just followed 'accepted practice'—'when in doubt form more committees'.[3] The reverse of that coin was the postulated flexibility of voluntaryism:

'The more this work is brought under State control the more difficult will become the administration of supplementary grants. However carefully rules may be drawn, there will always be hard cases . . . The adjustment is easy so long as there is a voluntary service administering private or semi-private funds, but when State servants are administering public money all applicants are equal, and it is not easy to show why such grants should be given to one and not to others.'[4]

It was a common belief: the Prince of Wales, among others, expressed it and so did the Statutory Committee itself.[5]

The belief in the flexibility of voluntary action may have been bound up with notions of public accountability, but it rested partly on the view that voluntaryism introduced 'a cheerful human element into a concern where constant freshness of outlook and sympathetic study of individual cases are essential to success'.[6] This was probably what Bailward had in mind in putting forward his fantastic suggestion that 'regiments or groups of regiments' [rather than local

[1] Jan. 1917, 156 and 157.
[2] Gildea, op. cit., pp. 209 and 210.
[3] ibid., 210.   [4] 225 Ed. Rev. Jan. 1917, 157.
[5] Cd. 8750 (1917), pp. 2 and 13.
[6] Basil Williams, *Raising and Training the New Armies*, 1918, p. 312.

committees] should be used 'as the medium for the assessment and payment of these pensions'. The old soldier, he thought, would prefer to deal with such organizations than with 'semi-municipal civilian committees'.[1] The proposal, absurd as it was, is interesting as an indication that older habits of thought survived even a fundamental transformation of scene.

Just as, in terms of the objects of government, a movement towards a new consensus could be discerned, so also was there a tendency towards a new consensus about the modes of government. Generally, the organization of a people-war gave added impetus to a trend noticeable even before 1914. But the groups within the community made their adjustments at varying speeds and with varying degrees of acceptance, so that the movement towards a new consensus was neither rapid nor uniform. For this inquiry, the first important breach in the defences occurred when all the older ex-service societies other than the Patriotic Fund were displaced by the Statutory Committee, and when, at the periphery, S.S.F.A. was unceremoniously thrust aside and superseded by local war pensions committees. The essential point about these committees was that they were representative, *i.e.*, the older, 'self-elected' societies were replaced by bodies that were basically elective.[2] It was this feature that interested contemporaries found 'striking', and that some found disagreeable and even alarming.[3] The representative character of these committees varied from place to place, appearing in London almost 'as sub-committees of the borough council'[4]; everywhere most of the members were drawn from the appropriate local authority. Significantly, too, there was provision for the representation of women and of Labour.[5] Clearly, the new democratic values were being to some extent incorporated in our system of public administration.

[1] 38 C.O.R. 1915, 276.

[2] Cmd. 14 (1919), 1st Report, Ministry of Pensions, p. 6.

[3] 10 *Progress* 1915, 142–3.

[4] ibid.

Departmental Committee of Inquiry into the Administration of the Ministry of Pensions, 1921, 24 (66).

V

THE AGENTS OF CHANGE

VALUES and beliefs, then, were changing, but at different rates among different groups. The tendency to prescribe a wider role for government was gaining strength but in relation to ex-servicemen it was nevertheless, in certain respects, resisted by the highest official groups and by some unofficial groups. Even within groups there were deep divisions. Thus as late as the autumn of 1916 the Lords was opposed to the Commons, while within the Commons the back benchers were ranged against the Government on the major (relevant) issue of the day. As for a share in the decision-making process, those deemed good enough to die for Britain were not yet considered wise enough to cast a vote for Britain's Parliament, though the actual opportunities to vote were in fact few. And within the ex-service field itself, the returned soldier was throughout 1916 not even represented on the local war pensions committees.

Of course, cultural values are never uniformly spread within a community despite the 'strain for consistency' there must always be incompatibilities and even conflicts. In Britain in (or about) 1916 the conflicts were perhaps of sufficient severity to be called rifts in the culture. Why should these rifts have emerged? The immediate answer is that the older values were a long time a-dying, while new values were being urgently pressed upon the community's attention. Despite the then recent change in values[1] implied in the Liberal Government's 'welfare state' legislation (*e.g.*, the introduction of national health insurance and old-age pensions), the voluntary principle must still have commanded wide support. In recruiting for the Armed Forces, for instance, the voluntary principle was retained until 1916, despite our being locked in a war of the Titans. On the other hand, the fundamentally new situation of a nation-in-arms produced and forced consideration of a new set of values.

Such an answer, of course, raises the question in another form, but it is not to the purpose of this inquiry to go on to ask why the older values were cherished for so long. Yet the 'other half' of the re-

---

[1] Cultural change is an immensely complicated subject. In this study the phrases 'change in values', 'new values', etc., include a re-emergence of older values long neglected as well as a 'tilting of the balance' in favour of values that, although to some extent in opposition, are concurrently held.

formulated question is highly relevant to this study, for among the instrumentalities that thrust forward the new values, organized ex-servicemen in all probability rank high. The new values were, so to speak, carried on the shoulders of a new, determined, self-confident generation of returned soldiers and sailors. That being so, one is obliged to sketch in the background to the role of ex-servicemen as agents of cultural change in this period.

At least three factors contributed to a new set of values and beliefs: the nature of the weapons, the character of the soldiers (and hence of the returned veterans), and the quality of their experiences. Already gunpowder had made 'all men alike tall', by which Carlyle meant that it 'democratizes fighting'.[1] This is perhaps what Adam Smith had in mind when, discussing one effect of the invention of firearms, he wrote:

'The nature of the weapon, though it by no means puts the awkward upon a level with the skilful, puts him more nearly so than he ever was before.'[2]

The Lee-Enfield rifle, the Lewis machine-gun and the 25-pounder gave added point to these remarks: universal weapons imply universal suffrage, or at least a wide participation in the decision-making process.

There were more fundamental considerations, which may be brought out by adapting Adam Smith's famous discussion of defence.[3] In an advanced economy, there are only two methods by which the decision-makers 'can make any tolerable provision for the public defence': by a militia or by a standing army. The 'essential difference' between these 'two different species of military force' is that:

'In a militia the character of the labourer, artificer, or tradesman, predominates over that of the soldier; in a standing army, that of the soldier over every other character . . .'[4]

He had in mind the military virtues, as had Friedrich von Bernhardi writing in this century,[5] but the distinction may also be extended to the civic virtues of *ex*-soldiers who have been drawn from the 'militia' in a broad sense, even if the militia as a formal institution has been discarded.

Although standing armies were known to the ancient world, as a characteristic institution they are of fairly recent origin. The first regular standing army since Roman times was established in France

---

[1] Quoted in J. F. C. Fuller, *Armament and History*, 1946, p. 83.
[2] *The Wealth of Nations*, 1893 ed., p. 548.
[3] Book V., ch. I, Part I.   [4] 1893 ed., p. 547.
[5] *On War of Today*, English ed., 1912, Vol. I, p. 62.

in the middle of the fifteenth century.[1] Generally, 'before the end of the sixteenth century it was realized that the practice of disbanding and paying-off regiments at the end of each campaigning season, and re-enlisting them the following spring, was an expensive way of doing business'.[2] For this reason and other (essentially military) reasons, mercenaries tended to be kept on for the winter, and so there 'arose the modern standing army'.[3]

Our own standing army emerged but slowly. 'Tudor rule was unsupported by any large professional army'.[4] Authorized by the Bill of Rights in 1689 and regulated by the Mutiny Acts and other statutes, it became sufficiently significant to be called 'a new feature of English government' only about the middle of the eighteenth century, when apart from the Irish establishment, it had a strength of about 19,000, which soon after the accession of George III was about doubled.[5] In this way, within a century, a standing army was built into the Constitution.[6]

Standing armies naturally vary in size and composition. Taking for granted a powerful Navy, we relied primarily upon a small force of volunteers serving, after Cardwell had spent himself in his reforms, the well-known 'six and six' (with the Colours and in the Reserve), and until the South African War it was they who bore the heat of the day in many a foreign land. Our wars were fought

'By a class of men set apart from the general mass of the community, trained to particular uses, formed to peculiar notions, governed by peculiar laws, marked by particular distinctions; who live in bodies by themselves, not fixed to any certain spot, nor bound by any settled employment; who "neither toil nor spin"; whose home is their regiment; whose sole profession and duty it is to encounter and destroy the enemies of their country, wherever they are to be met with, and who, in consideration of their performing that duty and the better to enable them to perform it, receive a stipend from the State exempting them from the necessity of seeking a provision in any other mode of life.'[7]

The 1914–18 War, on the other hand, was fought essentially by the 'general mass of the community'. Beginning with only a small force,

---

[1] 1445. Richard A. Preston, Sydney F. Wise and Herman O. Werner, *Men in Arms*, 1956, p. 89.

[2] Michael Roberts, *The Military Revolution 1560–1660*, Queen's University of Belfast (an inaugural lecture), n.d. (? 1956), p. 18.

[3] ibid., p. 19. I have followed Professor Roberts against those other interpreters of the rise of standing armies to whom he himself refers in text and footnote.

[4] Sir Lindsay Keir, *The Constitutional History of Modern Britain*, 3rd ed., 1947, p. 36.

[5] ibid., 305.   [6] ibid.

[7] Quoted by Wilfrid Ashley in *Comrades' Journal* Feb. 1919, 4.

we recruited a million by the end of November 1914,[1] and in the four agonizing years in which Europe ate up 'her own young',[2] nearly five million men 'went or were fetched', representing some 11 per cent of the populations of England, Wales and Scotland, or between one in four or one in five of the male population of those three countries.[3] This meant that about eleven amateurs were recruited for every professional (*i.e.*, members of the Regular Army, Reserve or Special Reserve) who had been available at the outbreak of war.[4]

Thus our professional army was engulfed by the incoming civilian tide, *i.e.*, in effect by the 'militia' of Adam Smith's conception, even though the militia as such had already disappeared. Their values were the values not of a standing army with its strict hierarchical arrangements and special loyalties but those of relatively well educated men with civic roots, some independence of thought and political experience. Like Cromwell's men, they were no 'mere mercenary army': they were 'Englishmen' who would have readily agreed—indeed asserted—that 'surely our being soldiers hath not stript us of that interest . . .'[5] And among 'Englishmen' the idea of democracy was already growing.

The war experiences of the men of the New Army must have reinforced these original notions, or given them a new sense of urgency and meaning, or shocked men into receiving or creating such ideas where none had existed in that rapidly retreating Golden Age 'before the war'. That there was a comradeship of the trenches only a few, overcome perhaps by the horror and misery of it all, would wish to deny: it was the source of a number of ex-service associations, and of one (in Germany) confined solely to front-line fighters. In the trenches officers and men were brought together by the daily crucifixion, 'by the wet bond of blood',[6] by 'whiz-bangs' and 'minnies' (*minenwerfers*), by giant rats and tiny but ubiquitous lice, and by their sense of separateness from 'the staff, Army Service Corps, lines of communication troops, base units, home-service units, and then the civilians down to the detested grades of journalists, profiteers, "starred" men exempted from enlistment, conscientious objectors, members of the Government'.[7] And if they went home on leave, it was to an England that trench-soldiers scarcely understood, where people talked 'patriotism', a 'remote' sentiment, 'fit only for

---

[1] British Army Reports, Cmd. 1193/1920, p. 60.

[2] H. M. Tomlinson, *All Our Yesterdays*, 1930, p. 421.

[3] Cmd. 1193, p. 60. Ireland: 3 per cent; 1 in 16 of the male population.

[4] ibid.

[5] Quoted in C. H. Firth, *Cromwell's Army*, 2nd ed., p. 355, n. 1.

[6] Robert Graves, *Poems 1914–26*, 1927, p. 62.

[7] Robert Graves, *Goodbye to all that*, 1929, p. 241.

civilians'.[1] It was at home too that a gallant officer, having been first given a hearty welcome at his club, found himself left alone. 'The fact is, I was unpatriotic, if you please, and hadn't known it. One has to go home to find that out'.[2] Doubtless he would have felt at home only when he returned to his own kind in that 'continuous ditch of hidden men' which meandered over the hills and through the valleys of France like 'raw interminable wounds in the green of the earth'.[3]

There was in a sense a democratic flavour about life in that continuous ditch, as also in Gallipoli, where a youthful A. P. Herbert found that each officer had his own private hole, set democratically among the men's . . .'[4] Yet the trenches, and the army generally, had another face. To John Campbell, later a prominent figure in the Scottish Federation of Discharged and Demobilized Sailors and Soldiers, it seemed that

'. . . there was no comradeship in the trenches. It was simply a case of members of the working classes held down by brutal and iron discipline. Different rations, different pay and different risk. The class line was as clear in France as it is at home; there was no comradeship in the trenches to perpetuate.'[5]

This was an extreme view, but setting aside 'different risk', which for second-lieutenants could easily be turned against its author, it was true that rations, pay and conditions were different. As Siegfried Sassoon was to say later, '. . . we were in clover compared with the men.'[6] On a troopship, when the bugle rang the Officers' Mess call, the men hummed:

'Officers' wives have pudding and pies,
Sergeants' wives have skilly',

which was a 'cynical' though 'tolerant' comment 'on the fine meal to which their officers were now strolling.'[7] The point need not be laboured since the army is, of course, essentially a hierarchical society, with clearly differentiated statuses and rewards. It is obvious too that since the soldier's real trade is killing and since the occupational hazards are therefore extremely high (of which sudden death

[1] ibid., p. 240.

[2] Tomlinson, op. cit., p. 419.

[3] ibid., pp. 336, 337 and 335.

[4] *Secret Battle*, 1919, p. 25.

[5] *Ex-Service Men at Grips*, (pamphlet), 1920, p. 29, (record of a debate at Paisley in Oct. 1919 between Dr. Alexander Jamieson, Glasgow, of the Comrades of the Great War, and John Campbell, Paisley).

[6] *Memoirs of a Fox-Hunting Man*, 1929 ed., p. 345; also Herbert, ibid.

[7] Ernest Raymond, *The Jesting Army*, 1930, p. 10.

itself may be the least disagreeable), discipline must always be strict if not severe. But the inevitable may still be unacceptable, and there must have been many discharged men whose thinking was different from John Campbell's only in being rather less extreme. Indeed the National Federation itself bore witness to it until 1919 by deliberately barring officers (other than rankers) from ordinary membership.

If contrasts between the treatment of officers and men in France and elsewhere must have set many soldiers (and hence ex-servicemen) thinking (or thinking still more) along democratic lines, what of contrasts within the commissioned ranks themselves? Between Special Reserve commissions and temporary commissions in the New Army there lay a great gulf. The old retired regular officer who got Sassoon into the Special Reserve 'wanted me to do the thing properly. Greatly as he admired their spirit, he couldn't help looking down a bit on those Kitchener's Army battalions'.[1] At camp in May 1915 these 'new' officers 'to some extent' clashed with 'the more carefully selected Special Reserve commissions (like my own) and the public school boys who came from the Royal Military College'. The New Army officers were different in manners, accents and style of dress, and as late as September 1915 the one who reported with Sassoon to the 1st Battalion of the Royal Welch Fusiliers was 'received with reservations of cordiality'.[2] Before the war one of the company commanders had lived on unearned income; one of his (first-rate) platoon commanders had been a clerk in Somerset House, who 'had never hunted. He could swim like a fish, but no social status was attached to that'.[3] Earlier that year, Robert Graves, having joined the 2nd Battalion of the same regiment, was surprised to find the two regular battalions playing a polo-match, and that in his battalion subalterns who could not ride had to attend riding-school every afternoon when in billets.[4] To his obvious question whether there was a war on, he received the superb reply: 'The battalion doesn't recognize it socially.'[5]

Graves's experience cannot be taken as typical if only because the 2nd Battalion were not typical; they had been a lucky battalion (in a lucky brigade) and so they had not yet buried their professionals. Nor, of course, must one make the elementary error of assuming that Graves, Sassoon, Herbert, Blunden and the rest were a representative sample of the soldiers of the day. But some such contrast between the

[1] Sassoon, op. cit., p. 324.

[2] ibid., pp. 331, 335 and 345. Sassoon uses, as a disguise, 'the Royal Flintshire Fusiliers'.

[3] ibid., p. 348.   [4] *Goodbye to all that*, p. 167

[5] ibid., pp. 167–8. It deserves to be called 'superb' rather than 'silly' because the battalion were not skilful on the polo field only; they were magnificent in the trenches too.

new officers and the old, and perhaps, up to 1916,[1] between two kinds of new officers, probably left a mark on those who were made to feel just a little inferior, or who in other ways became conscious for the first time of class distinction. The officers 'who had never given orders to servants, let alone soldiers'[2] are likely to have returned to civilian life with some notion, however vague, that they wanted to have a hand in that general order-giving in the community at large which is here called decision-making. That does not mean that their experiences made them move Left, though this may have been true of Federationist Ernest Thurtle, later to become a Labour M.P. Other ex-officers with 'order-giving' aspirations chose other parties, while many became indifferent or even hostile to party. But whatever their party attitudes might be, they could all be active in the associations precisely because these conferred participation in the decision-making process. In general, we might indeed liken the Old Army to the Roman Church and the New Army to the Reformed Church.[3] In the Old Army, 'the dogmas were firm, the discipline strong, the procedure stereotyped . . . A weak individual in a position of authority was protected by the full strength of the system. But the men of the New Army were strangers to discipline, and cherished notions of personal liberty. They jibbed at harsh, arbitrary rules'. Hence the New Army officers had to develop the qualities of real leadership, which they could later bring to bear on the problems they encountered in civilian life.[4]

There were thought-provoking contrasts not only between the treatment of officers and men, and at first between the social origin and prestige of officers themselves, but also between those in France (especially of course in the trenches) and those at home. One contrast has been already noted: the difference in war 'fever'. Another was the inequality of sacrifice. There was not merely the well-known contrast between a soldier's shilling a day and the earnings of a munitions worker, but also that other contrast implied in Sir Ian Heathcoat-Amory's vow, at the close of 1916, that the Tiverton Foxhounds, of which he was Master, would not meet again until we had defeated the Germans.[5] For him this may well have been a considerable sacrifice, but the contrast between it and the sacrifices made a few months earlier at High Wood and Delville Wood is striking. Few soldiers would have known about the Tiverton Fox-

---

[1] ibid., p. 341: from 1916 onwards, few of the new officers were 'gentlemen', but 'their deficiency in manners was amply compensated for by their greater efficiency in action'.

[2] E. S. Turner, *Gallant Gentlemen*, 1956, p. 277.

[3] E. S. Turner, p. 278, citing Donald Hankey, *A Student in Arms*.

[4] ibid.   [5] *The Times*, 30th Dec. 1916.

hounds, but they all knew about the profiteers. And ex-soldiers could easily compare their own pensions with the standard of living that some people enjoyed even in wartime. Just before Christmas 1916, attention was drawn in *The Times* to 'the extravagance flaunted in shops and advertisements': 'quite a good *table d'hôte* luncheon' for 5s.; tea for 2s. 6d.; and dinner for 7s. 6d.[1] Only some three months earlier complaints had been made in Blackburn that two soldiers had been discharged with a mere 5s. 3d. *a week*.[2] Less than two months earlier married men there had been discharged with 4s. 8d. and 6s. 8d. a week,[3] while in near-by Burnley a man who had earned 30s. a week before enlistment was said to be receiving 4s. 8d. a week for himself and his wife, although 'totally unable to follow his employment owing to injuries in Egypt'.[4] The precise circumstances are not described but matter little for our purpose because such cases, especially seen against the background of other people's comfortable and sometimes even luxurious living, were certainly major factors in precipitating the Blackburn and District Discharged Sailors' and Soldiers' Association, the first significant group in the ex-servicemen's movement in this country.

In short, there were more senses than one in which some members of the community could be said to enjoy 'different rations, different pay and different risk'.[5] Such differences in the distribution of the burden of war must have strengthened the democratic aspirations of soldiers and ex-soldiers not merely in the individual voting sense but also in the desire to substitute either their own associations or official groups for the older ex-service societies. But Snowden's view that the soldier ought to be an elector, not as a soldier but on the general ground that 'every man and woman should have the vote'[6] would not have been universally shared, while S.S.F.A., understandably resented and resisted its replacement by local representative committees. Since such differences were manifestations of differences in values about the modes of government, here was another conflict within the political culture.

When differences in values about the objects of government are taken into the reckoning, it may be enough, cumulatively, to permit one to speak of a rift in the culture. Men whose very lives had come under Government control were, with bitter exceptions, likely to be predisposed to invoke Government action when some essential decision or policy touching them as returned soldiers was required.

[1] 23rd Dec. 1916.

[2] *Northern Daily Telegraph* (Blackburn), 14th Sept. 1916.

[3] ibid., 1st Nov. 1916.   [4] ibid., 16th Oct. 1916.

[5] See above, p. 42.

[6] *Northern Daily Telegraph*, 9th Oct. 1916.

Emotional attitudes tended to widen the gap. That emotion has a fundamental role in any political order is one of those old truths that has to be perpetually rediscovered. Aristotle knew that it lay at the very basis of political union.[1] Burke found emotion lodged in the interstices of the political structure and with a majestic sweep placed it in the forefront of his philosophy; but the contemporary discussion probably owes most to Graham Wallas's adaptation to the realm of politics of what was in his day the new psychology.[2]

Wallas's emphasis on emotion was part of his general attempt to free political science from the 'tendency to exaggerate the intellectuality of mankind'. In order to demonstrate that political impulses are not simply intellectual inferences from calculations of means and ends, he was led to single out emotions such as affection, fear, ridicule and the desire for property.[3] With his general theme we are not concerned: our interest is focused on emotion in so far as it maintains the stability of a political system, the 'solidarity' of a 'loyalty area'.

The strength of the emotional commitment of the British people to the prosecution of the 1914–18 War is well known. Whatever divisions within our ranks might have been revealed had Germany not invaded Belgium were prevented from becoming serious by that callous turn of events and by the cynical destruction of the 'scrap of paper'. The astonishing rush to the colours reflected the national mood: on 4th August it took twenty policemen twenty minutes to clear the recruiting officer's path to his office in Great Scotland Yard.[4] The first hundred thousand spoke for millions, for almost everybody except one wing of the Labour Party. That proviso has its importance, however, as we shall see, because some people thought that the Blackburn Association was run by 'Pacifist M.P.s'; but the main consideration is that a rift in the lute did in time appear. It was not so much that the rush to the colours, once artificially checked to give the administrators and clerks a chance to recover their breath,[5] then had to be revived by methods more appropriate to a circus or jamboree, although this was a portent. It was not so much the white feathers in Piccadilly; it was rather that as the soldiers, burrowing like rabbits into the earth, settled down to the long years of apparently useless slaughter, they were slowly drained of emotion at the very time when civilians at home, for obvious psychological reasons, were becoming more and more emotionally aroused until in the Election

---

[1] *Ethics*, Bk. VIII, ch. I; Graham Wallas, *Human Nature in Politics*, 2nd ed.. 1910, p. 30.

[2] op. cit., introduction, esp. pp. 14–15 and 18–19.

[3] ibid., ch. I.

[4] Basil Williams, op. cit., p. 6.

[5] ibid., p. 10.

that followed on the heels of the Armistice the slightest reference to a 'tough' German policy would win an easy round of applause.

That the civilian population reacted in this way is not in the least surprising; on the contrary, if they had remained calm and rational (were that psychologically conceivable) it would have been astonishing. Equally it would have been astonishing if the men in the trenches had not undergone a profound emotional change. There was still a patriotism of the trenches, but, as we know,[1] it came to have almost nothing in common with the patriotism of the West End clubs, or with that of humbler establishments. Standing on Paddington Station, Robert Graves and Siegfried Sassoon felt that England was a foreign land, where a different emotional language was spoken.[2] Sassoon's famous acts of renunciation (the almost ceremonial casting away of his Military Cross and that letter to the authorities which would have recoiled on the head of a less well-connected man) were not characteristic, yet the emotional barrier between the men overseas and most civilians at home was obvious enough. And whereas in the realms of values and beliefs, soldiers, and hence ex-servicemen, were to some extent separated from the rest of the community, in the domain of the emotions they tended to be isolated. For the emotions of which they had been drained were the 'ordinary' civilian emotions; in another sense they were more emotional than the people at home because they bore the image of their dead comrades, perhaps even of the way they had died.

Set off, then, from the rest of the community by their values, beliefs and emotional attitudes, ex-servicemen founded their own associations. Specific circumstances provided the occasion for their emergence as well as the substance of their early claims, but the cultural factor has to be married to the circumstantial if the origin and character of such associations are to be fully understood. To a large extent these associations were precipitates of the soldiers' (and veterans') values, beliefs and emotions.

In turn the new associations helped to spread the new values. Doubtless there were other forces at work, but the intensity with which ex-soldiers held their views probably put their associations high among the important agents of cultural change in this period. In a sense, therefore, ex-servicemen, by striving to realize their own values and to solve their own problems, went a long way towards closing the gap in our political culture, and so towards solving a basic community problem—how to reconcile change with stability.

[1] Se above, p. 42.   [2] *Goodbye to all that*, p. 283.

VI

ECONOMIC FACTORS

DOUBTLESS the men of Blackburn who, about the end of September 1916, were groping their way towards organization,[1] and, later that year, the Londoners who used to meet each week in an old shop in High Street, Poplar,[2] were also the product of particular circumstances. These may be resolved for convenience into economic and non-economic components. The 'economic situation' is a handy phrase that requires interpretation in context. Risking over-simplification, one may interpret it for ex-servicemen in 1916 as meaning employment and (war) pensions. The general employment position remained remarkably good. Within a year of the outbreak of war, unemployment in insured industries had fallen below 1 per cent and generally remained at that level until the Armistice.[3] In October 1916, when the Blackburn Association was under way, unemployment in insured industries was only a half of 1 per cent.[4] Thus the administrators of the National Relief Fund found employment conditions 'exceptionally good'; except for the East Coast seaside towns, there was 'practically no distress among the industrial classes as a whole'.[5] Such conditions persisted.[6] In these 'exceptionally good' employment conditions ex-servicemen generally fared quite well as long as the war lasted. Up to early December 1916, about 175,000 had been reported to the employment exchanges as discharged, of whom rather less than half responded to an invitation to present themselves for work.[7] Of those who presented themselves, over 38,000 were placed. The 90,000 or so who did not arrive either went back to their old jobs or found new ones as soon as they were physically fit, a 'large number' going into munitions.[8] This presum-

[1] *Northern Daily Telegraph*, 14th Sept. 1916, and interviews with writer.

[2] Letter to writer from G. W. Nash, the chairman, 24th Sept. 1955.

[3] International Labour Office, Studies and Reports, 1922, No. 6, Unemployment Series, p. 18, Table 1. This was in all industries in the U.K. covered by the returns, but it should be noted that the statistics for successive years are 'not altogether comparable' (ibid. p. 28).

[4] ibid.   [5] Cd. 8621 (1917), p. 4 (7).

[6] Cd. 8921 (1918), p. 4 (5).

[7] Cd. 8750 (1917), p. 20. Effective date: 8th Dec. 1916. 175,193 reported, 85,161 responded, of whom 38,776 were placed.

[8] ibid.

ably is what happened to the men (43,000 or so) who were not placed by the employment exchanges; on 8th December, only 2,919 soldiers remained on the register.

It follows that up to late 1916 about 13 out of every 17 men reported as discharged found jobs for themselves.[1] In so far as the official statistics accurately represented the ex-servicemen's employment situation, it is obvious that there was no general problem at the time.[2] Yet there were particular problems, partly because here and there particular disabilities may have been inhibiting but more fundamentally because many returned soldiers were unskilled. Before the war some had found themselves in blind-alley jobs; others had no doubt enlisted before they could learn a trade. A social worker, L. V. Shairp, who had been in touch with some 250 discharged soldiers on the books of Soldiers Help in a big industrial city in the North found that about one third of them were shown as labourers.[3] It is significant that the Blackburn men had drawn attention to themselves by standing about day after day at the top of Church Street.[4] And at a very early stage in its history the Blackburn Association was appealing to the local authority to stop engaging women and to arrange technical classes for training discharged men.[5]

This request for training is some confirmation that the problem was largely a problem of the unskilled or semi-skilled worker, which far from being confined to Blackburn was a matter of general importance. It was a familiar theme in contemporary discussion, from which, up to 1917 at least, one receives an impression of unsatisfactory provision. Part of the responsibility for that must no doubt be placed on the shoulders of the men themselves: in the 'abnormal condition of the labour market', many men who should have sought training were tempted by 'high wages' into temporary jobs, setting off their present gain against the future.[6] But, as the same observer noted, if that was the one of the two main reasons for the 'disappointing' response to such opportunities for training as existed, the other one essentially concerned the Government.[7] Since, up to March 1917, the rate of pension was related to the assumed loss of earning capacity, men already receiving an award feared that, once

---

[1] 90,032 did not turn up; add 43,466 [85,161—(38,776 + 2,919)] who did respond but were not placed through the exchanges: 133,498. The register may of course have been faulty.

[2] In 1915–18 the 'majority' of discharged men found work for themselves, the employment exchanges placing rather less than a half of those who registered. Cmd. 14 (1919), p. 54.

[3] 225 Ed. Rev. 1917, 120–1.   [4] Interviews with writer.

[5] *Northern Daily Telegraph*, 1st Nov. 1916.

[6] Shairp, ibid. See also Williams, op. cit., p. 285.

[7] Shairp, ibid., p. 121.

trained, they would either lose their pension or have it reduced, while men who had 'expectations' were loath to compromise them.[1] Moreover, there was 'often long delay before a man knew whether he was to get a pension or not . . .'; there were also other delays and mistakes, resulting in 'considerable hardship', and so the men's 'own resentment was a further barrier to training'.[2]

In other instances, 'stern necessity' may have prevented men from training for a new career. For although, on the recommendation of the local committees, extra allowances could be granted to men undergoing training, and although training fees could be paid, 'each case had to be investigated on its merits and there was no definite promise made by the State that this assistance would be given'.[3] 'Many maimed soldiers' may have felt that they could not afford an unremunerative period of training 'before the certainty of assistance had been made clear to them'.[4] What the official groups ought to have done from the first was to offer 'generous inducements to a maimed soldier to train himself for skilled work', and as claimable rights from, not supplicatory requests of, some local committee; but these reforms did not come about until March 1917.[5]

If there were obstacles to the acceptance of opportunities for training, the opportunities themselves were either not well enough known or simply inadequate. It sometimes happened that 'men who had been anxious to train themselves for good work have left hospital ignorant of the existence of Local Committees and of panels of employers and workmen ready to give them advice and provide help, and have drifted away and become lost before they could be told of the advantages within their reach'.[6] Nor were the facilities fully adequate. Shairp agreed that the local war pensions committees had not achieved much in this respect,[7] and the continuing muddle over the Statutory Committee even in 1917 doomed 'the treatment and training of disabled soldiers' to failure.[8]

The issue of training for work, then, was a basic factor in the specific (economic) circumstances that helped to precipitate at least one association of ex-servicemen. Even ex-servicemen in employment, however, sometimes found it expedient to band together, *e.g.*, one of the main sources of the National Federation was the deputation that F. A. Rumsey led to his North London employers in 'protest against the way the discharged men were being treated by them'.[9] What the

---

[1] ibid.

[2] ibid., p. 122.

[3] Williams, p. 285.

[4] ibid.

[5] ibid., p. 286.

[6] ibid., p. 284.

[7] ibid., p. 129.

[8] London correspondent, *Liverpool Post and Mercury*, 30th June 1917.

[9] H. Jellicorse, *The History of the Ex-Service Man Movement*, 1919, p. 5.

issue was on that occasion is not recorded,[1] but it is at least clear that the conditions of employment were among the catalysts of the ex-servicemen's movement.

The other major factor in the economic circumstances that stimulated ex-servicemen's associations was the inadequate scale of pensions and the peculiar conditions under which awards were made. The very small pensions that some discharged men in Blackburn and Burnley were receiving in the autumn of 1916 have already come to our notice in another connexion.[2] These may have simply been hard cases in which the men had failed to fulfil the conditions of the current Royal Warrant (or pensions code). A sharp distinction was drawn between a disability due to war service and one 'merely' aggravated by it, and correspondingly there were two different scales. Pre-war earnings were not taken into account, which may have been partly why the Burnley man who had earned 30s. a week before enlistment felt aggrieved.[3] On the other hand, the current earnings that a pensioner could be expected to receive were put in the balance,[4] a provision which was obviously unworkable.

In this context, however, the main impetus to organization probably came from the steady decline in the value of the pensions scale itself. Taking July 1914 as the base, one finds that by September 1916 the general index-number (including food) of retail prices had risen to 150; for food alone it had reached 165.[5] The rate of increase in the late summer and early autumn of 1916 was startling. Between August and September, retail food prices went up five points; in September/October the increase was more moderate—a mere three points—but the following month saw a spectacular jump of no fewer than ten points, which up to that time was the greatest single monthly increase of the war.[6] This was indeed a 'great acceleration', as Arthur Shadwell noted;[7] ex-servicemen and their wives may have used stronger language to describe it. Altogether, in 1916 alone,

---

[1] Just after the war ended, one of the issues was whether a firm could be expected to carry disabled men 'on its back'. The dismissal of two disabled men from a tobacco factory on the ground that 'they were no longer efficient workmen', which seems to have meant 'efficient' at normal market rates of wages, led to a strike. *The Times*, 10th and 11th Dec. 1918; *Halifax Daily Guardian*, 12th Dec. 1918.

[2] See above, p. 45.   [3] ibid.

[4] J. M. Hogge and T. H. Garside, *War Pensions and Allowances*, 1918, p. 129; Devine, op. cit., pp. 167–8.

[5] Arthur L. Bowley, *Prices and Wages in the United Kingdom, 1914–1920*, 1921, pp. 69–70.

[6] Bowley, p. 70.

[7] *The Nineteenth Century and After*, April 1917, 738.

retail food prices rose by thirty-nine points, and general retail prices (including food) by thirty points: these were the greatest increases in any (calendar) year during the whole of the war.[1] No wonder an M.P. told a meeting in London in December 1916 that 'there was not a single member of the House of Commons who did not daily receive from his constituents despairing appeals for help from men who had been discharged from the Army'.[2] Jellicorse, too, the first historian of the ex-servicemen's movement, noted a flood of bitter complaints throughout 1916[3].

Thus economic factors operating within the matrix of ex-servicemen's values, beliefs and emotions tended, late in 1916, to precipitate associations that were *of* them and not merely *for* them. But there were other factors, too, of which some account now becomes necessary.

[1] Bowley, ibid.

[2] *The Times*, 18th Dec. 1916.

[3] op. cit., pp. 3–4.

VII

NON-ECONOMIC FACTORS

IN order to understand the non-economic factors it is essential to consider in outline the course of recruiting during the first two years or so of the war. For this inquiry, two phases may be distinguished: the period of (more or less) voluntary recruiting that lasted from the outbreak of war to the end of 1915; and the period of compulsion that opened the following January.

Within the first period, four sub-phases are discernible. There was the first five weeks or so of delirious enthusiasm. The recruiting officer's struggle to reach his office in Great Scotland Yard has already been recounted.[1] There were similar scenes all over Britain.[2] Four weeks after the declaration of war, over 30,000 recruits were attested in one day—as many as were expected in a whole year in peacetime.[3] In a single month the Army 'received ten times the number of men that the machine had been designed to receive in a whole year'. Under such 'tremendous pressure', the recruiting machine came to 'the point of breaking down';[4] that explains why, after their enlistment, the youthful Vernon Bartlett and his two companions sat 'day after day on the hot sands of Branksome'.[5] Amateur recruiters came to the rescue by cutting through the regulations (one M.P. in a Midlands city even abolished the bath that recruits were required to have), but on 11th September the War Office, bowing to the inevitable, raised the standards in order to restrict the supply.[6]

The fire so roughly if unavoidably damped down was not easily revived; when the recruiting figures showed to what extent enthusiasm had cooled, standards were reduced, but to persuade men to join now required the fairground methods of the Parliamentary Recruiting Committee and their local party stalwarts, canvassing every household as they had never canvassed before even for themselves, dispatching eight million letters, issuing fifty-four million posters,

---

[1] See above, p. 46.   [2] Williams, op. cit., p. 6.

[3] ibid., p. 7.

[4] H.C. 126 and 185, Select Committee on Military Service (Review of Exceptions) Act 1917, Mins. of ev., Q. 2; Williams, pp. 7–8.

[5] Vernon Bartlett, *This is my Life*, Evergreen Books ed., 1941, p. 38.

[6] Williams, p. 10.

leaflets and other literature, holding 12,000 meetings and making 20,000 speeches[1] that were destined to become part of the ex-service-men's 'oral tradition', to be recalled even today with a wry smile or with bitterness according to mood and temperament. By July 1915 the Government had succeeded in enlisting more than two million men in the land forces of the Crown by what Williams innocently called 'purely voluntary methods'.[2] The Government had also succeeded not only in disrupting industrial production by taking 'tens of thousands'[3] of our essential workers for the Army and Navy but also in ensuring, so far as humanly possible, that our fittest should on no account survive.

The National Registration Act of 1915 marks the opening of another, more orderly phase within the period of voluntary recruiting (it also initiated the procedure for converting Britain into a nation-in-arms). Registration began in the middle of August, and when it was completed a month later, the local authorities were required to hand over to the recruiting authorities the cards of all men aged 18 to 41.[4] Thus the scene was set for what in the language of a later war might be called 'Operation Round-Up'. The orators of the Parliamentary Recruiting Committee refurbished their perorations; invitations hung from every hoarding; military bands tried to set the feet tapping (in a rhythmic movement leading to the recruiting office).

In October, Lord Derby was brought into the War Office by Kitchener to be head of the recruiting drive. Derby introduced the group system of recruiting under which men attested but were then placed in reserve according to age and marital status to await calling-up on that basis. If most of the single men failed to attest, compulsion would be applied to that category before married men were taken.[5]

The immediate result of the Derby Scheme was that about two and a quarter million men attested and another 275,000 anticipated their fate by direct enlistment in the Army.[6] Once again the machine was overwhelmed.[7] The Military Register was 'extremely elaborate', and worked properly only if a man enlisted where he was registered; otherwise he was not marked off. Under the Derby Scheme 'enormous' numbers attested in London who had registered elsewhere, perhaps five hundred miles away in Aberdeen. Nor was mere physical proximity sufficient to ensure accuracy: if a man who had registered in Finchley (north London) attested in Whitehall, the records were

---

[1] ibid., pp. 15–16. [2] ibid., p. 19.

[3] Col. Herman Beukema, in Jesse D. Clarkson & Thomas C. Cochran (ed.), *War as a Social Institution*, 1941, p. 121.

[4] Williams, pp. 22–24.

[5] Williams, p. 24. [6] Williams, pp. 27–28.

[7] H.C. 126 and 185, Mins. of ev., Q. 6.

just as far off being collated as if he had registered in Aberdeen.[1] There were complications, too, arising from the ingenuity of man: in London many 'were seized with a fever of attestation', going through it five, six or seven times—at 2s. 9d. a time.[2] Multiple attestations naturally made the records chaotic, especially when there were so many 'William Smiths' ('the commonest of English names'), and in some places so many 'Abraham Cohens', of whom there were fifty-three in the Stepney sub-area alone.[3]

The Derby Scheme did not stave off conscription, which came for single men in January 1916 and for married men four months later.[4] Every man who was not in a 'group' (*i.e.*, who had not attested) fell into a 'class' (*i.e.*, was liable under these two 1916 Acts). But if a man had attested elsewhere than in his own home (and had not been traced through the collation of documents), he, too, was placed in a 'class'; thus there arose duplication between groups and classes. By May 1916 there were, on the Director of Recruiting's own estimate, about 'a million errors in the military registration'.[5]

This was muddle on a grand scale, indicating, undoubtedly, an unfair distribution of the military burden as between individuals. If so, it reinforced the unfairness inherent in the attempt to convert the recruiting machine from a 'receiver' into a 'thinker'. For it was not simply that the recruiting system had been subjected to unprecedented strain. Its essential feature at the outbreak of war was that of being 'merely a machine for receiving men who were in fact recruits'; it had been 'designed, primarily not to collect men, but to receive' time.[6] But in the spring of 1915, 'the Army was instructed to begin discriminating between the men who came forward to it', (*i.e.*, to say whether a man could be spared locally or not). In intention, it then ceased to be a receiving machine, and was supposed to become, at the periphery, a thinking machine; but it had not been designed for that purpose. In retrospect, a later Director of Recruiting commented, that was 'a very dangerous step', which 'has landed us in very great difficulty ever since'.[7] It was the beginning of a process of selection and exemption that had gone on ever since. From trying to make the machine at the periphery a thinking machine 'every sort of difficulty had ultimately arisen'.[8]

These difficulties, too, almost certainly implied the unequal treatment of equals; and there were still other sources of such inequality.

[1] ibid. [2] ibid.
[3] ibid. The administration of separation allowances in South Wales was at one time complicated by the profusion of David Evanses.
[4] Williams, p. 28.
[5] H.C. 126 and 185, Mins. of ev., Q. 6, p. 3.
[6] ibid., Q. 2. [7] Qs. 3 and 4. Also Q. 6.
[8] Qs. 5 and 6.

The sub-division of the original three medical categories (A, B, C) that resulted in the formation of nine categories had not been made for medical reasons but 'purely for administrative convenience'.[1] It is clear that the examining doctors were thereby given an extremely difficult, 'almost hopeless', task. Apart from the absolutely fit, 'no two boards would put the same man into the same category'.[2] In placing men into categories, there was 'ample room for differences of opinion' . . . 'Medicine is not an exact science'. 'Medicine is not like engineering; you cannot express fitness mathematically . . .' A former senior physician at Charing Cross Hospital was even more emphatic: he thought not only that the fine categorization had set the medical profession an 'impossible task' but that it was 'the basis of nine-tenths of a very large proportion of the difficulties we have to face . . .'[3] And the War Office saw to it that the task was made still more difficult by requiring doctors to classify a man *not* as he appeared before them but as he *would become* after fresh air and exercise, *i.e.*, after the drill sergeant and 'gym' instructor had worked their magic on him. Thus their medical judgement had to be 'to a certain extent prophetic'.[4]

Nor was this all. The very fine categorization was a fundamental difficulty; another was that the medical standards as such were lowered as the war dragged on. The suggestion that such a lowering had taken place was at first denied by the Director of Recruiting, the Director-General of Army Medical Services, and others, as it had been repeatedly denied in the House of Commons by Ian Macpherson, the Under-Secretary of State for War.[5] It was the President of a Travelling Medical Board who had been examining recruits since the outbreak of war who admitted:

'I think we have taken a more generous view as the war has gone on, in view of the necessity of getting men. . . . In the beginning we were extremely

---

[1] Qs. 170, 129, 394. When Surgeon-General Bedford (D.D.M.S., Northern Command) said there were as many medical categories as there were colours in the rainbow, he must have meant the seven categories of fitness. Q. 1126.

[2] Q. 129.

[3] Q. 394. The sub-division of A, B and C into nine categories had other unhappy consequences. Outside the War Office, it was at one time not realized that B.2 and B.3 came after C.1 and not before; hence more muddle when orders were given that men of certain categories were to be taken and others not to be taken, for a particular industry. ibid., Q. 34.

[4] Q. 129. Qs. 129, 2040, 3953–56, 4093–97 and 4673. This practice meant, *inter alia*, that a man with V.D., otherwise fit, was passed fit. Qs. 2085 and 2087. Also 94 H.C. Deb., c. 2000.

[5] Qs. 5002–4; 92 H.C. Deb., c. 349, 1144–5, 2017.

strict according to the old standards, and as the necessity for men arose I do not think we were quite so strict.'[1]

A Member of Parliament had made that very point in the House of Commons about three months before when he said that the idea at first had been to take the 'very best men you could get' but:

'We have got past all that. If we can get a serviceable man in we must have him, although he may not come up to pre-war standards.'[2]

The Deputy Director of Medical Services, Northern Command was even more candid. In his view, the civilian doctor had 'never raised his eyes to the horizon of his country's needs'.[3] Certificates of unfitness were being given to men who could have been usefully employed in the army even though they were not sound, so he had pointed out to Presidents of Medical Boards in his Command that a man found permanently unfit 'disappeared from military usefulness'. His idea was to get more men classified C.3 instead of being permanently rejected.[4]

This admission (to the Select Committee on Military Service, 1917) made it comparatively easy to establish that, early in September 1916, a special meeting had been held at the War Office and that it had been followed by a special War Office circular (16th September 1916) remarking that 'rejections continue to pour in' and requiring D.D.M.S.s to instruct Medical Boards not to reject totally a man who could perform any other work without danger to himself or to others.[5] 'Every man who can earn a livelihood in civil life can do something in the Army. . . .'[6] This cat leapt out of the bag. Macpherson had to explain to the House and to the Select Committee that he had never heard of the September circular until the Committee brought it to light.[7]

One revelation was followed by another. There also came to light a confidential letter, dated July 1915, again from the Director-General of Medical Services, stating that it was essential to get more men for garrison duty abroad and, therefore, many disabilities should from then onwards be ignored. Further, as there were so many civilian doctors on the Boards, they might have to be overruled.

[1] Qs. 150, 286, 592, 676–84; Qs. 5002–4. The introduction of the nine sub-divisions was of course a lowering of standards of a kind, but this was not the point at issue. Col. John Lewtas, ex-Indian Medical Service. ibid., Qs. 1045–6.

[2] Sir Christopher Johnston in a maiden speech, 92 H.C. Deb., c. 654.

[3] Surgeon-General Bedford. H.C. 126 and 185, Mins. of ev.,, Q. 1171.

[4] ibid. Q. 1177.

[5] Q. 1197.

[6] Q. 1825.

[7] Qs. 5002–4, 5006–7, 5043–45, 5049.

The whole matter, it was urged, was one of 'primary importance' about which Kitchener was 'very anxious'.[1]

The embarrassment suffered by Ministers and Departments is no part of our inquiry. What concerns us is that although the public were unaware of these special instructions, they knew enough about the Medical Boards to regard their work, in the words of the Select Committee, with 'grave distrust and suspicion'.[2] The percentage of errors may very well have been small, but the very large 'base' meant, of course, a 'large volume of individual injustice and individual hardship'. And so 'almost everyone' knew of and was affected by some such case.[3] The Medical Board procedure, then, worked capriciously both in space and time: so much of what one was required to do for King and Country depended on where and when one was subjected to medical examination.

This sense of injustice was heightened when it was realized that somehow or other, for no obvious reason, some people were escaping military service altogether. For many a man took a hand in arranging his own destiny. There was the man, for instance, who would buy (and no doubt use) at an average price of only £15, the official blue printed forms marked 'Not Accepted' that had been issued in the early attestation period.[4] The switching of identities at the medical examination was an imaginative stroke worthy of a better cause.[5] It resulted in obviously unfit men reporting for duty: in the north of England a man with two wooden legs once turned up and even a blind man.[6] Doping (to affect the heart) was a fairly obvious (and fairly common) device; rancid oil or condensed milk running from the ears, merely a silly one.[7] The 'numerous' civilians who infected their sputum from some extraneous source revealed how keen they were to remain civilians; while the cases of false urine induce a sense of wonder.[8]

There were also achievements that illustrate a fruitful partnership between amateur and expert. Doctors gave 'unfair' certificates—in favour of the man, and showed 'a want of judicial detachment'.[9] Early in 1916, classification cards were being 'forged on a great scale'; turning out such cards 'became an industry'. Cards were even stolen ('abstracted') from the files; 40,000 disappeared in one county alone.[10] The 'cleverest' move was none of these: it was to volunteer for one of the select corps whose social standards were high and be rejected on personal, not medical grounds. Since the grounds officially

[1] Qs. 1805–6.
[2] ibid., Report, para. 5.
[3] ibid.
[4] ibid., Mins. of ev., Qs. 7 and 8.
[5] Q. 14.
[6] Q. 31.
[7] Q. 32.
[8] Q. 396.
[9] Qs. 912 and 1003.
[10] Qs. 8, 9 and 10.

stated would be medical ones, a man would thus arm himself with a protecting medical certificate.[1]

This, then, is the background to the ex-servicemen's reception of the Military Service (Review of Exceptions) Bill presented to the House of Commons on 28th March 1917: muddling on the part of politicians and civil servants caught unawares by a new kind of war, and cheating by some men determined not to take part in war of whatever kind, new or old, the effect of which was to distribute equal obligations unequally. Now the tendency of one part of the Bill was to aggravate that unfairness, for the 'exceptions' to be reviewed included not only those previously rejected on medical grounds or declared unsuitable for foreign service but also men who had relinquished, or been discharged from, naval or military service.[2]

Bonar Law asserted, when he opened the Second Reading debate the following day, that the military situation made the Bill an 'absolute necessity'. The 'increasing severity of the submarine menace', and the consequential labour needs of agriculture and shipbuilding, had deprived the army of the men promised as recruits; as a result, from the beginning of 1917, the number of recruits had fallen short by 100,000. By reviewing the million 'exceptions', the military authorities hoped to put their hands on that 'missing' 100,000.[3]

Nevertheless, as Bonar Law himself admitted, there was 'great hardship' in the measure he was introducing. It was a 'very great hardship' that men who 'by accident, or by want of proper foresight, obtained commissions', as well as former non-commissioned officers, could be recalled as privates. Nor could he imagine any case harder than that of a man who 'had served his country, had been wounded, had gone back to work, and was under the impression that he had done his share and would not be called upon again'.[4] It would indeed have been a hard case even considered in isolation, but seen in the context of so much administrative confusion in the use of manpower, and of sufficient 'dodging' to have come to people's notice, the proposal appeared to ex-servicemen as monstrously unjust and therefore intolerable.

The response of the Blackburn Association was swift and vigorous. In the first of its leaflets, it described the Bill as one 'to conscript the *Wounded Discharged* men back into the Army', and characterized it as 'the meanest and most dispicable [*sic*] Bill that ever any Government introduced'.[5] Their violent criticism of it from soap-boxes in the market-place at Blackburn drew a warning from the local police.[6]

---

[1] 94 H.C. Deb., c. 2012.
[2] 92 H.C. Deb., c. 432.
[3] ibid., c. 636–8.
[4] ibid., c. 639.
[5] *Lest We Forget!* (leaflet, n. d.).
[6] Interviews with writer.

For the disparate groups of discharged men in Poplar and North London[1] the Bill was in several senses even more significant. In the first place, the Bill welded those two groups into a London organization, which, as the National Federation, spread rapidly throughout the country. There is no doubt that this Bill was the most important single factor in precipitating the second of the great ex-servicemen's associations. It 'was the reason the Federation came into being', declared J. Shepherd, the President of the Stockport Branch and a member of the N.E.C.[2] The Federation (an official leaflet said) 'was born out of the storm of protest raised by wounded ex-servicemen against the clause in the Review of Exceptions Act, 1917, which sought to conscript wounded men back to the Colours'.[3]

The Act was also significant for the Federation in that, once founded, its opposition was carried into the Parliamentary field. The men took the opportunity of a convenient by-election in Liverpool in order to press home their opposition to the Act. Hurriedly improvised and fought against a Stanley on his home ground, the campaign was a failure, but that intervention gave the Federation men a taste for Parliamentary action, and led on to their campaign in the General Election of the following year.

The Review of Exceptions Act was even significant for the ex-servicemen's movement as a whole in giving rise indirectly to the third of the great associations, the Comrades of the Great War. The circumstances in which this body made its appearance have already been briefly described,[4] and a further discussion will become appropriate at a later stage in this inquiry.[5] For the present one need observe only that the National Federation grew rapidly under the tutelage of two Liberal M.P.s., and that since the Blackburn Association had Labour connexions,[6] the ex-servicemen's movement seemed to be going 'left'. The Comrades of the Great War was in large measure a right-wing counter to an apparently 'left-inclined' movement. Thus the Review of Exceptions Act consolidated the Blackburn Association, precipitated the National Federation and led indirectly (though there were other considerations) to the Comrades of the Great War.

[1] See above, pp. 48 and 50.

[2] *Bulletin*, 27th Nov. 1919.

[3] Leaflet no. 8, n. d. (probably Spring 1919).

[4] Hist. B.L., pp. 3–5.   [5] See below, chs. IX–XII.

[6] Hist. B.L., p. 2; *Northern Daily Telegraph*, 14th Sept. 1916, and interviews.

PART TWO

The Associations (1917-57)

VIII

CHARACTER, STRUCTURE AND GOVERNMENT

THE very number of general ex-servicemen's associations that suddenly emerged during and immediately following the First World War is significant: it is a rough indication of the rifts in the political culture and of the gravity of the situation. These societies included the Blackburn (later, the National) Association (1916), the National Federation (1917), the Comrades of the Great War (1917), the Silver Badge (1918) and the National Union of Ex-Service Men (1919). The British Legion emerged in 1921 as an amalgamation of the first three of these.[1] The National Union and the Silver Badge soon disappeared from the scene, leaving the Legion in command of the field.

During the inter-war period, the Legion, which absorbed several very tiny societies irrelevant to this study, remained in command of the field until 1927, when the Labour League of Ex-Servicemen was launched. Alternatively, since that body consisted not so much of ex-servicemen who incidentally exerted political influence as of political animals who also happened to be ex-servicemen, one could say that the Legion was alone until the early 1930's when, the L.L.X. having meanwhile died, the Legion was joined by the Comrades of the R.A.F., (1930), ancestor of the R.A.F. Association, and by the Limbless Ex-Service Men's Association (1932) (the predecessor of BLESMA). All three 'benefited' from a second world war within a generation, the Legion reaching new heights and the other two becoming really viable and to some degree influential for the first time in their history. After the 1939–45 War only the Ex-Service Movement for Peace could be represented as new.

Some of these associations need be mentioned only in passing. The R.A.F. Association hardly features in this inquiry: it played its part in the post-1945 campaign for a basic pension of 90s. a week,

---

[1] In an administrative sense the Legion also absorbed the Officers' Association (1920), which, however, remained a distinct legal entity with its own governing body. There were other general societies, *e.g.* the Veterans' Association (London, 1917), but these do not fall for mention here because they did not grow or even impinge, however faintly, on the political process.

but its aims are more social than political even in the ordinary interest group sense. The L.L.X. and the Ex-Service Movement for Peace were political in every sense and hardly social at all: neither deserves much attention. Thus of the ten groups that have a *prima facie* claim to be discussed, only five are really relevant and of these not more than three come under scrutiny: the British Legion, the National Federation and BLESMA. The first selects itself; the other two will be shown to be worthy of selection, even though BLESMA, embracing only the limbless disabled, is not a general association. It would, however, be foolish to exclude it on those grounds, for unlike many specialist societies such as Old Comrades' Associations, its role does cast some light on the nature of the political process in Britain.

It cannot be too strongly emphasized that the R.A.F.A. is not alone in harbouring social as well as political aims: all the major associations have combined the two but in varying proportions. Of the contemporary associations, BLESMA puts 'unity and comradeship' first among its nine objects.[1] British Legion activities have been described by an acute observer, H. G. Nicholas, as '*surtout sociales et non politiques*',[2] but that was in the context of a discussion of the impact of public opinion on *foreign* policy. In matters of home policy the emphasis would have to be different. Nevertheless, the implied reference to good fellowship and 'welfare' is important. It should always be borne in mind that the political aims of the Legion (as of BLESMA) constitute only one side of its work, although it does not follow at all that the Legion cannot hold a political candle to the N.F.U., N.U.T., B.M.A., T.U.C. or F.B.I.

The description of any part of their work as 'political', on the other hand, would be rejected outright by many members of ex-servicemen's associations and regarded with disfavour and distaste by most of them. Yet they have always been 'political' in the sense of seeking to influence those who take decisions in the name of the community. This confusion about the meaning of 'political' has had its parallel, too, in the almost automatic rejection of the term 'pressure group', despite the undoubted fact that the language of pressure (to say nothing of attitude and conduct) has been in use from the outset and by all the associations.[3] Such a rejection is certainly not surprising because the term is undoubtedly emotive,

---

[1] Constitution and Rules, May 1957, 2 (a).

[2] In J-B. Duroselle (ed.), *La Politique Étrangère et Ses Fondements*, 1954, p. 121.

[3] See my thesis, *The Political Influence of Organized Ex-Service Men in England and Wales, 1917–57*, pp. 11–14, in the University of London Library, Senate House, for the evidence.

carrying with it echoes of the 'cohesive power of public plunder'.[1] But J. D. Stewart[2] is surely right to maintain that it is too late now to try to dislodge the term, which simply means 'any non-party group that seeks to affect the formulation or administration of public policy'.[3]

These associations have differed not only in the proportions in which they have combined their social and political activities, nor only in the degree to which they have been prepared to be political, but also in general character, size of membership and financial resources. Except for the Federation between 1917 and 1919, when officers, other than ranker officers, were barred, they have been open to all ranks with war service from August 1914 onwards, without the distinction between 'home' and 'abroad' that characterizes the Veterans of Foreign Wars in the United States, or between 'front line' and 'the rest' that was the mark of the German *Stahlhelm* organization. Only BLESMA, whose members are very conscious of being for the most part battle casualties, has something approaching a front-line pride and ethos. On the other hand, the proportion in which officers and men have actually joined these associations has varied much more considerably. The Comrades of the Great War had many officers, the Association and Federation (even after the change of rule) had few; the N.U.X. had fewer still. Today BLESMA resembles the Association and Federation in being basically a ranker organization, while even the Legion has probably recruited fewer officers than one might have expected, doubtless because the Officers' Association, which has its own Royal Charter, its own funds and its own system of government, is a strong counter-attraction. On the other hand, officers have figured prominently in both the presidency and the chairmanship of the Legion. As between the three Services, relative numbers alone would ensure that the associations are made up very largely of Army men. Certainly among the leaders one rarely finds either dark or light blue; the dominant colour is khaki.

The outstanding association of course is the British Legion. It has four elements jostling inside it: a benevolent society, an Old Boys' Association, a quasi-religious cult and a pressure group of considerable vigour. Many Legionaries prefer to speak of 'service' rather than 'benevolence', which, however, is appropriate for much of what they do. The capacity to exercise what would usually be called

[1] Albion Small, *General Sociology*, 1905, p. 287, apparently quoting Ratzenhofer. See also: E. E. Schattschneider, *Party Government*, 1942, p. 37.

[2] *British Pressure Groups*, 1958, p. 1.

[3] Allen Potter, 9 Parl. Aff. 1956, 418. Cf. N. C. Hunt's '. . . any organization which seeks to influence government policy without at the same time being willing to accept the responsibility of public office'. (12 *Occidente* 1956, 114.) There is of course a fairly wide choice of acceptable definitions.

'benevolence' was indeed put forward in December 1920 as a reason for amalgamation. Sir Frederick Maurice then told the Third Joint Conference on Unity that a sum of about £170,000 was 'waiting for the relief of the very prevalent distress among ex-servicemen today, waiting for a united body to deal with [it]'.[1] Certainly over the years vast sums have been spent for benevolent purposes; by 1956–7 such (direct) spending was of the order of £600,000 a year.

Old (Army) Boys like to talk about that day on Vimy Ridge or Salerno Beach, or more generally, to rest upon a foundation of shared experience, a certain good fellowship and even conviviality. The Legion's Clubs are a built-in recognition of this predilection, which however shows itself no less intensely (at the time) in the reunions and on other special occasions.

The concept of an Old Boys' Association seems to accord ill with that of a quasi-religious cult, but the two, as it were, meet without incongruity in a substantial part of the membership. At the one end of the scale, it appears as a simple Christian faith, perhaps especially noticeable among the former 'hired assassins', as retired regular soldiers sometimes ruefully describe themselves, but not of course confined to them. In such company the description of the Legion as 'a Christlike enterprise' (as a Canon of Windsor once said in a sermon in St. George's Chapel) is altogether fitting. At the other end of the scale is a cult of the dead, of which the Remembrance (formerly known as Armistice) Day ceremony is the most obvious manifestation. The ritual at the opening of every Legion meeting, however, is almost as significant. In this ritual all stand, heads bowed, while the chairman intones the Legion *Exhortation*:

> 'They shall grow not old, as we that are left grow old:
> Age shall not weary them, nor the years condemn.
> At the going down of the sun and in the morning
> We will remember them.'

To which all respond by repeating with fervour the last line—'We will remember them'; as they say it, one can almost catch them in the act of remembering. (At the opening of BLESMA meetings, too, members stand 'In Silent Memory of Fallen Comrades').

Of the Legion as a pressure group it is unnecessary to say anything here, for this is the concern of other chapters. In size of membership the giants of the 1917–21 period were the Comrades of the Great War and the National Federation of Discharged Sailors and Soldiers. The latter liked to claim a million members in the four countries,[2] but although a million men may have passed through its hands, they were certainly not retained. No one now knows (or at least admits to

---

[1] Hist. B.L., p. 30.   [2] *The Times*, 16th May 1919.

knowing) what the total was in, say, 1919, but from its financial accounts it is possible to estimate that the real 'live' membership may have been of the order of 100,000.[1] The Comrades of the Great War was certainly larger. The leadership claimed upwards of 680,000 in 1919,[2] but this included members overseas, and its accuracy cannot be judged from the accounts because most of the money came from the world of commerce and industry. But no one doubts that it was a large organization.

Only the British Legion has been of comparable stature to the Comrades of the Great War, and even it did not reach a million until as late as 1948. Since then, despite great exertions, numbers have steadily declined to the level of some 700,000 members.[3] (With the 250,000 in the Women's Section, the grand total approaches one million, but then the comparable figure for 1948 is almost a million and a quarter). By comparison the other associations have been small or even tiny, ranging from 500 (the Silver Badge) to perhaps 50,000 (the National Association). It does not follow that effective political influence is ruled out by smallness, for BLESMA (between five and six thousand paying members in 1957 and only some 12,000 *in all* at its peak in 1947-9) may be cited to prove the contrary, but it is plain that smallness is an obstacle to be overcome by factors such as skilled leadership, the sympathy of the public at large and especially of some of the highly-placed, and by external sources of finance. Generally, these countervailing influences are not in operation.

In financial resources the associations have ranged from the very rich to the very poor. Neither the N.U.X. nor the L.L.X. (to say nothing of the Ex-Service Movement for Peace) can have had any money from the start, while the Association withered away for lack of it. The Federation went from clogs to clogs within three years. Only in 1919 was it in really good fettle. The Comrades was rich but not in its own right; it had a very good run on what the City and the industrial magnates provided. The Legion, on the other hand, is rich on what the public, through Poppy Day, provides. Of course its members pay affiliation fees, which may be notionally placed against the cost of administration, but the proportions may be gauged from the 1956-7 figures: affiliation fees fell just short of £57,000 but Poppy Day (1956) yielded over a million pounds. With interest on investments and other receipts, its total income was about £1,300,000.

---

[1] Income and Expenditure Account and Balance Sheet for 1919.

[2] Annual Report for 1919, p. 11.

[3] 700,000 was the total in 1959. It is not comparable with the membership figures given in Appendix 5 to my Hist. B.L., being based on an analysis not of the national accounts but of actual 'returns' made by branches to headquarters. Cf. p. 218 below, n. 1.

Of course, in its 'Poppy Day' role the Legion resembles the 'millionaire' charities such as the Oxford Committee for Famine Relief and the National Spastics Society rather than the N.F.U. or the B.M.A. Obviously, a high proportion of its income is virtually earmarked for an array of benevolent purposes. On the other hand, such a large income does presuppose a powerful organization which can be used for the purposes that are the subject of this inquiry. The Legion is also a great property-owner. Over 800 branches own their headquarters. Nationally, the Legion owns freehold and lease-hold properties worth over half a million pounds; its total assets are put at three millions, including investments with a value (at cost) of about £1,700,000 (in 1957, when their market value, however, was no more than about £1,300,000).

BLESMA, naturally, is less well endowed with this world's goods. Its total assets in 1956 amounted to less than £200,000 (including its homes and endowments). The assets in its general fund were worth no more than some £37,000; its income for the year was but £11,000. On the other hand, given its commitments and role, it is undoubtedly viable.

If ex-servicemen's groups have varied in some major respects, they have been rather more alike in their internal structures and modes of government. The administrative structure has generally been three-tier: a national executive, area committees, the branches. Typically, the executives have not been chosen by and directly responsible to the 'Parliaments', or annual conference of branches, although this is true of BLESMA. But more often the executives have been mainly drawn from the intermediate bodies, which have put forward to 'Parliament' names for selection (Federation), for approval (Legion) or simply for acceptance (Association). Such national executives have strong provincial roots.

All the executives have been composed essentially of lay members. The full-time officers have always been in attendance, but never, in intention, as (internal) decision-makers. But two variations on the lay executive may be noted. For a short period some trade unionists served on, or perhaps with, the executive of the Blackburn Association; since 1946 BLESMA has had an advisory committee of non-members elected by Conference and parallel to the executive, to which it is linked chiefly by the general secretary. On certain crucial issues of strategy the advisers have been the real decision-makers.[1]

Of the intermediate bodies generally, nothing need be said here, but three observations about the territorial basis of the associations are required. Unlike the early societies and BLESMA, the Legion,

[1] See chapter XXV.

thanks largely to Earl Haig, does not cover Scotland, where there exists an indigenous variety known as the 'British Legion, Scotland' but in fact a different species. On the other hand, the Legion (proper) covers the whole of Ireland. Two groups have made special efforts to rest their organizations upon the traditional counties. The Comrades was partly launched by the Lords-Lieutenant of the counties, where, unlike the Federation (at bottom, an urban group), its potential strength no doubt lay. But the Comrades also had sufficient imagination to try to harness the emotional loyalty still surrounding the counties and maintained to this day in sport (notably in county cricket) if less warmly in local government. The Legion, too, now makes great play with its county organization, though this is a relatively recent development and emphasis. The effect is to make the Legion basically a four-tier structure, with the counties coming in between those 'bloodless categories', the Areas, and the local branches. These branches are of course territorial, but room has been found for the 'functional' principle, of which branches in Government Departments, industrial establishments and, until 1955, the House of Commons are examples. The Legion even has one branch (the Earl Haig, in London) which defies classification, being neither territorial nor 'House' but a vehicle for bringing together some of those who have rendered signal service in its cause. But here and generally the territorial branch has been the 'primary unit'.

All national executives have been powerful but the Legion's N.E.C. occupies an exceptionally strong position, which is inherent in, if not fully explained by, its Constitution.[1] Administratively, it can control the area conferences (of branches) through the power of the purse, and so indirectly the area councils, or 'provincial executives'. It can suspend or expel a branch, either for going against the Charter or Rules or simply for refusing to obey the area conference [in practice, the area council] or its own instructions 'when requested in writing to do so'. It can suspend or expel any member whom in its opinion after proper inquiry it 'shall consider to have acted disloyally or dishonourably towards the Legion'. Provided that at least two-thirds of the N.E.C. hang together, officers at all the subordinate levels can be made to hang separately, *i.e.* suspended or removed from office. The various provisions for appeal in no way detract from the power of the N.E.C., for some of these (*e.g.*, the expulsion of a branch) lead back to the N.E.C. itself.

On the other hand, one 'appeal-route' (where an officer has been suspended or relieved of office) leads to the next national conference, which raises the question of the relationship between the N.E.C. and the 'Parliament'. This body rests of course on the branches: one

[1] Royal Charter 1925 and Schedule of Rules, as amended.

delegate for each branch up to 500 paid-up members, with the reward of another delegate for branches boasting more than 500. On that basis, conferences of the order of 700–800 delegates came together in and around 1957. They had the support of another 50–60 delegates from the area and county conferences, in discussion though not in voting. It is the votes of the branch delegates[1] that, ostensibly, govern the Legion, since 'conference shall so far as the law will allow have supreme authority in all matters affecting the Legion; and its decisions shall be final.'

In this clause, however, there is more, or rather less, than meets the eye. Administrative decisions have to be excluded, conference being restricted to 'deciding questions of general policy'. Even in this realm, however, the N.E.C. has the advantage over conference, not only for the well-known reasons but also for two reasons specific to this form of private government. In the first place, this executive is not responsible to this 'Parliament'. Out of an executive of rather than more than thirty (in 1957), 'Parliament' controls precisely four—those principal officers which it elects each year, *i.e.* the president, chairman, vice-chairman and treasurer. Apart from the past-chairmen, the rest of the executive are derived from the area conferences. 'Parliament' could refuse to approve such nominees, but that would only pass the initiative back to the area conferences. 'Parliament' might pass a vote of censure on the executive, which, however, would prick the skin without drawing blood. Accordingly, it cannot in practice hold the executive to account. Nor, secondly, can it achieve that result by refusing 'supply', for the N.E.C. controls both the general and benevolent funds.

An executive that cannot, in practice, be dismissed or starved of money is an executive that is free to take policy as well as administrative decisions. Even so, constitutions do not, in the last resort, so much explain as demand to be explained. Why did Legionaries accept such a 'balance of power' in the first place? One should not rule out the possibility that some or even many of them did not understand the significance of the constitutional provisions, but fundamentally one must seek the explanation in the political culture. Even more than the British generally, ex-servicemen like to talk Radical but act Whig. In other words, their conception of authority, shaped particularly (one supposes) by their experience of discipline and command in the Services, permits and even encourages strong, centralized leadership within their own associations. One may even detect an element of charisma in their attitude to their leaders, most obviously in the veneration of Earl Haig by some of the first genera-

[1] One vote per delegate. Motions: by show of hands. Election of officers and amendments to Charter and Rules: by ballot.

tion of Legionaries as, almost, the Lord's anointed of ancient prophecy. Of course, there have been dissentients: the forty-nine (or some 7 per cent) who voted for Colin Coote and therefore against Haig for the presidency in 1921, and those who left the ranks because they had so little influence on policy. And for sometime after the Second World War the tail wagged the dog on one issue. But over the whole period under review Legionaries generally have let the N.E.C. 'get on with the job'.

Thus, over the years, the N.E.C. has had the predominant voice in the government of the Legion. The policy of doubling the basic rate of pension, carried in 1946 and sustained against the real wishes of the N.E.C., was an exception to the rule, but the rule is that the N.E.C. governs, if not through conference motions then by virtue of decisions taken in between conferences. Later protests can be overriden, as in 1925 when the Leyton Branch protested about the policy of making contacts with the ex-enemy ex-service organizations.[1] On the other hand, conference resolutions that cannot be stopped can be ignored, as in 1948, when the N.E.C. blandly (and, as I think, rightly) refrained from implementing a resolution to start a Legion football-pool. At the next conference it arranged to have the decision reversed. So much for the 'supreme authority' of the national conference and the finality of its decisions.

Nor is this all. The power of the N.E.C. extends into every corner of the structure, not only administratively but also in terms of policy. One of the very earliest rules accords branches 'full local autonomy', with power to adopt and declare 'a definite policy' upon local matters and to take 'any action considered necessary in pursuance of it', provided that it is both constitutional and consistent with the Legion's objects. The rule concludes: 'The decision as to what are or are not local matters shall rest with the National Council of the Legion'.

So far, it has been convenient to speak simply of the power *of* the N.E.C., but what of the distribution of power *within* the N.E.C. itself? Of course, its work is done through its committees and officers; the committees are more powerful than the N.E.C. as such, and the officers more powerful than either. The principal honorary administrative officer is the chairman, who presides over the N.E.C. and conference, and attends headquarters probably two days a week. At times the president emerges as a rival centre of power. He is *ex-officio* a member of the N.E.C. and all its committees, and *opens* conference with a major speech. Earls Haig and Jellicoe, as great wartime leaders, were content to be ornaments, but Sir Frederick Maurice was very much a working president. That he should fly to Germany

[1] Hist. B.L., p. 117.

to interview Hitler during the Munich crisis in 1938[1] was symbolic
of his career as president. Sir Ian Fraser, too, was a working president.
If the president works, does the chairman cease to? He may be
content to play a relatively minor role; or spheres of influence may be
demarcated; or there may be friction, as between Sir Ian Fraser and
S. H. Hampson, chairman 1953–56. But somehow or other a working
compromise is reached and the work gets done.

The vice-chairman and the treasurer are also important in this
context, for they, too, attend headquarters regularly, probably once
a week at least. But there is one person who is on hand every day:
the general secretary. What is his role? Officially he is a subordinate,
appointed by the N.E.C. and responsible to it, but as everyone knows
these roles tend in many organizations to be reversed in practice.
Certainly J. R. Griffin, the second general secretary, was an immensely
powerful figure, not only for the well-known reasons of general
application but also because he had been active in the field since 1917
and an administrator (general secretary of the Federation) since
March, 1920. By definition, no successor can ever carry that weight
of (pioneering) experience, but he will be in daily touch with the
work and will eventually be the repository of a great fund of
'departmental' knowledge.

Where precisely, among these lay and professional officers, power
resides it is impossible to say with any confidence; it would always
be wise to look first to the chairman and general secretary, but the
location will vary according to circumstances and to the personalities
of those who occupy the various offices (or statuses). All one can
venture to say is that somewhere within this circle of officers
(including in some periods the president) a high proportion of the
important decisions will be taken. In theory such decisions will be
reached within the context of conference policy, but policy has to be
interpreted and often enough there is simply no declared policy.
In practice someone has to take on the decision-making burden.

That burden will be the easier to bear the longer the officers remain
at the helm; in fact, a striking feature of the national leadership is its
stability. Between the wars the Legion had only three presidents,
four chairmen and one general secretary. From 1945 to 1957, the
elected offices changed hands rather more often but a stable pattern
was still preserved. No officer has ever been unseated by the rank and
file. The only possible exception to the rule occurred in 1956, when
some leaders of the Southern Area privately urged retirement on the
president, Sir Ian Fraser. Their objection was not in the least personal
but simply that his role as an active party politician was embarrassing
to a non-party organization, and that his role as a Government

[1] Hist. B.L., chapter XXIX and appendix 21.

supporter inhibited the campaign for a basic war pension of 90s. a week. But their willingness to carry the fight into the open was never put to the test because, some eighteen months later, the president did retire.

This was a special case, not only because it was, almost, a 'palace revolution' but also because Sir Ian had been elected president in 1947 against the wishes of the incumbent leadership. As with BLESMA (*e.g.*, two presidents only between 1937 and 1956), an unchallenged continuity in office has been the almost invariable rule. How is this characteristic to be explained? In part no doubt it reflects the strength of the N.E.C. as a whole, but the Michelsian 'rules'[1] also have their specific application. The organizational and psychological factors are obvious enough; what also has to be taken into account is the educational, intellectual and sometimes social 'gap' between the leaders and the rank and file not only in the Legion but in the movement generally. In the Comrades the social gap existed from the beginning: the founders were aristocrats or plutocrats almost to a man. In the Legion, too, the difference in social class (as measured, for instance, by occupation) between the honorary officers and the rank and file has been wide. It is most obvious in the presidency (as distinct from the office of patron, which is filled by the Sovereign or some other member of the Royal Family). Between 1921 and 1957 there were four presidents: one field-marshal, one general officer, an admiral of the fleet and a member of parliament, who had defeated the N.E.C.'s nominee, another admiral. (Since 1957, another general officer has become president, and he is also Gold Stick in Waiting to the Queen). Of the ten chairmen between 1921 and 1957, all but one had the status of Army officers, mostly of field rank or above, at the time of their election. Perhaps one or two of them were old soldiers whose commissions came only in the 1939–45 War (Home Guard), but they had the rank when elected, and were in any case 'balanced' by the two general officers and the three colonels. (Since 1957, another general officer has been in command.) Alternatively, if a somewhat different criterion is used, one finds that, apart from four retired regular army officers, the Legion chairmen included an insurance inspector, a man of independent means, an architect, an accountant, a provincial newspaper owner and a school headmaster (retired). Both treasurers were men of independent means, one rich, one perhaps less well endowed but a peer of the realm. (They were succeeded after 1957 by an accountant.)

With the two general secretaries of the period, the social gap was not quite as distinct. The first had been an Army 'coach', *i.e.*, a kind of schoolmaster, though at the time of his appointment he was indeed

[1] Robert Michels, *Political Parties*, 1915.

a colonel. The other, a very young man when he joined the Army, had been training to be an architect. In these cases an intellectual distinction yielded a social distinction, for their advancement within the ex-servicemen's movement naturally yielded very substantial, even high, salaries, and a mode of life quite different from the rank and file's.

All in all, the unchallenged continuity in national office causes no surprise; only instability would be news.

PART THREE

Aims and Methods (1917-39)

BROAD AIMS (A) 1917–21 : CHAPTERS IX–XIII
BROAD AIMS (B) 1921–39 : CHAPTER XIV
METHODS 1917–39 : CHAPTERS XV–XIX

IX

THE TWO TARGETS: DOMESTIC AIMS

BETWEEN the autumn of 1916 and the summer of 1917, then, the discharged men's values, beliefs and emotions, and the economic and other circumstances in which they found themselves, induced a number of men in different parts of the country to lay the foundations of an ex-servicemen's movement. But of course it is not only the foundation of such bodies that should be seen in those terms: it is clear that the political aims of the new associations should also be viewed against the background of the prevailing political culture and the specific circumstances of the time. Bearing these factors in mind, one may divide the original political aims into two broad categories, taking as a text a passage from Sir Harold Nicolson's novel, *Public Faces*. Describing the character of Walter Bullinger, Sir Harold wrote that in spite of political success he

'was not a man at peace with himself. There was his outside self—confident, convivial, voluble: there was his inside self—dispirited, self-critical, tongued-tied. He was painfully aware of this divergence. It was as though he possessed two separate charts of his own individuality: he visualized them vaguely as two targets painted in concentric circles of red and black. The Bullinger target was contrived of stiff white cardboard: it was highly ostensible: the central bull's-eye was plumb and emphatic: the surrounding circles were unwavering and firm. . . . The Walter target was of a different quality: now that he came to think of it, it wasn't a target at all. It was like a Japanese flag printed on tissue paper: it was a splotch, a protest, a disavowal.'[1]

The political aims of ex-servicemen in the period 1917–21 may be likened to those two targets. The aims designed to confer benefits upon (or to ward off, or remove, disabilities from) the ex-service community as such correspond to the Bullinger target: 'the central bull's-eye . . . plumb and emphatic'. Obvious examples are pensions and allowances, training for and preference in employment. In pursuing such aims, ex-servicemen were, so to speak, inward-looking; hence those aims may be conveniently called 'domestic'. But they were also, in the beginning, making protests and disavowals that reflected general movements of opinion and schools of thought in the community at large, such as the demand for 'justice, not charity',

[1] *Public Faces* (Penguin ed., 1945), p. 14.

which, applicable in their eyes to the (war) pensions system, obviously had wider implications. Such aims may be called 'external'.

The distinction may be alternatively expressed by extending the line of thought set out in chapter I. If a pressure group accepts 'its place' in the universe of groups, *i.e.*, the terms of its relations with official groups and unofficial groups, and merely tries to advance its claims for a bigger share of the national product or for some change of rule relevant to its own situation, then it is inward-looking, and the aims are 'domestic'. On the other hand, such a group may not accept the terms of its relations with other groups. The Cabinet may not know of its existence; the relevant Ministry may know only to ignore, or to treat with scant respect. A department, such as the War Office in 1918–19, may wish to persuade the associations to accept paternalism when only democracy of a kind will satisfy the men.[1] Similarly, a group may strive to get some function or other transferred from voluntary bodies into the hands of the Government on grounds of general principle. Above all, a group may reject the whole political and social framework within which pressures are being exerted, thus tending to make its own organization a vehicle for viewpoints and actions of a fundamentally challenging kind. In each of these instances the group is outward-looking, staring beyond the immediate and 'customary' limited claims to some fundamental re-arrangement. Such aims are here called 'external'.

It will be argued that organized ex-servicemen, like Walter Bullinger, had to set aside the one kind of target before they could be at peace with themselves, or indeed with the rest of the community. That setting aside of the external aims was largely, though not entirely, achieved in 1921, through the formation of the British Legion. Thus the period here surveyed falls into two parts: 1917–21 and 1921–39, which together form a convenient framework for the discussion that follows.

Domestic Aims (1917–21)

The Blackburn (later, the National) Association's domestic aims are by now familiar in outline. Of the aims having an economic basis, one of the two characteristic types was illustrated at the inaugural meeting on 13th September 1916, when it was announced that, as a result of representations to the authorities, allowances for two discharged soldiers had been raised from 5s. 3d. to 16s. 3d. a week.[2] Those representations had been made by the local Trades and Labour Council, who had sponsored the meeting in order to suggest that soldiers' associations should be formed throughout the country for

[1] Interviews with writer. See chapter XI below.
[2] *Northern Daily Telegraph*, 14th Sept. 1916.

the purpose of exerting influence of that kind.[1] A start was made at Blackburn that very night.

The Association grew on a diet of pensions grievances that were slowly 'universalized' into aims. A number of instances has already come to our notice.[2] There were also cruel anomalies so far unremarked upon: a wounded man was apparently proceeding on leave from hospital; on the way to the station he was knocked down and killed. As he was not killed on 'actual [? active] service', a pension was not awarded.[3]

The other characteristic type of aim arising out of the economic circumstances reflected, as we know, the specific employment situation. The Blackburn men, as we noted, were out of work, and wanted to be trained in a trade; hence this statement in the first of their leaflets:

'We hear a great amount of talk about training schemes for the disabled men's future, but this is taking place in very very small sections. 90 per cent of the men are still awaiting [? training] owing to the authorities leaving the question to Local Committees instead of attacking the whole problem nationally with the National Executive of all the allied Trade Unions.'[4]

As for non-economic factors, the Association men, we already know,[5] were vehement in their denunciation of the Review of Exceptions Act, and although that did not in itself constitute an aim, it nevertheless implied one. In this respect the National Federation's policy was very much more clear-cut: it required nothing less than 'immediate repeal'.[6] Similarly, the policy formulated in response to the economic circumstances was very much more comprehensive than the Association's, and more ambitious than that of the Comrades of the Great War. The Federation intended to 'prevent the exploitation of labour in connexion with discharged men': the Comrades, to 'press the claims of discharged sailors and soldiers to State and public employment; to enlist the co-operation of employers for the same object; and to support undertakings for the suitable training and employment of disabled men'. The Federation wished to see pensions granted on the principle of 'fit to fight, fit to pension':[7] the Comrades never accepted that approach, and, as for the amount, merely required pensions to be 'adequate', whereas the older body stood out for generous treatment.[8]

[1] ibid. [2] See above p. 45 and 51.
[3] *Northern Daily Telegraph*, 16th Oct. 1916.
[4] *Lest We Forget!* [5] See above p. 59.
[6] *Liverpool Post*, 25th June 1917; Object (i) 1917.
[7] Federation: Objects 2 (c) & 2 (f), 1917. Comrades: Object (4), 1917.
[8] Comrades: Object (5), 1917. Federation: Object (c), 1917, T. F. Lister's Election Address 1918, and Demobilization Programme, 1919.

It would be tedious to catalogue the end-of-the-war and post-war programmes of the 'Big Three'.[1] A discussion of some of their important objectives follows at a later stage.[2] What now needs to be noted is that by 1919 the policy differences still distinguishing the 'Big Three' were small in comparison with the differences between them and the newly-formed National Union of Ex-Service Men, to which I have made some reference elsewhere.[3] If the three original associations were still separated at various points by a narrow crevasse, then between them and the N.U.X. lay a yawning chasm. The N.U.X. went further than even the Federation in setting out to prevent 'the exploitation of the disabled and demobilized men by unscrupulous employers'; the Federation had implied that at least some employers were unscrupulous, but the N.U.X. said so explicitly. Similarly, the Federation had asked for payment of war gratuities at least on the scale enjoyed by colonial troops, but the N.U.X. urged that every man who had served during the war should 'receive as "back-pay" the difference between what he actually received and the rate of 6s. a day'.[4]

Only one of the important pre-Legion organizations remains to be mentioned: the Officers' Association (1920).[5] Its policy (1921 formulation) is very easily stated:

'The primary object of the Association shall be to aid and assist and promote the interests of all those who have at any time held a Commission in Our Naval, Military or Air Forces and the wives, widows, children and dependants of such persons, by grants of money, loans, guarantees, and other financial methods, and by any other means whatever.'[6]

But this of course is only a statement of general intention; it is silent about the aims here called domestic. The reason for this vagueness was partly that the Officers' Association bore, and bears to this day, the least resemblance to a pressure group, even in the relatively innocuous terms of our earlier discussion,[7] but also that its real *raison d'être* has to be sought in the field of external aims. Although it has given ex-officers of two wars valuable help, the Officers' Association must be seen primarily in the context of an ex-servicemen's movement considered, at best, to have 'got out of hand', and, at worst, to have moved alarmingly to the left.

[1] See appendices 5, 6 and 8 of my thesis.
[2] See below Parts Five and Six.
[3] Hist. B.L., p. 10; 29 P.Q. 1958, 29. See also ch. VIII above and ch. XII.
[4] *Aims and Policy*, n.d. (See appendix 7 of my thesis for a reproduction of this leaflet).
[5] Hist. B.L., pp. 14, 22–3.
[6] Royal Charter, 1921.
[7] ch. VIII.

X

EXTERNAL AIMS

(1) JUSTICE, NOT CHARITY

THE values that discharged men came to hold about the objects of government were never made more explicit than in the policy epitomized as 'Justice, not charity'. It is well known that the word 'charity' has come down in the world. In most people's minds it has come to mean almost the opposite of 'love'; or, at least, the dispensing of benefits in so chill a spirit and so patronizing a manner that the 'love' in it is obviously dying at the roots.

Sensitiveness to 'charity' is not of course confined to this country. In 1957, an American business man who had deposited $25,000 in an Indian bank in order to help enterprising young men felt it necessary to characterize the plan as 'business, not charity'.[1] Professor Rushbrook Williams has noted the wish to make the early agricultural settlements in Israel 'self-supporting and self-respecting communities deriving their living from the land. It was no longer considered right that Jewish immigrants into the Promised Land should subsist on charity...'[2] But the hatred of the Poor Law system and the revulsion against 'charity' was perhaps a peculiarly English experience; at any rate it was exemplified soon after the outbreak of the First World War, when, as already observed, the Local Government Board took steps to ensure that families forced temporarily to seek Poor Law relief should have their names struck out of their records.[3] Yet so insensitive were some social workers that one of them could comment on the Local Government Board's action: 'This is attaching a stigma to the Poor Law relief with a vengeance'.[4] Other social workers were more perceptive. Bernard Bosanquet, for instance, in an address to the Charity Organization Society at Oxford in 1915, recalled how impressed he had been by the chance remark that the wage-earning class would not 'look at you as long as you have the word charity in your title', an attitude he had come across himself and which he considered quite natural. 'Charity suggests to them "Almsgiving"', which 'means to them a

---

[1] *Manchester Guardian*, 14th Aug. 1957, leader.
[2] *The State of Israel*, 1957, p. 23.   [3] See above, p. 22.
[4] 38 C.O.R. Sept. 1915, 301.

violation of their independence, an admission that wages are inadequate for proper life, and that supplementation of them is at the discretion of a different class'. Wage-earners also took the view that charity was normally dishonest because it was undertaken, at bottom, for the good of the alms-giver, not of the recipient. Their attitude might be expressed: 'Don't come saving your soul on me'.[1]

How far their criticism was generally valid need not be discussed here. No doubt charity was a form of alms-giving. Miss Octavia Hill herself had said at Fulham in 1889 that 'if you want to see really wise, sufficient, helpful alms-giving, you will find it, if anywhere, at your Charity Organization Society's committee'.[2] The fundamental point for this inquiry is Bosanquet's inference that 'charity' suggested the supplementation of wages 'at the discretion of a different class'. For the traditional ex-service societies were essentially charities; the S.S.F.A., the Soldiers Help and the Royal Patriotic Fund Corporation were almost the Charity Organization Societies of the ex-service (and serving) community. That the founders and active members of such bodies were kindly people who did good work was true but in this context unimportant; the supplementation of pensions 'at the discretion of a different class' was repugnant to the men discharged from the New Army.

The demand for 'justice, not charity' took a number of forms. It was, for instance, reflected in the policy of making the right to a (war) pension statutory and no longer, technically, an expression of the royal bounty. Under Elizabeth I and again under Cromwell, and indeed as late as 1826, the right of a disabled soldier to a pension seems to have been a statutory one and not 'a claim on personal charity or public funds in the shape of Royal Bounty distributed at the discretion of Government officials'.[3] After 1826, however, that statutory right seems to have lapsed and a pension became again an emanation of the royal bounty.[4] Once again it appears to have been true that 'The Army looks to the King and not to the Parliament'.[5]

The men back from the New Army equated 'bounty' with 'charity': for their pensions they looked to Parliament rather than to King George. They therefore demanded a statutory right to pension, so abolishing at one stroke (in the Federation's words) 'the idea that the State was granting anything' and ensuring 'the carrying out of every obligation entered into by the State without the degrading and demoralizing recourse to charity'.[6]

---

[1] 38 C.O.R. Nov. 1915, 381.   [2] 39 C.O.R. Mar. 1916, 137.

[3] Judge Edward Parry and Lieut. Gen. Sir Alfred Codrington, *War Pensions: Past and Present*, 1918, pp. 5–6, 18–28.

[4] ibid., p. 27.   [5] ibid., p. 22.

[6] Federation pamphlet No. 1, *What we think*, n. d., p. 2.

The revulsion against charity and the claim for justice was still more explicit in the policy adopted by most (organized) ex-servicemen towards the King's Fund (*i.e.*, towards an aspect of voluntaryism). The King's Fund was formed on the initiative of John Hodge, the Minister of Pensions, who, in July 1918, appealed to the public to subscribe three million pounds to help to rehabilitate discharged men. At the end of that month he was able to announce that the King had not only become patron but also proposed to hand over to the fund the Silver Wedding Gift of £53,000 presented to the King and Queen by the City of London,[1] together with a personal subscription of £25,000. Added to the balance of voluntary funds held by the Minister, these gifts formed the nucleus of the King's Fund, which, vigorously backed by the Press, grew almost to the level of a million pounds by March 1919.[2]

It was quite certain that at least the Federation would attack that method of raising money for the assistance of discharged men because it smacked too much of the methods practised by the great ex-service societies, *i.e.*, of charity. Even in the 1890's S.S.F.A. had become aware of the stigma of charity. Whereas in 1887, two years after S.S.F.A.'s foundation, a very gallant admiral could say at its annual general meeting that one of its two objects was the principle of charity, seven years later another admiral felt called upon to interpret its benefactions in terms of friendship:

'No one with any self-respect would wish to be in receipt of charitable Funds, but I think all of us at times like to have the assistance of our friends.'

He emphasized the Secretary's remark that 'the assistance given by the Society should not be looked upon as charity', but 'should be understood to be the ready help given by *friends to friends*'.[3]

With the best will in the world, such a relationship was hard to establish. As late as January 1917, a writer in the *Edinburgh Review* who was distinctly favourable to the Society, implied that such friendship had been achieved only during the course of the war. Discussing S.S.F.A. visiting by officers' wives, he wrote that most of them:

'... became real friends to the women. It was not the patronizing lady who called to give some little charity. War had wiped out, or had deadened, that pride of class. The New Army recognizes no class distinctions; the risks and honours are common to all, whether officers or men, and the

---

[1] Ultimately, £56,648. H.C. 39 (1920), p. 40.

[2] £994,940. ibid., p. 41.

[3] James Gildea, *Historical Record of the Sailors' and Soldiers' Families Association*, pp. 17, 43.

officers' wives, having breathed something of this same spirit, have—sometimes at the request of their husbands—thrown themselves wholeheartedly into the work of helping their poorer sisters'.[1]

Even if that 'friendship' attitude had become general during the war, replacing the 'pride of class', the men had emerged from the war with a heightened sense of class, although in general they would not have described it in such terms. The most extreme expression of it has already been quoted.[2] But the whole Federation, by excluding officers (other than rankers) from membership,[3] was in effect saying much the same thing in administrative terms. And, in a sense, correspondingly, they took the view that the discharged man (*e.g.*, in industry) was

'... exploited by charity-mongers, who run flag-days and cigarette fêtes. Recognize him as the honourable ward of the State that he may "buy his own cherries"'.[4]

It was only to be expected, therefore, that the Federation should give John Hodge's proposal a warm welcome. The original proposal elicited a 'strong letter of protest' from the Executive Committee.[5] And thereafter the Federation never tired of criticizing the King's Fund. Hodge was characterized in a Branch resolution as:

'... not a fit and proper person to hold office as Minister of Pensions because he has failed to obtain the necessary money to place the disabled men in their rightful position as citizens of the country they have helped to save, and that he realizes his own inefficiency to obtain this by starting a voluntary fund to dole out charity in place of that justice which was promised by responsible Ministers of State, and which is right.'[6]

When James Hogge, M.P., the Federation President, declared that 'the root principle of the immediate needs of the men is State compensation from State funds. Charity is abhorrent', he was criticizing voluntaryism in general and perhaps the King's Fund in particular.[7] Sir Frederick Milner in fact wrote to various provincial newspapers

[1] 225 Ed. Rev. Jan. 1917, 143–4.

[2] See above, p. 42.

[3] Until the spring of 1919, when the rules were changed. Before that time officers could be made honorary members but could not take part in the government of the association.

[4] Federation pamphlet No. 1, *What we think*, p. 5. Early in 1919 the leaders were upset when they found that some branches had been running their own flag days. *Bulletin*, 24th April 1919.

[5] Minutes, 19th July 1918, Min. 18.

[6] Agenda, General Council Meeting, Nottingham, 28th–29th Sept. 1918, resolution 14 (Bishop Auckland).

[7] *The Ex-Service Man*, 25th Sept. 1918. See also 112 H.C. Deb., c. 452.

complaining that Hogge was 'trying to prejudice the Fund by stating it is a charity. I beg to point out it is nothing of the kind. It is a free-will offering on the part of those who had to stay at home; an expression of their gratitude . . .'[1]

Appropriately, in the middle of January 1919, a 'Gratitude Week' was held throughout the country for the purpose of boosting the King's Fund.[2] It evoked an angry protest from the 950-strong Stoke Newington Branch of the Federation, who condemned:

'. . . lock, stock and barrel the effort of the Minister of Pensions to organize a "Gratitude Week", in order to raise funds for the King's Fund and so relieve the State of its obligations to men who have been disabled in the Great War. Discharged men know they have the public gratitude and do not want charity to prove this. The silver badge is for services rendered. You cannot pay for services rendered by charity. The discharged men ask the public not to subscribe to the King's Fund.'[3]

The Association was no less severe than the Federation in its denunciation of 'charity'. The Association men in Gloucester proclaimed:

'We set out with certain definite aims and objects. We have never lost sight of those aims and objects to get JUSTICE AND RIGHT, NOT CHARITY, for those who have answered the Country's call. Surely the Discharged Men have the energy and brain power to stand fast together and not be hoodwinked and deluded into blind-alley organizations, which are today giving out charity in shovelsful. Begone! we say to charity . . .'[4]

By the spring of 1918, this attitude had been embodied in one of the three main objects of the Association:

'to educate public opinion to the belief that the maintenance and welfare of the disabled sailor and soldier and his dependants is the direct duty of the State and should be its first care, and that they should in no way be dependent upon charity for their livelihood.'[5]

In view of the discussion so far, it would be natural to conclude that the 'charity' said to have been given out 'in shovelsful' was a reference to voluntaryism, but although that would have been perfectly in character, the criticism was in fact directed against the Comrades of the Great War. To the Association (and the Federation), the Comrades was hardly different in kind from the traditional ex-service societies, and if their attitude failed to embrace the whole

---

[1] *e.g., Grimsby Gazette*, 11th Jan. 1919.

[2] 113 H.C. Deb., c. 206.

[3] *Hackney & Stoke Newington Recorder*, 24th Jan. 1919.

[4] Gloucester Branch leaflet, n. d.

[5] Poole Branch leaflet, n.d. (a note written in ink at the bottom of this leaflet is dated 24th April 1918). See also Folkestone Branch leaflet, n.d.

truth about the Comrades, it was nevertheless soundly based. The Comrades collected money from the public in the old 'charitable' manner, which offended against the discharged men's principle that the State should provide whatever was deemed necessary. It also dispensed money in ways ('beer, buns and billiards') that were at least reminiscent of charity.

Far from denying these charges, the Comrades' original leaders would no doubt have claimed them as virtues. It cannot be said, therefore, that every ex-servicemen's association exhibited a revulsion against charity in all its forms. On the other hand, the Comrades was far from being a typical association: in origin an imposition from above[1] and not a spontaneous growth from below, it was one of those exceptions that proves the rule. And later, in 1919, the N.U.X. was without any equivocation to take up its position, for this purpose, at the side of the first two associations. In an article that was not an official expression of N.U.X. policy but gave an impetus to the organization and may be accepted as representative, a writer declared that the men 'detest the payment which bears the stigma of a "dole" and makes them appear to be recipients of outdoor relief'.[2] Moreover, 'the creation of a vast reservoir of cheap labour must menace the position of all workers and strengthen that of the Capitalist as a buyer of flesh and blood'.[3] By the time the Officers' Association appeared in 1920, the relevant issues were largely settled, so, on balance, it can be said that the ex-servicemen's movement generally did adopt the position attributed to it in the title of this chapter.

[1] Constitution, 1917. See below p. 89.

[2] *Daily Herald*, 9th June 1919.

[3] ibid.

XI

EXTERNAL AIMS

(2) DEMOCRATIC REPRESENTATION

THE values, reinforced by beliefs and emotions, that discharged men came to hold about the modes of government crystallized as a series of claims for more democratic representation. Throughout 1916, as previously remarked,[1] ex-servicemen as such had no voice on the local war pensions committees; the Naval and Military War Pensions, etc., Act, 1915, had provided places for various voluntary bodies but not for organized ex-servicemen.[2] It therefore became one of the aims of the Federation, and apparently other associations as well, to make these committees representative of discharged (disabled) men and of widows.[3] They urged their view upon the Minister of Pensions and succeeded in getting it accepted, whereupon in 1917 the Minister introduced a short Bill under which every local or district committee was to have at least two discharged (disabled) men on it as well as one woman in receipt of pension as a widow or dependant of a man who had died in consequence of service in the war.[4] Sub-committees and joint committees were also to have at least two disabled ex-servicemen among their members.[5]

The demand for representation was not confined to formal structures such as committees. Late in 1918, for instance, the Federation was bold enough to write to the Prime Minister asking for representation at the Peace Conference.[6] This was perhaps the first occasion on which the common soldier had acted on the belief that he had something to contribute to the peace he had helped to establish. It need hardly be said that Lloyd George felt able to carry on without his assistance.

The typical claim, of course, was for representation at home wherever ex-servicemen felt their interests to be involved. When, for instance, late in 1920, a departmental committee of inquiry was set up to investigate the administration of the Ministry of Pensions, the authorities failed to provide direct representation for ex-servicemen:

[1] See above, p. 38.   [2] Devine, op. cit., p. 137.
[3] Cmd. 14 (1919), p. 6.   [4] ibid.
[5] ibid.
[6] G.P.C. Minutes, 15th Dec. 1918, Min. 9.

the House of Commons and the Local War Pensions Committees were well represented but the 'consumers' (ex-servicemen) were expected to be satisfied with a former editor of *The Service Man* who was also honorary secretary to the Disabled Society.[1] But they were not satisfied. The Federation leaders discussed the position at a meeting of the General Purposes Committee on 11th December 1920. They heard that other [unspecified] organizations had already refused to give evidence, whereupon they, too, decided to follow suit 'until such time as the composition of the said Committee was duly altered in order to give direct representation to the Federation'.[2] And the leaders made doubly sure by asking branches as well to refrain from giving evidence.[3] Confronted with this opposition, the Minister gave way, and accordingly the Federation agreed to give evidence.[4]

So all-pervasive did this democratic spirit become (or, as some preferred to say, so shrill the democratic cry) that the ex-servicemen's organizations themselves had to pay tribute to it in their internal structure, and to proclaim (on letter-headings and in their literature) that they were 'democratic' (as well as 'non-party' and 'non-sectarian'). Undoubtedly, the Federation was proud of its democratic constitution, and in the first issue of its journal the Association announced itself as 'a strictly democratic body. No member's vote is greater than another's, and each member is directly concerned in the election of the officers'.[5]

Even the Comrades of the Great War dared not ignore the democratic values. The association was 'created to inaugurate and maintain in a strong, stimulating, united and democratic comradeship all those who have served in any capacity in the Sea, Land, and Air Forces during the Great War . . .'[6] As one of the founders recalled, '. . . from the very first it was recognized that . . . the Movement should be democratic and non-party in character'.[7] The Comrades even criticized the Federation for its exclusion of officers from ordinary membership on the ground that it was undemocratic,[8] which was carrying the war into the enemy's camp and using the enemy's own password.

[1] H.M.S.O., Departmental Committee of Enquiry into the Machinery of Administration of the Ministry of Pensions, 1921. The Disabled Society was a society *for*, not *of*.

[2] G.P.C. Minutes, 11th Dec. 1920, Min. 8 (b); Monthly Circulars, Jan. 1921.

[3] Monthly circulars, Jan. 1921.

[4] Monthly circulars, March 1921.

[5] *The Bayonet*, Vol. 1, No. 1, Sept. 1920.

[6] Constitution, p. 3.

[7] Annual Report, 31st Dec. 1918, p. 4.

[8] *Comrades' Journal*, Jan. 1919, 4.

Indeed, all that the Comrades lacked (until 1919) was a democratic practice to match its democratic affirmations. The first Constitution provided that for at least a year after registration under the War Charities Act and until a general meeting of representatives of Divisions had taken place, 'the policy and management of Headquarters shall be controlled by a General Committee, with power to add to its number, of whom not less than four shall be non-commissioned officers, privates, petty officers or seamen.'[1] The General Committee appointed the Executive Committee with, technically, unlimited power.[2] It was not until February 1919 that the self-nominated and self-sustained Executive handed over the leadership to the elected representatives,[3] and even then among the elected were a considerable number who had previously nominated themselves, *e.g.*, five members of the immediately preceding Executive Committee re-appeared, three of whom had been in from the start.[4] Thus the chairmanship of the General Committee and of the Executive Committee remained in the same hands as before. But, at least, a democratic procedure was introduced in 1919.

In one important matter the ex-servicemen's demands went beyond mere democratic representation as far as democratic control. The issue was the disposal of the surplus canteen profits.[5] The official plan to administer those profits through a quasi-official Empire Services League foundered on the rock of determined ex-service opposition: despite all the careful preparatory work between 23rd October 1918 and 6th February 1919, the authorities deemed it advisable to give way. So much is already known.[6] But the precise nature of the ex-servicemen's opposition has not been recorded.[7] The dispute was essentially one of democratic control. The exact status of some elements in the total canteen profits had been the subject of inter-departmental discussion from January 1916 onwards.[8] As early as June 1918 the Army Council was considering in what legal form some of the profits would be held, how these would be

[1] Constitution 1919, XI (a).

[2] ibid., XI (b).

[3] Minutes of First Annual Meeting of the elected Grand Council, 15th–16th Feb. 1919, p. 3.

[4] ibid., and Constitution, 1917.

[5] Hist. B.L., pp. 6–7 and 12–14.

[6] ibid., p. 7.

[7] The best generally available sources are Major H. Jellicorse, op. cit., and the official journals of the ex-servicemen's associations. The Ashley Papers furnish some corroborating evidence.

[8] Army Appropriation Account 1915–16, Public Accounts Committee 1917, Mins. of ev., p. 156; P.A.C. Report 1918, pp. 140–1; Report of Comptroller and Auditor-General, 1917, on Army Account of 1916–17, para. 40.

disposed of 'and on what objects'.[1] The problem needed early consideration partly because of its scale (it could already be seen that altogether several millions would be available), and partly because of the source of those millions. As the Select Committee on National Expenditure observed:

'. . . before the war we had a small professional Army; after the war our forces will be reduced to whatever peace establishment it may be found necessary to maintain; during the years of war the Army has been expanded to include a great part of the adult manhood of the nation. It is from this vastly larger body that this fund has been drawn, and the disposal of it should take these differences into account.'[2]

That disposal problem had two aspects: participation in the decisions about disposal as well as the nature of the decisions themselves. What was decided? The War Office[3] recognized the interest that the men had in the decision-making and was ready to grant representation, but, not unnaturally in view of its traditions, it tended to think of representation in terms of Commanders-in-Chief and of others officially nominated rather than elected. The objects on which the canteen funds were to be spent were implied in the declared purpose of the Inter-Departmental Conference held on 5th November 1918, which was to consider and report upon the best method of fostering the spirit of comradeship and mutual help among all those who had served, or were serving, in the Navy, Army and Air Force.

Thus the Service Departments' approach to the problem was paternalistic: they would decide *for* the men. The Conference set up a Consultative Committee which met for the first time on 21st November: among the nineteen who attended were W. G. Clifford, who had written extensively on ex-service matters, and six army 'other ranks' as well as a naval chief-writer. But these were either official nominees or co-options of those nominees: no member of the Committee had been elected. The ex-service organizations as such were not represented, although the Committee did decide at that meeting to ask the Federation, Association and Comrades to appear before them. They would have been astonished, even incredulous, if they had been told that, within twelve months, those three organizations would have not only reversed the roles but also have been put well on the way to taking sole control of the canteen funds.

The scheme that the Consultative Committee first recommended

---

[1] P.A.C. mins. of ev., pp. 138–9 (2977).

[2] S.C.N.E., 5th Report 1918, p. 48 (11).

[3] All three Service Departments were affected but for obvious reasons it was the War Office that had the greatest responsibility. That was why the Chairman of the later Inter-Departmental Conference was a military officer.

to the Service Departments had paternalism built into its structure.[1] It certainly visualized a permanent organization based on the elective principle, but for the time being there was to be a Provisional Executive established under the authority of the Service Departments. Ultimately, the whole organization was to be 'entirely self-governing' —except that the principal governing body, the Central Council, was to have a nominated Patron, Patroness, President and three Vice-Presidents, 'and such other Honorary Officers as may be recommended by the Central Council'.[2] Even this degree of control seemed inadequate to the War Office, who wanted to ensure proper financial supervision of the new body's activities. The right of the Service Departments to appoint financial experts to the Central Council was conceded, as indeed it had to be so long as the Army Council remained trustees for the canteen funds.[3]

In reserving ultimate power to themselves, the Service Departments were not only giving expression to a paternalism that was natural to them; they also wished at one fell swoop to eradicate the political character of the three great ex-servicemen's organizations, to unite them and to make use of the machinery that would be so inherited. This was the real meaning of the object expressed as 'to co-ordinate the work of all voluntary and unofficial bodies, both inside the services and outside of them, which are working on behalf of those who have served'.[4] No doubt in Whitehall generally the ex-servicemen's movement was feared as a potential political instrument. The Assistant Secretary to the Cabinet, Thomas Jones, confided to his diary on 8th February, 1919:

'Bolshevik propaganda in this country is only dangerous in so far as it can lodge itself in the soil of genuine grievances. There is no doubt that large numbers of workpeople are expecting a big and rapid improvement in their social and industrial conditions. . . . Much of the present difficulty springs from the mutiny of the rank and file against the old-established leaders and there seems to be no machinery for bringing about a quick change of leaders.'[5]

To a substantial degree the ex-servicemen's movement represented such a 'mutiny'; perhaps even the word is a kind of Freudian slip. At any rate, the Service Departments seem to have been of like mind.

Success, however, was not easily attained, and never came in the form that the Service Departments intended. A conference at the

---

[1] Memorandum on the Amalgamation of the Existing Ex-Service Men's Organizations, published by the National Association, n.d., p. 9.
[2] ibid., p. 10.   [3] ibid.
[4] ibid., p. 9.
[5] From the late Thomas Jones's *un*published diary. Entry made available by him to this writer.

Horse Guards Library on 5th February 1919 failed entirely to win the ex-servicemen's co-operation, which was also the fate of a further attempt on 22nd March.[1] The Comrades took a very strong line. Hamar Greenwood, by now installed at the Home Office, made it plain to Churchill, the new Secretary of State for War, that if the scheme were pursued the Comrades would put up the fight of its life.[2] The influential Wilfrid Ashley was also distinctly hostile. His attitude was clearly expressed in the House about this time when, intervening at Question Time, he asked the War Secretary:

'Ought not the decision regarding the allocation of money derived from serving soldiers to rest with service and ex-service men, seeing that it has nothing at all to do with civilians?'[3]

And beyond any doubt at all he would not have stood by while the Comrades, which had flourished thanks largely to him, was undermined; two years later he withdrew temporarily to Spain rather than hand over the Comrades to the embryonic British Legion.[4]

In the event, the ex-servicemen's views prevailed (although the decision actually reached did help to bring about, in 1921, a united and politically neutralized body). On 26th July, it was publicly announced that the Government had approved an organization for the disposal of the canteen profits accumulated during the war.[5] The sums involved (it was announced) were considerable[6] and would be devoted to fostering the spirit of comradeship and mutual help among those who had served in the Armed Forces. It was recognized that many organizations existed which had some of the same objects in view, and it was the intention of the new body to further the interests, and make the greatest use, of existing machinery. General Sir Julian Byng would leave the Army to become Chairman of the Board of Management; the Executive Committee would include representatives of all ranks. The Government (the statement concluded) had decided to delegate the task 'to this central authority which will be unconnected with any Government Department'.[7]

This was one great victory for ex-servicemen: another was achieved

---

[1] The Association was not represented. An invitation sent to Blackburn would probably not have reached the president, James Howell, who lived in Abercynon, South Wales.

[2] The Ashley Papers, Greenwood to Ashley, 10th Mar. 1919.

[3] 113 H.C. Deb., c. 202–3.   [4] Hist. B.L., p. 26.

[5] *The Times*, 26th July 1919. No doubt a War Cabinet decision had been necessary.

[6] A masterly under-statement: it was already clear that some ten and a half million pounds would be ultimately realized.

[7] ibid.

the following October when, after Byng had held his first meeting with the ex-servicemen's representatives,[1] an M.P. tried to ask four questions about the United Services Fund. Byng became very angry and made it clear that, as the Fund was in no sense under the War Office, he considered it most inadvisable that the Secretary of State should answer questions about it in the House. His view prevailed, and in due course a Royal Charter guaranteed the independence of the Fund for the future.

Thus ex-servicemen achieved one of their main objectives. They also won independence in a different sense. The intention had been to have representatives of both S.S.F.A. and of Soldiers Help on the Executive Committee of the Fund. But Byng had formed an unfavourable view of both organizations: he told the representatives of the three ex-servicemen's associations:

'Our trouble has been that we find that these two Associations have not fulfilled the conditions that they claim; that is to say, they have not been able to do the work we expect them to do, and they have rendered themselves very open to criticism by having the wrong people administering and the wrong people doing the local representing. We have therefore sent them a very drastic memorandum of which the gist is that these organizations should consist in future of 20 per cent voluntary workers, 20 per cent ex-Officers, and 60 per cent ex-service men. That is a complete revolution, as you know, of the whole of their organization, which up to the present rather has been on the lines of patronage and voluntary workers. We have put that memorandum to them. If they accept it, they practically become us . . .'[2]

These proposals, of course, constituted an ultimatum, a term which Byng himself used in this connexion on at least three occasions.[3] It had been agreed by both the Comrades and the Federation before being delivered on 24th October. Its effect was perfectly clear. The executive committees of the S.S.F.A. and Soldiers Help 'would be practically our nominees; at all events they would be so organized by us as to be us', Byng explained.[4] And when Lister asked: 'If they come on, they take our instructions?', Byng answered: 'They become us. They come and sit here and take their orders'.[5] Naturally, S.S.F.A. and Soldiers Help refused to do so; and the upshot of it was that the United Services Fund came under the virtual control of the three ex-servicemen's organizations, and, in due course, therefore, was *in effect* inherited by the British Legion, who over the years acquired something like one-fifth of the ten million pounds.[6]

---

[1] Hist. B.L., p. 13; Minutes of United Services Fund Conference.
[2] Minutes of United Services Fund Conference, pp. 17–18, 14.
[3] ibid., pp. 14, 15 and 45.   [4] ibid.
[5] ibid., p. 45.   [6] Hist. B.L., p. 13.

Thus what began as a demand for democratic representation eventually expanded into a demand for democratic control: at first, ex-servicemen were merely to be consulted about the proposals; in the end, they were sitting firmly in the saddle, and were able to ride away, leaving behind not only the Service Departments but also the traditional ex-service societies. The whole episode illustrates both the transition from societies *for* to societies *of* and the rise of democracy.

XII

EXTERNAL AIMS

(3) ATTITUDES TO CAPITALISM

MONSIEUR RENÉ RÉMOND has speculated on the extent to which ex-servicemen's associations in certain countries have been used to defend the existing economic order,[1] usually, of course, referred to as 'capitalism'—one of those chameleon-like phrases that in different hands display quite different colours. His interesting reflections did not extend to Britain, where he could have found some support for his thesis but also examples of organized ex-servicemen who were highly critical, to say the least, of the *status quo*. The Association and Federation, for instance, were opposed to some features of the socio-economic order, and even seemed to the Comrades of the Great War to be subversive of it. The N.U.X. was undoubtedly hostile to the whole social order. The local councillor who suggested that the men standing about at the top of Church Street, Blackburn,[2] should organize themselves was a keen Socialist who had been associated with Philip Snowden for thirty years and whom Snowden later described as 'my devoted friend and helper . . . who gave the whole of his spare time to working for the movement'.[3] For a short time Snowden himself played a part in the Association,[4] and the very first meeting in 1916 was held under the auspices of the local Trades and Labour Council.[5] Moreover, the movement was developed by using the machinery of the Trades Councils in the industrial areas such as Lancashire itself, Yorkshire and South Wales.[6] The original Executive had four Trades Council representatives on it in an advisory capacity.[7]

It was therefore only to be expected that in 1917 the Executive Committee should announce that the Association was to be 'a purely working-class organization' and 'that the discharged men should not be exploited by the capitalist class. This will certainly happen if the

[1] 5 *Revue Française de Science Politique* 1955, 287–8.
[2] See above p. 49. Interview. The councillor was James Frankland.
[3] Viscount Snowden, *An Autobiography*, Vol. 2, 1934, pp. 554–5.
[4] Jellicorse, op. cit., p. 6; interview.
[5] *Northern Daily Telegraph*, 14th Sept. 1916.
[6] H.Q. Circular, 1st June 1917.
[7] Leaflet, Series No. 2, n.d.; Gloucester Branch leaflet, n.d.

Trade Union movement does not actively interest itself in getting the men together'.[1] This attitude came to be embodied in the declared objects of at least some branches of the Association, as when Folkestone Branch announced that one of its aims was 'to prevent any advantage being taken of the disabled man's labour in the way of lowering of wages'.[2]

This oblique criticism of the economic order, implied in the first quotation at least, did not, however, find either a notable or a permanent place in the policy of the Association. At their second annual conference in April 1918, the men of the Association broke with the Labour movement, and in effect moved towards the political centre. Accordingly their policy became more 'neutral', *i.e.*, more narrowly concerned with ex-servicemen's issues.

Like the Association, the Federation set out to 'prevent the exploitation of the discharged man's labour', which was one of the three principal aims elaborated in an early policy statement.[3] But a more radical attitude tended to emerge out of the demand for higher pensions and allowances. If the value of a husband to a wife was 13s. 9d. a week (the writer commented) and the value of a father to a child was 7s. a week when the man had been 'killed in defence of the liberties to [*sic*] the State, it becomes an open question as to the worth of the liberties'.[4]

Such attitudes do little more than hint at the Federation's early policy *vis-à-vis* the social order. That policy became rather more explicit when they expressed their views about discharged men and the land. They argued that since there were men who desired to go on the land and since land was available, it was the Government's business to make suitable provision to meet the demand. But access to land should not be 'denied or made possible only upon terms of servitude'. If land-owners refused to co-operate, the land should be taken from them and paid for on the basis of a 'rental equal in amount to the valuation upon which he pays taxes'. The land could then 'be handed over to the discharged men under State supervision'. There was no intention of placing on the land men incapable of using it, but on the other hand men should not be so placed 'as appendages to a decrepit land system, nor as serfs, the sole purpose of whose labour is that they may exist from day to day'.[5]

In their 1919 general programme, the Federation men went further. 'Land being the chief monopoly', the 'ultimate aim' was public

---

[1] H.Q. Circular, 1st June 1917.   [2] Folkestone Branch leaflet, n.d.

[3] Pamphlet No. 1, pp. 2 and 5.   [4] ibid., p. 3.

[5] Leaflet No. 4, *Discharged Men and the Land*, n.d. (from internal evidence about autumn 1918).

ownership.[1] This was in line with their general policy of advocating the 'public ownership of all Monopolies'.[2] Among their constitutional aims they sought the abolition of the House of Lords and its replacement by an elected second chamber.[3]

In its early years, then, the Federation favoured some fundamental changes in the existing economic and political order. But it never advocated wholesale reconstruction: indeed, its general programme was a hotch-potch bearing the obvious imprints of *ad hoc* pressures and was not the emanation of a consistent philosophy. The real 'radicals' were the men who broke away from the Federation in 1919 to form the National Union of Ex-Service Men.

The N.U.X. was the only ex-service organization to recognize explicitly the distinction between 'our special interests as ex-servicemen' and 'our general interests as ex-servicemen'.[4] The purpose of the association was partly to 'watch over' those special interests, *i.e.* to secure justice for the disabled and to look after the dependants of the fallen.[5] But the association also existed 'to fight shoulder to shoulder with organized labour in the general struggle to make this country "a good country to live in"'.[6] The same dichotomy between special and general interests was of course inherent in other ex-servicemen's organizations (illustrating the important phenomenon of overlapping membership),[7] but their leaders either could not or would not admit it. Obviously, ex-servicemen constitute a species of citizen and may therefore be pulled in different directions. But the nature of their general interests, on the other hand, are highly debatable. The N.U.X. interpreted such interests in something like Marxist terms. For over two years, their General Secretary, Ernest Mander, wrote in 1920, ex-servicemen as a body have been 'dupes of the privileged class'. Owners of land and capital 'recognized from the first in the ex-servicemen's movement a very serious menace to themselves'. Their interests were irreconcilably opposed to ex-servicemen's. They had to keep ex-servicemen as a 'subject-class', and so were determined, as far as possible, 'to bribe and bluff them into forsaking their own class and kind, thus converting the movement into the means of again helping them to make the world safe for plutocracy'.[8]

The policy of the capitalist class (on this analysis) was twofold: to divide and conquer, using ex-servicemen as a lever, and to play off

---

[1] General Programme, 1919, Section 9 (F).

[2] ibid., Section 4. [3] ibid., Section 3 (B).

[4] *Aims and Policy*, Sections 1 and 2.

[5] ibid. p. 3. [6] ibid.

[7] David Truman, *The Governmental Process*, 3rd ed. 1955, ch. 6.

[8] 1 *The New World*, Jan. 1920, 3.

organized ex-servicemen against organized labour.[1] But the capitalists made the mistake of starting too soon. 'In a flash, the class-conscious ex-service workers realized everything' and stopped short. Now they were breaking away from the old [so-called] independent organizations and throwing in their lot with all the rest of their fellow-workers. 'Instead of being the means of saving Capitalism, the organized ex-servicemen will now be the means of destroying it'. For neither the ex-serviceman's general interests nor his special interests could be met under the existing social system. The aim should be to produce a form of society in which the resources of civil life would be used to make life good. 'If it means smashing the system, why then, we'll smash the system.'

This was the kind of language that sent shivers down the backs of the members of the Comrades of the Great War—and of many people in authority. And although the Federation as a body had never used such language nor come within distance of taking such a stand, to men like Norton-Griffiths and Wilfrid Ashley and many others, it seemed almost as sinister and dangerous when it grew to national stature in 1917. The Comrades, James Hogge once wrote, was the outcome of an attempt to 'gas' the discharged man. For the Federation (he asserted) 'had become a political menace', and its demands 'awkward to the Powers that Be'. The discharged man 'was not to be allowed to become a power. He was instead to be taught what was due from him to his superiors. He was to be drilled into blessing the squire and his relations.'[2] Ignoring the rhetorical exaggeration, one may accept the charge as substantially true in the sense that the Comrades was undoubtedly launched as a counter to the Federation.

In retrospect and by comparison with the N.U.X., the Federation seems innocuous enough, hardly meriting the plans discussed privately in the Carlton Club, the House of Commons and elsewhere as to the best method of drawing its sting. But of course it was 1917: defeat was near and the reverberations of those momentous events in St. Petersburg could be heard all over Britain. The first of the two Russian Revolutions was followed by the launching of the National Federation, which was soon (June/July) holding its first annual conference. In reality the Federation, as we have seen, was not founded on ideology.[3] But a 'union' of ex-soldiers, suffused with grievances and led by two Liberal M.P.s who had been highly critical of some aspects of government policy, was bound to appear menacing to M.P.s like Norton-Griffiths, Wilfrid Ashley, David Davies, Hamar

[1] ibid.
[2] Federation, Bristol Branch Leaflet, n.d.
[3] See above, p. 60.

Greenwood and the rest, even though some of these (such as the last two mentioned) were themselves Liberals at the time.

Already these men would have found much in the domestic situation to give cause for alarm. As recently as the previous December, the editor of the *Trade Unionist*, who was secretary of the National Union of Catering Workers, as well as W. H. Watson, an honorary secretary of the Amalgamated Society of Engineers, had been charged at Bow Street with 'attempting to cause disaffection among the civilian population'.[1] Watson's article was alleged to have argued that the working classes were downtrodden dupes of the capitalists, and that they had only got to resist in order to remedy that situation. According to the counsel for the prosecution, the article included a reference to 'slitting gizzards' in Park Lane before long.[2] In his own defence Watson claimed that he wished only to cause disaffection among the civilian population when the rights and privileges of the organized workers were being taken away from them, but the alleged title of his article ('Forty millions—mostly fools') had wider implications. Another article, unsigned, in the same issue took as its theme 'The Three-Card Trick', *i.e.*, according to prosecuting counsel, 'that patriotism was a sham and a mere cloak for robbery, trickery, and oppression'.[3] This, too, on the face of it, had wider implications. Defendants escaped with fines and costs; as they left the court there was some cheering and Watson was carried shoulder high through a crowd of trade unionists.[4]

In the very issue of *The Times* in which that report was printed, Norton-Griffiths and the others could have read a letter from a man who described himself as an 'active Socialist for nearly twenty years' (Fred H. Gorle). He complained that for far too long Snowden 'and his colleagues in national disunity, Messrs. MacDonald, Morel, & Co., have been poisoning the minds of the people from their platform and their Press...'[5] The position taken up by Snowden, MacDonald and the other anti-war men is well known. They had considered the question formulated later by G. D. H. Cole in these terms:

'Here, then, is the problem which the revolutionary is compelled to face. Is allegiance due first of all to the nation, which includes some of all classes, or to the class, which includes some of all nations?'[6]

In effect, most of them, although certainly not all (*e.g.*, the 'pure' pacifists) had answered: 'to the class'.

This of course was not true of most of the Labour movement. At the Labour Party conference at Bristol in 1915, about five votes to

<hr>

[1] *The Times*, 4th Dec.1916.   [2] ibid.
[3] ibid.   [4] ibid.
[5] ibid.   [6] *Labour in Wartime*, 1915, p. 5.

two were cast in favour of the prosecution of the war.[1] *The Times* letter-writer's reference to Morel is significant for our inquiries because the Union of Democratic Control from the first appealed 'direct to the workers'.[2] By October 1915 not far off half the organizations affiliated to it formed part of the Labour movement. Among these were many trade union branches. As Gorle complained:

'Literature of an utterly dishonest character has been scattered in our industrial circles for many months. The so-called National Council for Civil Liberties, whose secretary was one of the founders of the Union of Democratic Control, and whose executive and committee were mainly composed of those who have never helped the nation in its greatest crisis, is planting down pamphlets and literature in the branches of our trade unions'.[3]

Such cases as these and the increasing effectiveness of the Union of Democratic Control in influencing trade union branches seem likely to have reinforced a fear of trade unions that already existed on other grounds. In June 1917 Norton-Griffiths, for instance, singled out the current leadership of the unions for strong criticism. He wished (he said) that the Government could sound public opinion other than through the leaders of the unions; he went on to blame the unions for preventing the Government from bringing in a Bill to compel every man up to a certain age to come forward for military service, referring darkly to organizations that had 'threatened the Government and dared them to do this, that and the other'.[4] Wilfrid Ashley, as the chairman of the Anti-Socialist Union, must have had a similar attitude to trade unions; so much indeed can be gathered from the oral tradition that has survived.[5]

In this matter, Norton-Griffiths would, in fact, have found some support even on the Labour benches. It was Charles Edwards, M.P. for Bedwellty, who complained that the Government had failed 'to recognize that the machinery of many of the trade unions has been deliberately captured by the caucus of the Independent Labour party and the Syndicalists, who do not represent the men in the industry', *e.g.*, the South Wales Miners' Federation.[6] The majority of the committee of the South Wales Miners' Federation did not, he claimed, represent the miners of South Wales.[7] What Norton-Griffiths (and no doubt others) feared in the summer of 1917 was that 'extremists

---

[1] Fenner Brockway, *Socialism Over Sixty Years*, 1946, p. 138.

[2] A. J. P. Taylor, *The Trouble Makers*, 1957, p. 135.

[3] *The Times*, ibid.   [4] 94 H.C. Deb., c. 2097.

[5] Interviews with Lt.-Col. G. R. Crosfield, former Chairman of the Finance Committee of the Comrades, and with Mr. S. T. Wilce Taylor, former General Secretary.

[6] 94 H.C. Deb., c. 2094.   [7] ibid., c. 2095.

and syndicalists' would succeed in capturing the discharged soldier for their political ends. He calculated that there were some 230 organizations working for such a purpose.[1] All soldiers should make a sustained effort to fight the pernicious propaganda and to keep soldiers clear of politics. As things were going the country would soon be face to face with discontent and revolution.[2]

Between that Defence of the Realm case at the end of 1916 and the summer of 1917, tremendous events had taken place. The Russian Revolution attracted the sympathy of Labour generally and gave a great impetus to the peace movement. Henderson cabled: 'Organized labour in Great Britain is watching with the keenest sympathy the efforts of the Russian people to deliver themselves from the power of reactionary elements which are impeding their advance to victory'.[3] Snowden addressed peace demonstrations almost every week-end, and on 16th May he opened a debate in the House on behalf of the peace group. The resolution attracted thirty-two votes.[4]

Meanwhile, an organizing committee, presided over by Snowden, composed mainly of representatives of the I.L.P. and of the British Socialist Party, had decided to arrange 'a great convention at Leeds' for the purpose of advocating 'peace without annexations or indemnities'.[5] The inspiration of the convention was obviously Russian: the circular dispatched to trades councils, trade unionists, local Labour parties and other units within the movement on 11th May was headed 'Follow Russia!'[6]

The convention was held at the Leeds Coliseum on 3rd June and was attended by some 1,100 delegates.[7] Its objects were epitomized in four resolutions, one of which, sponsored by W. C. Anderson, M.P., is particularly relevant to our inquiries. This was the resolution that called on constituent bodies to form Workmen's and Soldiers' Councils immediately 'for initiating and co-ordinating working-class activity in support of the policy' which would be decided at the convention. Their task would be to:

'concern themselves with questions affecting the pensions of wounded and disabled soldiers and the maintenance grants payable to the dependants of men serving with the Army and Navy, and the making of adequate provision for the training of disabled soldiers, and for suitable and remunerative work for the men on their return to civil life.'[8]

---

[1] He may have meant the branches of the Federation throughout the country and possibly those of the National Association as well.

[2] Hist. B.L., p. 3.

[3] Francis Williams, *Fifty Years' March*, 1949, p. 262.

[4] Snowden, op. cit., Vol. 1, pp. 440, 449.

[5] ibid., p. 449.   [6] ibid., p. 450.

[7] Brockway, op. cit., p. 264; Snowden, p. 452, gives 1150.

[8] Brockway, p. 153; Snowden, p. 445.

This resolution was indicative of 'the exhilaration that the Russian revolution had created'.[1] It had 'no practical result' because the organizing committee decided that such councils were unnecessary,[2] but it must nevertheless have sounded alarming in St. James's and Westminster and perhaps in humbler places too. For W. C. Anderson, who had taken the initiative in bringing forward that resolution, left no one in doubt what the convention meant to him: it meant 'the conquest of power by the hitherto disinherited class'.[3] At the same time, a writer in the *Bradford Pioneer*, postulating that war had 'made revolution necessary', added:

'We mean a fundamental alteration from the pre-war method of progress by small instalments to one of sensational and immediate change. The atmosphere is favourable.'[4]

Snowden thought a revolution not simply necessary but inevitable. Speaking at the annual demonstration of the Woolwich Branch of the I.L.P. towards the end of July, he said that the Russian revolution had helped to make vocal the inarticulate discontent which already existed. He was often asked (he said) by wealthy M.P.s if he thought there would be a revolution in England. He always answered that 'it was quite as certain as tomorrow's sunrise'.[5]

Norton-Griffiths, Wilfrid Ashley and their associates, then, may be reasonably assumed to have been men frightened by the prospect of revolutionary change. They were all wealthy or well-to-do men; the sources of their wealth ranged from land through coal, railways and constructional engineering to brewing,[6] and so had tended to produce different party allegiances, but all were naturally ready to take a stand against the 'conquest of power by the disinherited class'. So, it is reasonable to suppose, were the men and the business groups who subscribed such vast sums (by ex-servicemen's standards) to the Comrades of the Great War. A brief reference to the financial backers of the Comrades of the Great War has already been made elsewhere.[7] Many of them cannot now be identified.[8] Even when they can be identified, it is not now possible to determine whether the donation should be properly regarded as a personal contribution or as 'really' representative of some great industrial or commercial

---

[1] Brockway, p. 264. [2] ibid., Snowden, p. 456.
[3] Williams, op. cit., p. 264. [4] *Bradford Pioneer*, June 1917.
[5] *The Times*, 30th July 1917.

[6] Capt. Albert Smith, M.P. (Labour), one of the original six signatories of the letter that led to the formation of the Comrades, was an apparent exception to this generalization, but he was brought in only to provide an all-party façade. He never played an active part and soon disappeared from the scene.

[7] See my article in 29 P.Q. 1958, 30–31.

[8] The complete list is contained in Income and Expenditure Account, etc., 1917, and in Annual Reports 1917–20.

undertaking. The 'extremities' are obvious: Ethel M. Dell (£50) at the 'private' end, and Ellerman Lines (£1,000) at the other. But should Stanley Baldwin's £500 and David Davies's £1,000 (1917) be classified as a contribution from the coal, iron and steel, and railway industries?

For the purposes of this discussion, the distinction may perhaps be neglected. The David Davies who helped to found the Comrades was indistinguishable from the David Davies who was chairman of both the Ocean Coal and Cambrian Railway Companies,[1] so that in indicating how far economic interests supported the Comrades it would be permissible to classify a seemingly personal contribution as institutional. So too with Sir James Horlick's and Viscount Iveagh's £500 each: these contributions may be ascribed, in this context, to the concerns that, respectively, produce the cure for night starvation and the stout that is good for us. Even if that procedure were unacceptable, one could say with complete confidence that a very considerable proportion of the money subscribed or donated came from powerful economic interests.

It would be a mistake, however, to think of the founders of the Comrades of the Great War merely as defenders of their own narrow economic interests. It would be as natural for them as for other social groups to equate their own interests with the public interest. Lord Lansdowne might want a negotiated peace but for most men (of all classes) the 'public interest' meant a successful prosecution of the war. Now, the movement by the disinherited to conquer power, which threatened to enrol soldiers and ex-soldiers, was also a peace movement. The Second International's call for a world-wide conference, representative of 'both sides' of the fighting, to define war aims had been reinforced by the establishment of Workers' and Soldiers' Councils in Russia. The Labour movement here was divided about the nature of the response to that call, but decided to send to Russia two delegates each from the Labour Party and the I.L.P. in order to determine the precise objectives the Russians had in mind. Later the plan to travel to Stockholm by sea was thwarted, in the first instance, by the organized seamen, who had, in the words of their leader Havelock Wilson, said to the delegates:

'If you want to go to Stockholm to kiss your German brothers, you must swim there.'[2]

These events were of course indications of a ferment of ideas that moved men generally, but organized ex-servicemen had some share

---

[1] *Mining Manual and Mining Year Book*, 1917, pp. 483–4; *The Times*, 6th Nov. 1922. He was also a director of the Barry Railway Company.

[2] Havelock Wilson at Hull, *Yorkshire Post*, 10th Dec. 1918.

in it. Snowden's connexion with the Blackburn Association was in all probability still unbroken, for the Association later felt called upon to defend itself against the charge of being the tool of pacifist M.P.s.[1] And Snowden, in justifying the decision of the organizing committee of the Leeds convention to refrain from carrying out the resolution to set up Workers' and Soldiers' Councils, explained that 'the work of looking after the interests of the workers in industry and of the disabled soldiers was undertaken by an organization conducted by the Labour Party and the Trade Unions',[2] a description that might perhaps be stretched to fit the Blackburn Association. If the Federation lacked a leader of the Snowden type, they had two M.P.s who were highly critical of some aspects of the Government's policy, such as the 'Review of Exceptions Act', which both Hamar Greenwood and Norton-Griffiths, in particular, supported as essential to national survival.[3] Thus the Federation also tended to be an 'opposition' organization and could in any case have been expected in due course to be influenced to some extent by 'extremists and syndicalists'.

Thus the men who launched the Comrades of the Great War probably had two conditioning thoughts: fear of a revolutionary situation and fear of military defeat. It may well be true that some of them were aware of the historical (and Marxist ideological) inter-connexion between the two possibilities, so that in advocating measures to stave off defeat they were also warding off an extreme threat to their own personal role and position in society. But this is only to say that people's motives, even when identifiable, are often mixed: it is likely that those who founded the organization and many of the subscribers who backed it, were, in 1917, as much concerned with winning the war, which they would naturally assume to be the overriding public interest, as they were with defending their own private interests. That at least seems the best reading of the situation in 1917; large subscriptions, however, continued to be paid in 1919–20, and so must have had some other motivation than winning the war. Certainly it seems safe to conclude that the maintenance of the *status quo* was an external aim of the Comrades of the Great War.[4]

[1] Gloucester Branch Leaflet, n.d.

[2] Snowden, op. cit., p. 456.

[3] 92 H.C. Deb., c. 1167; 94 H.C. Deb., c. 2095–2100, 2105. They did not say so in such terms but their speeches implied that view, to say nothing of their voting records.

[4] How far the aims of the leaders coincided with the aims of the led within the ex-servicemen's movement is a general problem of considerable difficulty. In this context, where the distribution of power within organizations is not at issue, it has been assumed that the Comrades was 'monolithic'. So, too, with the other associations. Cf. my article in 9 P.S. 1961, 141-56.

The Officers' Association, formed only in January 1920,[1] had no place in the early rivalries. For the most part it did not exhibit external aims—with the one important exception that, in effect, it buttressed the Comrades of the Great War in its support of the existing economic order. To many such a statement will seem grotesque—not unlike charging a bishop with indecent exposure. At the inaugural meeting, the objects of the Officers' Association 'were declared to be to form a National Relief Fund' to help officers and their families.[2] That such a function has been discharged no one doubts, but historically the Officers' Association also discharged a very different one. On that score Haig was both clear-headed and unusually articulate. At a meeting of the Grand Council of the Officers' Association held on 10th November 1920, and attended, as the *Daily Herald* expressed it in a series of extremely accurate 'leaks', by 'thirty-three titled, decorated, and moneyed celebrities', he recalled that when he became Commander-in-Chief, Home Forces, he had been greatly disturbed by the revolutionary ideas which existed among societies of ex-servicemen. 'The only solution was to get those men back to their old leaders, the officers, and consequently I urged union amongst all ex-servicemen'.[3] The amalgamation of the various societies for officers and their dependants into the Officers' Association was a necessary step in bringing officers and men together.[4]

But who would finance this 'necessary step'? The Income and Expenditure Account for 1920 reveals that out of a total income of nearly £923,000, some £637,000, or roughly two-thirds, had been given in the form of 'donations from the public' (as distinct from members' subscriptions, which amounted to only about £20,000).[5] What the account does not reveal is that 'the public' was to a very considerable extent 'institutional'. As with the Comrades of the Great War, economic interests furnished significant financial support. How much of the £637,000 came from them is not now known, but it is easy to suggest the order of magnitude because the corresponding total up to the end of *October* 1920 was £574,000, and of that no less than about £288,000 was subscribed as follows:

[1] Hist. B.L., p. 14.

[2] Balance Sheet and Report of work to 31st Dec. 1920. *The Times*, 31st Mar. 1921.

[3] *Daily Herald*, 14th Jan. 1921. Haig spoke freely because 'there are no reporters present', but somebody later discharged a reporter's function. In three successive issues (14th, 15th and 17th Jan.) the *Herald* was able to print verbatim reports or inspired extracts. An edited version, omitting the references in the text above, was sent by the O.A. to the embryonic Legion on 25th Nov. 1920.

[4] ibid. *The Times*, 31st Mar. 1921.

[5] *The Times*, ibid. Totals rounded.

	£
Lloyd's	173,084
Baltic	28,400
Oil Corporation	61,900
Insurance Companies	25,500[1]

Thus the proportion of the whole year's 'donations from the public' furnished by these commercial groups cannot have been less than 45 per cent and may even have been greater.

It is plain, therefore, that one external aim can be ascribed even to the Officers' Association, however much it may have seemed to stand aloof from partisan conflicts. This does not mean that the professed (domestic) aims were simulated; on the contrary, Haig was deeply moved by the plight of the ex-officers, so many of whom, drawn from a different class from their pre-war predecessors, lacked private means but were still treated administratively as if they were comfortably off, *e.g.*, in not being eligible for the 'unemployment donation'. Haig and his associates were genuinely concerned; their sympathy *was* real. But to acknowledge their compassion is not to gloss over their political purpose. As with the rest of us for most of the time, their behaviour had many roots, not one.

[1] *Daily Herald*, 15th Jan. 1921. Lloyd's presumably means the marine insurance firm, not the bankers. The identity of the last two groups of donors is not revealed.

XIII

REMOVING A TARGET

THE terms 'left' and 'right' in political discussion have no precise significance, but can be given the degree of precision needed for this inquiry by equating 'left-wing' with a desire to change the whole socio-economic framework, leaving 'right-wing' to be applied to the wish to preserve it intact. 'Left centre' and 'right centre' then come to represent varying reform positions within an accepted framework.

From the discussion of the last three chapters it will have been observed that ex-servicemen's associations in the period 1917–21 may, as a rough generalization, be assigned to two categories, corresponding to 'left' and 'right' in politics generally. The N.U.X. was as unambiguously 'left' as the Comrades was obviously 'right' and the Officers' Association discreetly so. The National Association bivouacked in the left-wing camp at least until Easter 1918; while the Federation, up to early 1919, might be broadly classified as 'left centre'. Thus these organizations, while pursuing the domestic aims of ex-servicemen as such, also had external aims that virtually reproduced in miniature the political conflicts of the community in general. For the ex-servicemen's movement as an effective articulation of group interests it was essential that those external aims should be abandoned, and it was precisely that disengagement from the broader political conflicts which was signalized by the founding of the British Legion.

The *process* by which four of the five leading ex-servicemen's associations came together in 1920–21 to form the British Legion may be rapidly sketched.[1] Between the summer of 1918 and the summer of 1920, there were at least four attempts to induce the associations to unite. The first was unofficial in form but possibly official in inspiration: a former regular Army officer who had interested himself in war pensions work brought the leaders together under the chairmanship of General Horace Smith-Dorrien, but to no avail. The second attempt took place after the Armistice and was demonstrably official, deriving from the Service Departments, especially the War Office, with the Commander-in-Chief himself, Sir Douglas Haig, hovering in the wings. The return to peace had, as we know, presented

[1] For fuller details, consult Hist. B.L., chs. II to IV, and ch. XI above.

the authorities with the problem of how to dispose of the surplus profits accumulated by the Navy and Army Canteen Board and by the Expeditionary Force Canteens. These profits belonged in principle largely to the rank and file who had spent their money in the canteens, but the authorities tried to make the disbursement of the surplus funds conditional upon the achievement of a united ex-service body and the virtual voluntary liquidation of the separate associations. At the Horse Guards Library in February 1919, after some three months' careful preparation of the ground, the plan foundered, as we have seen, on the stubborn opposition of the ex-servicemen's leaders.

In August 1919 Haig himself renewed his efforts to achieve unity, this time by the roundabout route of first uniting the officers. With the formation of the Officers' Association in January 1920, his first trench was taken. This event, with its public appeal for funds, also had the unintended effect of weakening the financial position of the Comrades, which had been about to launch an appeal on its own behalf, and so making it better disposed towards amalgamation.

In the end, the ex-servicemen's associations united of their own volition to form the British Legion. Three predisposing factors may be discerned. In the first place, Lord Peel's sense of fair play and his flair for the possible led, in the autumn of 1919, to the transfer of the canteen profits to an independent agency (the United Services Fund) in which the ex-servicemen's associations had the dominant voice. Thus the ex-servicemen virtually acquired the funds (eventually about ten million pounds) and yet retained their identity.[1] The establishment of the United Services Fund was significant in that it compelled the leaders of the principal associations to work together, and so made amalgamation less unthinkable.

By 1920 it was not only the Comrades that was feeling the cold wind financially: the Association was, as usual, struggling, and even the vigorous Federation was beginning to experience difficulties. By 1920 also, the atmosphere was cooler politically (in the ex-service context) as well as financially. After the Armistice the Government had blundered badly in its demobilization policy, which, being so obviously unfair in its incidence, caused great bitterness and some disorder. For demobilization there was at least a policy, but the structure of war pensions resembled a half-completed building constructed from plans drawn up by different architects. For military (though not naval) persons, entitlement was in form a matter of royal grace and favour; appeal on entitlement was not genuinely independent; the rates of pension were inadequate in relation to the cost of living; pensions were—of all things—liable to income tax.

---

[1] Hist. B.L., p. 13. Between 1919 and 1947 something like £2,000,000 went to the British Legion Relief Fund. Peel was Under-Secretary of State for War.

Nor were ex-servicemen systematically consulted by the decision-makers either in these matters or in others.

Between August 1919 and February 1920, a series of Cabinet decisions transformed the situation by meeting the ex-servicemen's 'external' ambitions. The demand for democratic representation was conceded, and ex-servicemen, from being 'out-groups', came to be officially recognized and consulted:[1] the establishment in 1920 of the Government Standing Joint Committee for Ex-Service Questions marks the transition. Occasional lapses occurred, and some suspicion of a united ex-servicemen's organization seems to have persisted here and there, but in general ex-servicemen were no longer 'outsiders'. Already they had won status and official recognition and could make their voices heard; soon they were to be given four places on the newly-created Central Committee for advising the Minister of Pensions.

There are those ex-servicemen who would deny that 'justice' has ever been achieved, but by 1920–21 the less comprehensive claim for 'justice, not charity' could have been notched as a successful one. The pensions reforms that resulted from the report of the Select Committee in 1919[2] were of crucial importance generally in reducing the high 'temperature' of organized ex-servicemen. The grant of (war) pensions ceased to be a form of royal bounty and became a statutory right.[3] The concession of independent appeal on entitlement was of great significance. One Appeal Tribunal had been in existence since 1917, and another had been set up in July 1918, followed by three others in January 1919.[4] An appeals system had even been established inside the Ministry itself. But the Minister's judgement was final; even the 'external' Tribunal was at first 'a personal creation by the Minister of Pensions, and it is part of the machinery of the Ministry'. Its sole function was to determine questions of fact and to advise the Minister accordingly.[5] The War Pensions Act 1919, however, provided for a genuinely independent Tribunal whose decision was final.[6]

A sound financial basis for 'justice, not charity' was also provided: pension rates for disabled men, widows and parents were increased, and the men also benefited through the abolition of income tax on what they received. The rates were based on the cost of living, which began to fall from the end of 1920 and so the real value of the awards increased. These developments obviated the need for 'charity', and although the King's Fund survived, the charity issue faded into the background.

[1] Federation Annual Report, 1919–20, p. 10.
[2] See below, ch. XXIII.   [3] ibid.
[4] H.C. 39 (1920), p. 21.
[5] ibid.   [6] Section 8.

The *status quo* issue was also resolved with comparative ease. The National Association had already divested itself of its trade union connexions, and in effect moved towards the political centre. The Federation followed in the same direction: Pringle, the Liberal M.P., dropped out at a fairly early stage, to be followed by his colleague James Hogge in the spring of 1919; soon afterwards the 'sectarian' Socialists inside the Federation who had failed to attach it to the Labour Movement broke away to form the National Union of Ex-Service Men. The N.U.X. withered away partly because it was deliberately and very effectively isolated by the authorities and also by Byng, and partly because it isolated *itself* from the negotiations that led to the founding of the British Legion.[1]

Thus the internal dynamics of the associations had already tended to eliminate those men who were most dedicated to the external aims. That tendency was sustained by the 1919–20 concessions, which marked a closing of the (relevant) rifts in our political culture. Like the foundation and working of the United Services Fund and the financial difficulties that the societies increasingly experienced, these tendencies helped the cause of unity by producing a more homogeneous ex-servicemen's movement. It was, naturally enough, the left-wing elements that suffered most, but the right did not go unscathed. If it did not wither away, it was nevertheless called upon to compromise a little, though not fundamentally. Wilfrid Ashley, by this time the main (executive) leader of the Comrades, refused to compromise (in the sense of amalgamating with others of different views) and went off to Spain during the critical negotiations. Towse, the blind V.C., was also too rigid to accept a move, in effect, towards the political centre, and so he too ceased to be active. The Officers' Association, in this context, was unique in not having to compromise at all: while negotiating with the other three societies to form a united body, it was also secretly negotiating for a Royal Charter to perpetuate its legal independence. This it was perfectly entitled to strive for, but the concealment of its intentions was a discreditable manœuvre. The outcome was that the Officers' Association came to be regarded, for administrative purposes, as the Officers' Benevolent Department of the British Legion (so 'fulfilling' the unity requirement), while in fact remaining a distinct legal entity, preserved for all time by a Royal Charter obtained at the eleventh hour (the day before the Legion came into official existence). Thus the Officers' Association had the best of both worlds: unity, with the men back under their old leaders as planned; for itself, not only actual separation but legal independence of the united body. Here was a strategy (or stratagem) that really worked with complete success.

[1] Hist. B.L., pp. 18–19.

These, then, were the factors that predisposed the leaders of the associations to amalgamate. If, as they negotiated, they had entertained any doubts about proceeding further, the bursting of the economic bubble in the autumn of 1920, and the mounting unemployment figures, would have been sufficient reason for suppression. Now compromise became a still more urgent need. The first (1921) Constitution bears the marks of many compromises but for this inquiry the Rules dealing with Principles and Policy and with Aims and Objects are particularly significant.[1] The former throws light on the 'tone' of the new organization. The Federation, echoing the American Legion, had suggested that one of the principles should be 'to inculcate a sense of individual obligation to the Community, State and Nation'.[2] Both the Comrades and the Officers' Association successfully countered with amendments designed to make the Crown the first object of 'loyalty' (a term which at an early stage in the negotiations had replaced 'individual obligation').[3]

The 'tone' of the new organization may also be deduced from the reception of another principle put forward by the Federation (and also evocative of the American Legion), which was 'to combat the autocracy of the classes and the masses'.[4] But the new organization was designed to bring in some representatives of 'the classes', and so this suggestion, too, met with the same fate as the other one, being replaced in the Drafting Committee by the much milder clause, 'to promote unity amongst all classes'.[5]

Which organization was responsible for the amendment is not recorded, but the two changes had a somewhat 'right-wing' flavour. The insertion of 'Crown' in the statement of principles, with its evocation of a most powerful symbol,[6] emphasized national unity and loyalty, and, accordingly, the maintenance of the socio-economic framework. The other amendment suggested a rather less 'aggressive' approach to the problem of adjusting class differences. In putting forward the original proposal the Federation may have harboured no

[1] For further details, consult my thesis, appendices 13 and 14.

[2] First typed draft.

[3] Comrades' circulars, 7th Oct. 1920 and 25th Nov. 1920; first typed draft; first printed draft; *Comrades' Journal*, June 1921, p. 26; Second Joint Conference on Unity, Sept. 1920, *Proceedings*, p. 20. The Officers' Association amendment was the more subtle: '. . . to the Crown, and to the Community, state and Nation', emphasizing the primacy of the Crown and depreciating 'the state'. This was a misunderstanding of the (American) terminology, but their basic aim was achieved.

[4] First typed draft.

[5] Second Joint Conference on Unity, *Proceedings*, p. 20.

[6] H. D. Lasswell and A. Kaplan, *Power and Society*, 1952, ch. 6.

particular design and, if so, suffered no defeat, but on the whole it was the Federation that made the most significant compromises.

It was the Federation, too, that had to modify some of the important 'aims and objects' it had proposed (and which had been, in fact, taken over almost 'wholesale' from its own constitution). The Federation proposed the inclusion of the following clause among the aims and objects:

'to *prevent* the exploitation of discharged or demobilized sailors, soldiers and airmen's labour.'[1]

The Association, by now close to the Comrades in general outlook, wished to substitute the less critical (and more practical) clause:

'to ensure the employment of ex-servicemen at wages not less than the standard rates.'[2]

Alternatively expressed,[3] this clause was embodied in the first printed version of the *draft* constitution. The Comrades went much further, saying (in effect) that one could neither 'prevent' nor 'ensure' but only 'assist' the men, who should, in any case, be paid only 'in accordance with their ability'.[4] Thus the Comrades drew, at the very least, a penumbra of ambiguity about the whole clause, which now became:

'To assist ex-servicemen to secure not less than the recognized standard rates of wages in accordance with their ability.'[5]

Thus the rule tended to become innocuous.

Another aim visualized by the Federation was to secure the ex-servicemen 'State and Public Employment' as well as employment in private industry.[6] It found expression, if not altogether lucidly, in this clause:

'To press the claims of discharged and demobilized sailors, soldiers and airmen for State and Public employment and to enlist the co-operation of employers and Trade Unions for their employment.'

But again the Federation had to compromise, and in due course that aim became the less specific one of pressing the men's claims 'for employment', enlisting for that purpose the co-operation of employers and trade unions.[7]

---

[1] First typed draft. One of the earliest Federation rules. Constitution 1917–18, Objects, 2 (f).

[2] Correspondence, 26th Nov. 1920.

[3] 'To prevent the employment of ex-servicemen at less than the recognized standard rates of wages'.

[4] Comrades' circular, 7th Oct. 1920; Correspondence, 1st Dec. 1920.

[5] ibid.; 1921 Constitution; *Comrades' Journal*, June 1921, p. 6.

[6] First Typed Draft.   [7] First printed draft.

These aims had been specified, but even unspecified aims were, so to speak, restricted in advance. The Federation had proposed that there should be nothing in the Constitution to prevent the new body from 'declaring a definite policy on any public question' and from taking any action considered necessary in pursuance of it, provided that the matter had been considered and endorsed by a majority of the branches of the organisation.[1] But 'any public question' was narrowed down by the Comrades and the Association to 'any question directly or indirectly affecting ex-servicemen'.[2] It is true that the term 'indirectly' would still permit a very wide range of policies to be adopted, but the intention to limit the scope of the aims and objects that could be properly adopted by the Legion is plain.

The course of the discussion may be summarized in this way: as the price of unity, the Federation men were required to make substantial compromises, and in the amalgamating process, such external aims as remained had to be narrowed down if not entirely discarded. In that sense the founding of the British Legion in 1921 represents a 'neutralization' of the ex-servicemen's movement in this country. Like an American trade union, the new body could at last proclaim:

'We have no argument with the system. We just want our share....'[3]

It had taken the ex-servicemen's movement some four years to learn to 'stick to its knitting'.[4]

[1] First typed draft.

[2] Comrades' circular, 7th Oct. 1920; Correspondence 1st Dec. 1920; Second Joint Conference on Unity, *Proceedings*, pp. 18–20.

[3] George Meany, President of A.F.L.–C.I.O., *Labour News from the U.S.* 4th Jan. 1948, p. 1.

[4] ibid.

XIV

STICKING TO ONE'S KNITTING

THE lesson that one should stick to one's knitting, *i.e.*, harbour only domestic aims, was generally if not universally learned in the period 1917–21. This phase was therefore the crucial one, as vital to the new organization itself in conditioning its success[1] as to the general body of citizens saved from any possibility of a para-military force. Once the gap in the political culture had been closed, a general revival of external aims was unlikely and perhaps impossible, but the economic conditions of the early twenties did at least give rise to a tendency for the tide to flow in that direction. Later, towards the end of the decade, an association was founded that was more 'external' than anything else. Thus it was not until 1929 that the neutralization of the ex-service movement was finally secured beyond all question.

The period 1918–early 1920 had had the appearance of 'phenomenal prosperity'.[2] As late as April 1920, unemployment (in trade unions making returns) was below 1 per cent. But the following month saw a slight increase, and by the end of the year the proportion exceeded 6 per cent. From then onwards the rise was 'exceedingly rapid', and on the eve of the official foundation of the Legion, it was more than 23 per cent, the 'highest ever recorded' by the Ministry of Labour.[3] Transposed into absolute terms, these statistics meant that in June 1921 some 2,100,000 applied for benefit as totally unemployed, while another 830,000 or so were on systematic short time.[4]

Even at the end of 1923 unemployment was still of the order of nearly 10 per cent.[5] It is not surprising therefore that only two years after the Unity Conference in 1921, with its political 'neutralization' of organized ex-servicemen, the Legion adopted an essentially political, and exceptionally controversial, aim. On the initiative of the Paddington branch, Conference, by a 'big' majority and merely on a

---

[1] See Part Seven below.

[2] International Labour Office, Studies and Reports, Series C, No. 8, Unemployment 1920–23, p. 18.

[3] ibid., pp. 19–21. June 1921: 23. 1 per cent. These statistics are all based on the trade unions *making returns*.

[4] ibid., p. 21. Totals rounded.

[5] ibid., p. 106.

show of hands, amended the constitution significantly. The aim of pressing the claims of ex-servicemen for employment[1] was replaced by the intention 'to press that those who assisted to save the country in its hour of need be granted the right to work or be granted maintenance instead of appealing to the Poor Law Authorities'.[2]

This resolution was an adaptation of the Labour Party's policy 'of work or maintenance', and in that sense constituted an external aim, but it was adopted only because of the desperate plight of ex-servicemen generally. Seldom had such a controversial resolution aroused so little controversy at Conference. The only opposition came from the South Farnborough branch, who saw it as 'the thin end of the wedge'.

'They were demanding the right to work. If they demanded the right then they must force the right. How were they going to force the right? There was only one way and that was by armed force. The same cry had been made from political platforms for years. Who was going to pay for it? They must keep politics and everything relating to politics out of the movement or the movement would be broken up. If they wanted a policy they must have one of their own. They must not steal one.'[3]

The National Executive Council as such neither supported nor opposed the proposal, but one of its members spoke strongly in favour of it. The amendment (he argued) 'would be the first step in the making of the organization in the country. If they did not pass it, they [would] still be journeying on the same old way as in the years after 1854 when they found Crimean veterans dependent on someone in Fleet Street to keep them in bread and margarine'. 'The men who had saved the country were worth something better than lining up for the dole'.[4] And Conference delegates agreed with him.

Although the N.E.C. speaker was careful to warn delegates against thinking that 'they were being submerged into the Labour Party', it is obvious that the adoption of this amendment tended to upset the equilibrium so carefully established in the period 1920–21 and finally achieved only at the Unity Conference. When it is realized that an attempt was also made at that 1923 Conference to amend the constitution so as to permit payments towards electioneering expenses, the tendency towards 're-engagement' becomes unmistakable.

Yet the 1921 compromise was not undermined. The new 'work or maintenance' aim was embodied in the constitution, but in the meantime negotiations had been proceeding for the granting of a Royal Charter. The Petition to the Privy Council had in fact been

---

[1] See above, p. 112, text and note.   [2] Verb. Rep., 1923, p. 66.
[3] ibid., p. 68.   [4] ibid., p. 67.

lodged in July 1923, a few months after the Conference at which the important amendment had been passed. The new clause was accordingly part of the statement of 'aims and objects' included in the Petition to the Privy Council, but their lordships made it plain that they would not accept it as drafted, and indeed thought that it should be discarded altogether.[1]

The Legion leaders did not find the proposed alteration much to their taste, but they were also anxious, for domestic as well as general reasons, to receive a Royal Charter. They tried various compromises, including an attempt to retain the principle that ex-servicemen should be given 'an adequate and honourable alternative to the acceptance of Poor Law Relief', but this, too, was abandoned in the end, the new aim becoming the much more innocuous:

'to endeavour to obtain public recognition for the principle that ex-service men and women in accordance with their qualifications are entitled to preferential treatment in all matters relating to the finding or provision of employment.'[2]

This fundamental change was embodied in the draft Petition dated 5th January 1925, and at the Whitsun following the Legion at last received its Charter.

This was the most important example of the Legion's accommodation to the Privy Council in terms of 'aims and objects'; but it was not the only one. The rule 'to secure adequate pensions, allowances, grants and war gratuities' for ex-servicemen, their dependants, and the widows and other dependants of those who had fallen also failed to commend itself to their lordships. The grounds for their opposition are not clear; possibly they considered that pensions and other awards *were* 'adequate'. Whatever the reason, under their influence the clause was given a milder form:

'to assist ex-servicemen and ex-service women, and the widows, children and dependants of those who have served, in matters relating to pensions, allowances, grants and war gratuities.'[3]

In this way the overt, though still tentative, challenge to the 1921 compromise was resisted, and, with one exception, the character of the aims of organized ex-servicemen became set in a permanent mould.

The exception to this generalization is provided by a body that did not exist in 1925; the Labour League of Ex-Servicemen, to which brief reference has been made elsewhere.[4] The 'Labour' in its title owed far more to Marxism than to Methodism; it was in fact a

---

[1] G.P.C. Minutes, 6th Dec. 1923, and *Constitution By-Laws and Charter.*
[2] ibid.   [3] Royal Charter 1925.
[4] 29. P.Q., 1958, 31.

Communist organization, formed in September 1927 by an ex-officer who had the advantage of a D.C.M. but suffered the disadvantage of being named Snooks, so oddly inappropriate for a militant leader. Membership was open to men and women who had served in the armed forces and the auxiliary forces on payment of a subscription of 6d. a month.[1]

Though the L.L.X. (as it was sometimes referred to) commanded relatively little support, it cannot be disregarded as a mere 'paper' organization. It was certainly active throughout 1928. The members made their first appearance as a body in uniform in March that year at a women's demonstration in Trafalgar Square. Khaki-clad with red ties and armlets, and carrying heavy sticks, about 250 of them kept order while A. J. Cook, the secretary of the Miners' Federation, harangued the crowd.[2] The following month about 130 men and women marched from the Commercial Road to Epping Forest, where they gave a demonstration of drill.[3] By May the movement had spread to Tyneside, where the first 'District Command' outside London was established, and the occasion marked by a District Congress, attended by some two hundred people. Two interconnected themes in the discussions are relevant to our inquiry. The British Legion in Newcastle and Gateshead, pronounced the L.L.X. secretary, was 'dead': that was the Labour League's opportunity. But Snooks (now commander of the 'force') and others condemned the British Legion on different grounds: 'it was based on charity and run by the leaders of the capitalist class'.[4]

Thus criticism of the British Legion was linked to the theme of the class war. One delegate gave it defiant expression:

'We are comrades. Our flag is the Red Flag, and if we had to march from here to hell we would follow that flag.'[5]

A resolution was also passed repudiating the policy of the Labour Party and the T.U.C. and declaring support for Soviet Russia.[6]

The Labour League also gained some support in South Wales. In September, a Neath contingent interrupted the annual memorial service arranged by the Briton Ferry Branch of the Legion at the local cenotaph with cries of 'what about the ex-servicemen in the workhouse?' The British Legion representatives laid wreaths but the

---

[1] *Sunday Worker*, 18th Sept. 1927; *Daily Express*, 19th Sept. 1927. Mr. J. S. Snooks, ex-lieutenant, was a kitchen porter at the Poplar Institution.

[2] *Manchester Guardian*, 12th March 1928; *Daily Mail*, 12th March 1928.

[3] *Daily Express*, 30th April 1928.

[4] *Manchester Guardian*, *Daily Mail* and *Newcastle Daily Journal*, 21st May 1928.

[5] *Manchester Guardian* and *Daily Mail*, 21st May 1928.

[6] *Newcastle Daily Journal*, 21st May 1928.

L.L.X. men were not to be outdone. They came forward carrying wreaths which had the words 'Victims of Capitalism' printed on the ribbons. The attempt to lay these anti-capitalist wreaths was foiled.[1]

The aims of the L.L.X. were threefold: to work for the establishment of a Labour Government that would fight to abolish wage slavery; to fight against imperialism and capitalist militarism in all forms; and to combat all forms of Fascism and anti-working class action, and to protect the lawful activities and assemblies of the organized working classes.[2] Except perhaps for the reference to militarism, which partly echoed the earlier Federation attacks, there was nothing in those aims to appeal to ex-servicemen as such. In the terminology here used, the aims were almost entirely external, but it seems that there was at least an avowed intention 'to function as an organization to fight pension cases'.[3]

Early in 1929 the leaders of the L.L.X. bowed to the inevitable. Membership had fallen (according to one report) to about 3,500, and the National Command decided to open the door wider. They abandoned the restriction on membership and accordingly changed the title of the organization to the 'Workers' Legion'.[4] It was recognized (they announced) that most of the work could no longer be regarded as exclusively the responsibility of the men who were 'duped' in the Great War of 1914–18, and so the organization opened 'its ranks to all class-conscious workers who are willing to pledge themselves to support its aims and objects'.[5]

Thus, early in 1929, the organization passed beyond the range of our interest by ceasing to be ex-service; but it is doubtful in any case if there is much more to say. The L.L.X. may have been able to attract for a time some of the militant Legionaries critical of what they regarded as lack of 'push and go'. The year 1926 had been a period of great internal controversy, notably about the possibility of entering the Parliamentary lists virtually as a political party, and about the Legion's attitude to the General Strike.[6] The controversy about the General Strike had in fact cost the Legion some members. But on balance it seems more likely that the launching of the L.L.X. in 1927 represented an attempt by the Communist Party to carry the fight into yet another field.

By 1929, then, the 'neutralization' of organized ex-servicemen in terms of their 'aims and objects' had been achieved. Since then, with

---

[1] *Western Mail*, 17th Sept. 1928. Neath and Briton Ferry are contiguous.

[2] *Sunday Worker*, 18th Sept. 1928 and *Daily Express*, 19th Sept. 1928.

[3] *Sunday Worker*, 3rd Feb., 1929.

[4] ibid., *Manchester Guardian*, 5th Feb. 1929.

[5] *Sunday Worker*, 3rd Feb. 1929.

[6] Hist. B.L., ch. XIII.

hardly an exception, ex-servicemen's organizations in this country have been content to act as pressure groups in the narrow sense, officially ignoring those wider issues in which their domestic aims were once so deeply embedded. It is true, of course, that the British Legion has from time to time made pronouncements, as for instance on housing policy, that had wide 'civilian' implications, but that merely emphasizes once again that ex-servicemen can never divest themselves of their 'civilian' attributes. It is also true, and much more important, that, particularly between 1935 and 1938, the Legion's aims included approaches to German (and other former enemy) ex-servicemen that implied a general national *rapprochement* as well. How Legion leaders were led by Ribbentrop to meet Hitler in 1935, how they were cheated by the Nazis when visiting Dachau, and how (though not why) Sir Frederick Maurice, the President, flew out to intervene with Hitler during the Munich crisis—these events have already been described elsewhere.[1] In form merely ex-service, this policy certainly had deeper roots: the Legion was to a considerable extent accommodating itself to the Government of the day, as it had accommodated itself to earlier Governments in support of the League of Nations, and, during Ramsay MacDonald's second term of office, of world disarmament.

Of the other associations, only the Limbless Ex-Service Men's Association, a Scottish seed that flowered in English soil after 1932, had any appreciable stature in the inter-war years, and it seems to have been an interest group proper from its foundation. So far from concerning itself with external aims, it concentrated on only one (though an extremely important) segment of the ex-service field—that occupied by the very badly (limbless) disabled.

Thus the foundation of the British Legion in 1921 marks the virtual removal of the external aims, but between 1921 and 1929, there was some tendency towards restoration, which however came to nothing. Even this slight qualification is not required for the remainder of the period here surveyed, *i.e.*, 1929 to the outbreak of the Second World War. Indeed in the whole period up to the present, only one further example of an association with external aims could be cited. In general that early lesson has never been forgotten.

[1] Hist. B.L., ch. XXIII; XXIV, esp. p. 185, note 1; XXV; XXVIII; XXIX.

XV

EXTERNAL AIMS: PARTY LINES

SINCE two broad classes of aims have been distinguished,[1] there is a natural tendency to anticipate two broad categories in the methods adopted, but such an expectation founders on the rock of 'intellectualism'.[2] Organized ex-servicemen generally made no rational calculation relating means to ends: for obvious reasons, hardly anyone sat back in a cool hour to consider the best method of achieving particular objectives. Fumblingly, then with greater assurance, they tried out many methods until experience sharpened their sense of the appropriate. Thus in general it is impossible to identify certain methods as specifically orientated towards the achievement of external aims.

Yet, without doing violence to the facts, it is possible to discern that in practice the pursuit of the external aims did to some extent tend to have its specific method: alignment with a political party. This, of course is not surprising because a group that cherishes external aims is itself tending (in the degree that such aims are proportionate to domestic aims) to become a political party. External aims, that is to say, are of the same genus as party political programmes, and so it is natural that in trying to achieve them a group should work in harness with one political party or another.

In the period 1917–21 a clear illustration of such an alignment is provided by the N.U.X.[3] Making (though in their own language) a sharp distinction between external and domestic aims, they reserved to themselves the achievement of the latter, while attaching themselves unambiguously to the Labour Party in pursuit of the former. No other group at that time was so clear-headed (or, at any rate, so candid). It is true that, with the exception of the O.A., each had obvious connexions, if only for a short time, with one or other of the political parties, either through individual M.P.s or through party stalwarts in particular localities. Thus, as we know, the National (then the Blackburn) Association had a Labour tinge from the very start. The inaugural meeting was not only convened but also paid for by the Blackburn and District Trades and Labour Council, whose president, H. J. Harvey, took the chair, supported by James

---

[1] Ch. IX.   [2] See above p. 46.
[3] *Aims and Policy*, n.d.

Frankland, a devoted party man to whom Snowden later paid a glowing tribute.[1] As the Association was also developed through the machinery of the trades councils in some of the main industrial areas,[2] it naturally came about that the Executive Committee included four trade-union representatives, although that arrangement lasted only until Easter 1918, when the newly-returned soldiers staged a kind of 'counter-revolution' in order to eject those whom they thought of as 'the politicians'.

Similarly, the Comrades of the Great War was certainly sponsored by influential Conservative M.P.s. Other brands of M.P.s were in the shop window as well but the shop walker and the shop manager were Conservatives consciously countering what seemed to them a serious threat to the *status quo* (as well as to the successful prosecution of the war).[3] In effect the Officers' Association, too, was defending the *status quo*, but, so far as written records go, it seems to have had no formal connexions with any political party, or with identifiable party workers. There is no doubt what it stood *for*, but its connexions do not stand *out*.

As a going concern, the Federation was born in the National Liberal Club and sponsored by two Liberal M.P.s, and so might be said to have worked through the Liberal Party for certain purposes. And since several of the other Federation leaders, too, were Liberals, the Liberal connexion might seem to have been fairly close. Yet in reality the relationship was a tenuous one. The discharged men had grievances and two Liberal M.P.s were ready (more than ready) to help them: it was as straightforward as that.

Thus, directly or indirectly enjoying some degree of intimacy with a political party, some of the organized ex-servicemen of 1917–21 vaguely hoped to achieve their wider aims. But in only one instance (the N.U.X.) was that intimacy sufficiently close for it to be dignified here as a *method calculated* to achieve certain ends. Accordingly, to claim that ex-service groups in general *adopted* political parties as means to their ends would be going too far; it could even be argued, on the contrary, that in one instance at least (the Comrades) a party (represented by its M.P.s) was using ex-servicemen to achieve what it itself desired.

Nevertheless, for whatever reason, it remains true that in the early years there was some tendency to work in harness, if very loose harness, with a political party, and as with the logically-connected external aims,[4] that tendency had to be checked if the ex-servicemen's

---

[1] *Northern Daily Telegraph*, 14th Sept. 1916. See above, p. 95 for Snowden's tribute.

[2] p. 95.   [3] p. 104.

[4] See above p. 78.

movement was to be crowned with success, or even survive. Most ex-servicemen felt this necessity in their bones, and some of them took steps to 'disengage' (in this different but connected sense)[1] as early as Easter, 1918, when, as noted above, the Association cut itself off from the Labour movement. With the departure of James Hogge early in 1919, the Federation found itself politically fancy-free, but the consummation of this trend was reached only with the founding of the British Legion. This event, as we know, represented a neutralization of the movement in terms of aims; it also signified a virtual abandonment of inappropriate methods. In the first place, the Comrades in effect broke with its ultra-Conservative sponsors. Secondly, through a major tactical error, the most 'dedicated' group, the N.U.X., decided to keep aloof from the new body.[2] Finally, one of the many compromises underlying the emergence of the British Legion[3] was the elimination of any possible connexion with political parties. The original proposal was that the new body should not be 'affiliated to any political party or political organization',[4] but during the negotiations it was made even more restrictive by the insertion, after 'affiliated to', of the phrase—'or connected directly or indirectly with'.[5] In this form the restriction was embodied in the 1921 Constitution and has survived ever since.[6]

Happily for the ex-servicemen's movement, that compromise on methods has never been disturbed and scarcely even seriously challenged. Certainly in the Legion itself, whatever the political outlook and affiliations of its leaders, there has been no suspicion of an alignment with a political party. The only qualification that has a measure of importance is the Labour League of Ex-Servicemen's ink, already noted, with the Communist Party.

[1] See above ch. XIII.
[2] Hist. B.L., pp. 18–19.
[3] See above p. 111.
[4] First typed draft.
[5] Draft Constitution for United Organization (*i.e.*, first *printed* draft).
[6] 1921 Constitution; Royal Charter, 18th issue.

XVI

DOMESTIC AIMS:

(A) THE TECHNIQUES OF INFLUENCE (1917–39)

(1) THE CABINET

Introduction

IN discussing the pursuit of the domestic (*i.e.*, the 'proper') aims of ex-servicemen, we can no longer ignore the ambiguity of the term 'methods', which has been used in various senses, sometimes making an unexpected appearance as the method of 'the best information'.[1] It is customary to resolve 'methods' into 'strategy' and 'tactics', but as that usage tends to introduce a further degree of ambiguity,[2] it seems preferable to speak of 'strategy' and 'techniques'.

The distinction between these may be derived from the political 'model' already outlined.[3] At any given time, various claims, economically conditioned and 'politically cultured', are being put forward by unofficial groups and projected at the appropriate official group. These projections may be made directly, indirectly or by some combination of the direct and indirect. Thus, in principle, a group may 'apply' direct to the relevant decision-making group and to no other body; or it may try to 'hit' the decision-makers 'off' another group (or groups), as one scores a cannon in billiards. In this 'stroke', the more the 'hit' groups are themselves official, the greater the degree of directness attributable to it. For instance, an attempt to influence the Cabinet through Parliament is deemed, for the purposes of this discussion, to be more direct than an attempt to influence it through the press. Alternatively, of course, both approaches may be used, in varying proportions.

The pattern of the approach to the relevant (autonomous) decision-making group may be called the 'strategy of influence', which, alternatively expressed, is the general design for securing a required decision, usually entailing the 'mobilization' and 'deployment' of other groups, both official and unofficial. But 'methods' may also be taken to mean 'techniques'—an association's 'own' approach to any

[1] W. J. M. Mackenzie in 6 B.J.S. 1955, 142.

[2] Cf. the meaning of 'tactics' in Stewart, op. cit., p. 28; in Truman, op. cit. Part III; and in John H. Millett, 72 P.S.Q. 1957, 71–82.

[3] See ch. I.

one official group treated as if it were isolated from the whole complex of official groups.[1] In a study that attempts to survey the ex-servicemen's movement over a period of forty years, the focus of interest is inevitably on strategy, yet techniques can scarcely be neglected. On the other hand, since a detailed account would become a mere catalogue, only an outline is offered here and in chapters XVII–XIX and XXI. These provide the evidence and generally prepare the way for the analysis in chapter XXII of the strategy of influence from 1917 to 1957. Later the methods used in some actual attempts to exert influence will be recorded.[2]

THE CABINET

As a group, the Cabinet is out of immediate reach. M.P.s can be lobbied, the gallery of the House can be visited and made the launching site for 'interruptions' of various kinds, while interviews of varying degrees of formality with Ministers and senior civil servants are part of the established routine. But the Cabinet as such remains inviolate. Perhaps the nearest anyone has ever come to a successful invasion of the famous white and gold room (or any other Cabinet location) was in 1908, when Mrs. Drummond leapt from a taxi-cab and barged into No. 10.[3]

Denied face-to-face contact, ex-servicemen devised various methods of trying to 'reach' the Cabinet. They not infrequently sent communications direct to the Prime Minister himself as the embodiment of the Cabinet. Sometimes these were in the form of Executive Council resolutions, as with the Federation in 1919 and the Legion in 1921. At other times the source of the resolution was a Conference decision, as with BLESMA in 1938 when nine resolutions were embodied in a petition to the Prime Minister. Very rarely, and then only in the early history of the movement, an association entered the lists during a Parliamentary by-election for the purpose of sending the Cabinet a 'message'. Thus in 1917 the Federation carried to the Abercromby Division of Liverpool 'the fight on behalf of the discharged soldiers'. There a Federation nominee grappled unsuccessfully with a Stanley on his home ground.

The main techniques in the early part of the period under review were the demonstration and the deputation. The great exponent of the demonstration was the National Federation, which, at least in 1919–20, resorted to it as readily as less energetic bodies sat back and

---

[1] Cf. Stewart, ibid., and Truman, ibid. and Preface, x.

[2] See Part Five.

[3] Roger Fulford, *Votes for Women*, 1957, p. 174.

passed resolutions. When the Review of Exceptions Bill became law,[1] the opposition to it was sustained by a Hyde Park demonstration of 'considerable dimensions', which formed the model for a number of much larger gatherings after the war. The year 1919 saw two 'monster' demonstrations organized. The first of these in May brought together a crowd of perhaps ten thousand;[2] some of those who made a 'spontaneous move' towards the Houses of Parliament had their heads rapped by police batons for their pains. Four months later the Federation launched another 'Great National Demonstration', ambitiously designed in the first place 'to put the wind up Winston Churchill' (as Secretary of State for War) but really aimed, as time went on, at the Cabinet itself.[3] Another big demonstration was put on in the spring of 1920.

These demonstrations (whose 'subjects' varied from unemployment to war gratuities and training allowances) were not confined to London; on the contrary, they were in intention highly co-ordinated. In May 1919, for instance, branches were required to exert pressure on local mayors to initiate housing schemes for the purpose of reducing unemployment. Branches were also required to 'press' their local M.P.s to take action on the spot as well as in the House, and to send resolutions to the Prime Minister, Bonar Law and the Ministry of Labour. And apart from co-ordinated moves, Federation branches were active in all parts of the country: in 1919 there were demonstrations in Eastbourne, Edinburgh, Sheffield, where 20,000 men and 5,000 widows are said to have turned out, Durham, Brighton Cork, Portsmouth, Nottingham and elsewhere. Altogether, this was a substantial effort by one association, sustained for perhaps eighteen months after the Armistice.[4]

None of the other early ex-service associations emulated the Federation in its use of the demonstration technique for exerting influence. For reasons that will presently emerge, the Comrades of the Great War hardly required to use such methods, which many of its leaders would have disapproved of even if the need had been pressing. Even today the surviving Comrades' leaders retain vivid memories of the Federation's marches and especially of its conflict with the police.[5] As for the National Association, its original leaders would not have been averse to mounting a demonstration: as we know,[6] the criticism they made in the Blackburn market-place of the

---

[1] See above ch. VII.

[2] *The Times*, 27th May 1919. The Federation, however, claimed 20,000 *ex-servicemen. Bulletin*, 5th June 1919.

[3] G.P.C. Mins., 16th Aug. 1919, Min. 18.

[4] *Bulletin*, passim.

[5] Interviews with writer.   [6] See above p. 59.

Review of Exceptions Bill was sufficiently forceful to be countered by a police warning. But at that time the Association lacked the resources and organization to demonstrate effectively, and by one of those minor paradoxes in the history of unofficial organizations, when, after the war, it found itself in a rather stronger position, it had come under the control of leaders whose attitude to such methods was as disapproving as that of the leaders of the Comrades.[1]

Of the later associations, the N.U.X. would have been willing, even anxious, to demonstrate: probably many of its members had had experience of marching and carrying banners, especially on May Day. But it so happens that they do not seem to have done so as ex-servicemen, which is perhaps not surprising since their organization was always a weak one. The Officers' Association, on the other hand, would not have dreamt of demonstrating—that would have been completely out of character.

The compromise that the foundation of the British Legion represents entailed the abandonment of the demonstration as a method of exerting influence. But it is worth recording that the technique did not disappear without trace. At the 1922 Conference, the Lambeth delegate called on the Legion to 'use something approaching force' to get something done for the 'poor devils' suffering from tuberculosis,[2] which might perhaps be charitably interpreted as a plea for another monster demonstration. Three years later, the West Ham (North) delegate, in arguing for a 'more militant, progressive and extended policy and programme', declared that the Legion was 'practically a dead letter', and that demonstrations should be staged in Hyde Park, with Earl Haig put up to denounce the Prime Minister for the pensions 'scandal'.[3] To which the Sevenoaks delegate retorted that 'it was absolute piffle to talk of meetings in Hyde Park'. West Ham's motion was not carried.[4]

At the following Conference, too, Edgbaston and Balsall Heath branch tried to commit the National Executive Council to taking 'strong action, by means of demonstrations and mass meetings', as a protest against Government policy on pensions.[5] It succeeded—on paper, but nothing of the kind was done.[6]

It was not in fact until as late as 1929, nearly eight years after the establishment of the Legion, that those who still wished to revive the

---

[1] Interviews with writer.

[2] Verb. Rep., p. 17.

[3] Final Agenda, 1925 Conf., p. 16; Verb. Rep. 2a/14–15 (*read:* 2nd day, morning session, pages 14–15).

[4] Verb. Rep., p. 18.

[5] Final Agenda, 1926, resolution 132.

[6] RESAT, 1926 Conf., p. 38.

demonstration method were finally silenced. That silence was preceded by a deafening roar. For in 1928 the East Midlands Area and the Leicester delegates had persuaded the Annual Conference to resolve that Headquarters should 'place a stronger pensions policy before the public and launch a "National Demonstration on Time Limits and pensions questions"'.[1] But once again the N.E.C. not only blandly refused to follow suit[2] but the following January even dispatched the Assistant Secretary, J. R. Griffin, to Leicester, where he announced unequivocally that the N.E.C. would 'never agree to a National Demonstration'.[3]

The disappointed branches naturally carried the fight to the next Annual Conference, which followed some four months later. The East Midlands delegate introduced a motion that expressed 'profound dissatisfaction' at the failure of the N.E.C. to arrange a National Demonstration as instructed the previous year, and urged it to proceed without delay; the motion also 'emphatically' protected against the Assistant Secretary's speech at Leicester.[4] Speaker after speaker added fuel to the fire in one of the longest debates in the history of Legion Conferences.[5] Only one delegate—representing Swansea Branch—attempted to defend Headquarters but he was challenged, not for the first time, as a salaried official himself and he was prevented from proceeding by general interruption.[6] Inevitably, the East Midlands' motion was carried.[7]

The tempest died down, leaving the leaders windswept and somewhat exhausted but still in complete command of the ship. Technically they did not emerge unscathed because a critical resolution had gone against them, but they were able to bear their punishment with fortitude because Legionaries have never been prepared to make it hurt, *i.e.*, to vote the principal offenders (the honorary officials) from office. So from 1929 onwards one may say that even the idea of the demonstration as a technique of influence was clearly disposed of in the British Legion.

Of course, the Labour League of Ex-servicemen were essentially demonstrators. As a Communist organization, they had not the remotest chance of presenting their views through the regular

---

[1] Final Agenda, 1928, p. 22, resn. 111 and Verb. Rep., p. 26.

[2] RESAT, 1928 Conf., pp. 41 & 112–14. It was later claimed, and not denied by the platform, that this resolution was carried 'unanimously, and with great enthusiasm'. Verb. Rep. 1929/3/37–38.

[3] Verb. Rep. 1929/3/37–38.

[4] Provisional Agenda, 1929, p. 26.

[5] It occupies 11½ foolscap pages of the Verbatim Report, apart from one page taken to record the remarks of the Chairman of the Standing Orders Committee on a related matter.

[6] Verb. Rep. 1929/3/40.   [7] ibid./3/49.

channels, and it was therefore only to be expected that the members should march and counter-march, though the decision to march *out of step* in order to demonstrate their revolutionary fervour was an unexpected touch.[1] But, as we know, the L.L.X. ceased to be an ex-servicemen's organization in 1929, so it is safe to assert that from then onwards (in the period under review) the demonstration as a technique passed into oblivion. And as a weapon actually wielded by the important section of the movement, it had fallen into disuse in 1921.

Deputations

In all probability, no Cabinet has ever received a deputation from a pressure group as such; certainly it has not received one from an ex-servicemen's association. But it is not unreasonable to regard a deputation to a Prime Minister (or, less certainly, to a senior Cabinet Minister representing him) as tantamount to a deputation to the Cabinet itself. Certainly the intention of ex-servicemen has been to carry the argument as high as they could.

In between the wars there were perhaps four major approaches of this kind. Again the Federation was the first in the field. In 1920 eighteen of its leaders waited upon Lloyd George in a deputation that must surely rank as one of the most remarkable meetings in the whole history of pressure-group activity. In putting his case, T. F. Lister spoke for an hour and twenty-six minutes with hardly an interruption from the Prime Minister.[2] The Legion followed suit with deputations to three Prime Ministers: Baldwin (1929), MacDonald (1933) and Chamberlain (1938).

That the deputation was on occasion combined with the demonstration may be illustrated by the Federation's campaign to increase war gratuities. In January 1919 the leadership wrote to the new Secretary of State for War, Winston Churchill, in order to bring to his notice the 'widespread' dissatisfaction at both the amount and method of payment of war gratuities to other ranks. As the representative body of 'upwards of 500,000' ex-servicemen, it had been 'inundated with resolutions and complaints': there was 'seething discontent'.[3]

The Department's response was deemed to be unsatisfactory, and so on 16th August the General Purposes Committee decided to hold

---

[1] *Daily Express*, 11th June 1928

[2] Lister-Griffin correspondence, 8th Feb. 1920. The *Liverpool Daily Post*, 7th Feb. 1920 and *Lloyds Sunday News*, 8th Feb. 1920 have good accounts. See my thesis, appendix 29, for an almost verbatim report.

[3] *Bulletin*, 13th Mar. 1919.

a National Demonstration towards the end of the following month as a 'protest against the decision of the War Cabinet not to re-consider the amounts of War Gratuities. . . .'[1] As already noted, a great demonstration was eventually staged, although by then its scope had been considerably widened. But the Cabinet showed no sign of giving ground,[2] and so induced the Federation to begin all over again. On 15th October, the P.M. was asked to receive a deputation, but although he was 'always ready, notwithstanding the heavy and ever-increasing tax upon his time and attention, to give reasonable opportunities for bringing to his notice at personal interviews important questions of State policy', he felt that matters of regulations and administration such as the Federation was considered to have raised would be best dealt with by the Ministry concerned.[3]

The Federation leaders were angered by this reply. 'Even a Premier', the official journal pronounced, 'must remember that he is a servant of the people'.[4] And so early in December they decided to mount yet another demonstration the following month as a mark of their disapproval.[5] When Lloyd George heard of their plans he changed his mind and decided to receive a deputation after all.[6] The Executive accordingly 'postponed the demonstration', although they advised that Divisional Councils and branches 'should on no account cease their efforts to bring pressure to bear on local M.P.s on the subjects raised, and resolutions in support should be sent to the Prime Minister'.[7]

[1] G.P.C. Mins., 16th Aug. 1919, Min. 18.

[2] *Bulletin*, Xmas number, 1919.

[3] ibid.　　　　　　　　　　　[4] ibid.

[5] G.P.C. Mins., 6th Dec. 1919, Min. 7.

[6] Executive Mins. 3rd–4th. Jan. 1920, Min. 9; *Bulletin* 4th Mar. 1920, 1; Annual Report 1919–20, pp. 5 & 6.

[7] *Bulletin*, 8th Jan. 1920, 4.

XVII

DOMESTIC AIMS:

(A) THE TECHNIQUES OF INFLUENCE (1917–39)

(2) THE HOUSE OF COMMONS (i) ELECTIONS

ALMOST from the beginning of the movement, the relationship between ex-servicemen's groups and the Commons has been a close one. Two strands or phases may be distinguished: the 'ante-natal' and the 'post-natal'. 'Ante-natal' means the attempt to influence the embryonic House during the course of a General Election. 'Post-natal' denotes the impact on a House already elected. Obviously the two phases are inter-connected: M.P.s may arrive at Westminster 'under the influence', or even specifically committed, as some of them felt themselves to be after the 1918 Election campaign.[1] On the other hand, despite the 'intolerable burdens' of public life, M.P.s usually leave no stone unturned, no avenue unexplored, to get themselves re-elected. Nevertheless, the distinction has its uses.

'Ante-Natal'

A general election affords opportunities of two main kinds: risking its status as a non-party group, an association may put up its own candidates; it may also try to influence and, if possible, commit other candidates to a particular policy. In 1918 some ex-servicemen seized both these opportunities, but the hope of putting up their 'own' men was quickly abandoned. On the other hand, attempts to influence candidates in the 'chrysalis' stage of their Parliamentary careers continued to be made until 1929 (and, in an attenuated and half-hearted form, are still made even to-day). Logically connected with this second kind of activity but not always or even commonly uttered was the threat of sanctions, *i.e.* support for this candidate, opposition to that one.[2]

---

[1] See below, ch. XXIII.

[2] Journal, Dec. 1923, p. 176. See below appendix 1.

The House of Commons (Elections)

I. SPONSORSHIP

In the General Election of 1918, three associations were involved in sponsorship. One association strove whole-heartedly, another half-heartedly, the third almost absent-mindedly. Such is the perversity of fate that only the third enjoyed a measure of success.

The National Federation

The society that strove whole-heartedly was the National Federation. Parliamentary action had been visualized from the very beginning, as may be seen from the first Constitution,[1] where it was expressed as the seeking of 'direct representation'. That was a common desire but some members of the Federation had more ambitious ideas. The Bethnal Green branch, for instance, wanted 'a Parliamentary Party separate from all other organizations'.[2] Hogge himself had had such a vision. At Westminster there should be a 'small, resolute band of discharged men', his advice went, but neither they nor organized ex-servicemen outside should be isolated. Based on them he 'would far rather see another and powerful new party'.[3]

According to *The Times*, the Federation does in fact seem to have made some such effort to become a separate 'Parliamentary Party'. It recorded that twenty-three candidates were standing in the name of the Federation,[4] which looks at first glance like an appreciable effort at winning direct representation, tending to carry the society beyond the ranks of pressure groups proper into the realm of political parties. *The Times* also reported that one of their candidates was elected, and a later student, for whom this episode is of only marginal importance, has naturally followed *The Times*.[5] The Federation's own records, however, present a different picture. The decision the Executive Council took in June 1918 was to contest one seat in every Divisional Council area, which would have meant eight candidates; £5,000 was to be raised by means of a levy.[6] Just before the Armistice the Council approved, in some cases provisionally, seven candidates and four of their constituencies.[7] One of these candidates, a Dr. Blood, who was provisionally the choice for the Bristol Division, seems to

---

[1] Constitution, p. 4, item (8).

[2] Agenda for Special Conference, July 1918.

[3] *The Ex-Service Man*, 25th Sept. 1918. In founding the Naval and Military War Pensions and Welfare League in Jan. 1917, Hogge had visualized the representation of ex-servicemen in Parliament. *The Times*, 16th Jan. 1917.

[4] *The Times*, 9th Dec. 1918, supp. viii.

[5] *The Times*, 30th Dec. 1918, El. S. vi, and J. D. Stewart, *British Pressure Groups*, p. 165 and note 2.

[6] N.E.C. Mins. 4th June 1918, unnumbered.

[7] N.E.C. Mins. 2nd Nov. 1918, Min. 4.

have quickly disappeared from the scene, leaving six approved candidates.[1] How then can one reconcile the Federation's account with *The Times* report?

In attempting such a reconciliation one may start with *The Times* list of candidates. Of these, two ceased to be acceptable to the local Federation and were disowned.[2] A Welsh candidate, on the other hand, withdrew under pressure from the Whips at No. 12 Downing Street, ostensibly 'in the national interest and from a high sense of public welfare', *i.e.*, to avoid splitting the Coalition vote in Aberavon.[3] In Poplar (London) the candidate described by *The Times* as a Federation man was to local pressmen simply 'the unionist candidate'.[4] Above all, we may eliminate the one man that, according to *The Times*, was successfully returned in the Federation's interest. Major Robert Barker was undoubtedly returned for Sowerby Bridge but in the interest of the Federation's rival, the National Association. Even as late as 4th March 1919, *The Times* identified Barker with the Federation but he had always been connected with a rival firm.[5]

Five of the apparent Federation candidates, then, have to be eliminated from *The Times* list. Of the remaining eighteen, ten were certainly Federation men, five others wore the Federation colours, three have a penumbra of uncertainty about them but may be given the benefit of the doubt.[6] On the other hand, one of the candidates whom *The Times* regarded as 'Independent' should be counted as a Federationist.[7]

What this examination of local newspapers brings to light is not so much that, in the confusion of the 1918 Election, the local correspondents of *The Times* (or the news agencies?) were inaccurate[8] but rather that the Federation candidates were extremely hetero-

[1] ibid., these were: D. Brookes and A. E. Shakesby (with constituencies in the East Midlands and Yorkshire divisions respectively); J. H. Dooley, (Aston); G. G. Gebbett, (Southwark); W. H. Dawson, (Great Yarmouth); T. F. Lister, (Ashton-under-Lyne).

[2] John Thompson, Newcastle East. *Newcastle Daily Journal*, 4th Dec. 1918 and 11th Dec. 1918; W. H. Dawson (*Yarmouth Mercury*, 9th, 16th, 23rd and 30th Nov. and 7th and 14th Dec. 1918).

[3] T. G. Jones, *Western Mail*, 12th, 14th and 30th Dec. 1918; *Yorkshire Post*, 13th and 14th Dec., *The Times*, 9th Dec. Supp. viii, and 30th Dec. 325 electors chose Jones despite his withdrawal.

[4] *East London Observer*, 9th and 23rd Nov. 1918. See also his election address, ibid., 7th and 14th Dec.

[5] *Halifax Daily Guardian*, 2nd Jan. 1919; *Hebden Bridge Times*, 14th Mar. 1919; interview with Major Barker 1957; *The Times*, 4th Mar. 1919, p. 15 d.

[6] For details on this and the whole section, consult my thesis.

[7] Lister to author, 15th May 1957.

[8] But one wonders how much historians and others lose by leaning so much on *The Times* to the neglect in general of the local weekly Press.

geneous. Here was no embryonic Parliamentary Party of the kind that some Federation branches—and James Hogge—wanted. It was less a ship's complement than a pirate crew.

The result of the expedition was generally disastrous. Eleven of the nineteen candidates found themselves at the bottom of the poll and two others only just escaped joining them there. Twelve had their pockets hurt as well as their pride, being among the seventy-three 'other' (roughly, 'independent') candidates[1] who forfeited their deposits. In three constituencies where there were straight fights, the Federationists did quite well, especially at Liverpool (Everton), where A. Brooksbank came within 592 votes of success after a 'remarkably good fight',[2] and at Ashton-under-Lyne, where T. F. Lister, opposing a Minister, Sir Albert Stanley, came less close to success in terms of votes but doubtless achieved much more in terms of influence.[3] Elsewhere, Federationists, notably the future Labour M.P. Ernest Thurtle (Bethnal Green), acquitted themselves moderately well, but, obviously, the general exercise in sponsorship was a disastrous failure. Their intervention may have achieved something but certainly not the nucleus of 'a powerful new party' nor even direct representation in the House.

The Silver Badge Party

The Federation was, of course, well established by the time of the 1918 Election, and as we know, there were other societies competing for the ex-serviceman's allegiance, yet the resumption of ordinary political life (such as it was) evoked yet another ex-service association —the Silver Badge Party.

The word 'party' at once raises the question whether this was in fact a pressure group. *The Times* described it as 'a new political organization' and certainly it had a general political policy. Peace terms were 'to be dictated by the Allies, and made known before ratification'; the Central Powers were 'to refund the total war expenditure of the Allies, reconstruct all property damaged by them, and those responsible for inhuman acts' should be 'dealt with as criminals'; the repatriation of 'enemy aliens, naturalized or not'; a 'definite land policy' as well as housing and national health legislation.[4] In this the appeal was to citizens generally and not to ex-servicemen only, for whom there was nothing but the claim for

---

[1] D. E. Butler, *The Electoral System in Britain 1918–51*, p. 168. Altogether, apart from Ireland, 135 candidates (over 10 per cent) forfeited their deposits in 1918.

[2] *Liverpool Daily Post and Mercury*, 30th Dec. 1918.

[3] See below ch. XXIII.

[4] 30th Nov. 1918.

training facilities and the freeing of service and disability pensions from income tax.[1] Yet membership was apparently confined to ex-service men and women ('born of British parents'), which accounts for its being called upon to give evidence before the Select Committee on Pensions in the spring of 1919.[2] On the whole, it seems best to count the Silver Badge Party as an ex-service pressure group, though with wider political ambitions than are usually recognized or at least acknowledged.

Whatever its exact status, the Silver Badge Party remained minute: even by May 1919, it could claim no more than '400 or 500 altogether', it not having 'been extended further because of lack of funds'.[3] Branches had taken root only in London, Lincoln and Sheffield—not much of a base for its grandiose ambitions.[4]

Its performance at the polls was commensurate with its organization rather than its ambitions. The Press referred to its candidates[5] but it is very hard to identify those who were 'Silver Badge' as distinct from 'silver badge', a convenient—and accurate—label for those who had been discharged on account of wounds.[6] And those who can be identified hardly covered themselves with glory. In Lincoln, its candidate, Lieutenant Broughton Trower,[7] was reported to have been taken ill, and to have sent a telegram from York saying that, in view of his 'serious breakdown in health', he withdrew his candidature and advised support for Alfred Davies[8]— an eloquent and brave effort for one so severely stricken. In the Central Division of Portsmouth the nomination papers were promptly ruled out of order,[9] an anti-climax that may serve as an apt comment on the whole Silver Badge effort.

[1] ibid.

[2] H.C. 247, 1st and 2nd Special Reports of the Select Committee on Pensions, 23rd Dec. 1919, Mins. of ev., p. 202. The organization is not in fact named in this context, but it can be identified (a) by elimination (cf. 1st Report, p. iii) and (b) from internal evidence.

[3] ibid., Mins. of ev., Q. 4702.

[4] Q. 4703.

[5] *Liverpool Daily Press & Mercury*, 5th Dec. 1918.

[6] The descriptions used in the election were most confusing. Apart from Coalitionists who liked to tag on such labels as the 'Soldier Candidate' (*Yarmouth Mercury*, 7th Dec. 1918, p. 4) and the 'Soldiers' Friend' (*The Times*, 9th Dec. 1918, p. 10), there was a considerable number of hard-to-classify titles (*e.g.*, 'Discharged Soldiers and Independent'—*Newcastle Daily Journal*, 6th Dec. 1918, p. 5).

[7] *Grimsby Gazette*, 23rd Nov. 1918. See also *Hull & Lincolnshire Times*, 23rd Nov. 1918.

[8] ibid., 7th Dec. Davies, a wealthy London-born Welshman, was a company director who farmed 2,000 acres. His conservatism was outweighed by his friendship with L.G. ibid. 23rd and 30th Nov.

[9] *The Times*, 5th Dec. 1918.

The National Association

This society made no attempt to hold a candle to the Federation or even to the ineffectual Silver Badge. Nationally it did not stir; such movement as occurred was the result of local initiative. Of this the campaign in Sowerby Bridge was the only noteworthy instance, resulting in the return, for the first (and only) time in our history, of a candidate put forward by an ex-servicemen's association. As this was achieved against a candidate who had received the Lloyd George–Bonar Law 'coupon', it looks like a famous victory; but there is more in it than meets the eye.

The Sowerby constituency stretched along either side of the Calder Valley in the West Riding of Yorkshire, extending tentacles into six other neighbouring valleys.[1] Its electorate had increased from some 12,000 in 1910 to about 34,000, 'mainly industrial and middle-class voters'.[2] Of these, men outnumbered women by over 6,000, but as there were perhaps 5,300 absent voters, the disparity between the sexes was much reduced.[3] Some 1,700 (about a third) of the absentees cast their votes, rather lower than in the near-by constituencies of Elland and Halifax.[4]

Traditionally, the fight had been between the blues and the yellows, with the yellows invariably in the ascendant.[5] But for the first time, excepting only the second of the 1910 elections,[6] the Tories were not giving battle. It was not that they had lost heart. Late in November 1918, the local Conservatives, 'undaunted by three previous failures', had decided 'unanimously' to run their old candidate, Lieutenant W. A. Simpson-Hinchcliffe, in the expectation that he would 'receive official sanction for his candidature'.[7] But, as he himself said, 'strings' were pulled against him,[8] which was indeed true: as the chairman of the local party revealed, both the Central Office and the Yorkshire Unionist Association had brought 'pressure' to bear to secure his withdrawal.[9] So the unfortunate lieutenant was forced to descend on Todmorden Town Hall to sound not 'advance' but 'retreat'.[10]

So it seemed that J. S. Higham, the nominal Coalition Liberal candidate, would be again returned. The 'coupon' was slow to arrive

[1] *Halifax Evening Courier*, 14th Dec. 1918.

[2] ibid. Strictly, from 12,805 to 34,296.

[3] ibid.; also 31st Dec. 1918. That journal's earlier estimate of absent voters (14th Dec.) was 'about 5,400'. I have used their 31st Dec. total (5,297), though the *Halifax Daily Guardian* the previous day gives '3,600 absentees'.

[4] *Halifax Evening Courier*, 31st Dec. 1918.

[5] ibid., 14th Dec. 1918.　　　　　　　[6] ibid.

[7] ibid., 29th Nov. 1918.　　　　　　[8] ibid., 3rd Dec. 1918.

[9] *Halifax Daily Guardian*, 3rd Dec. 1918.

[10] ibid.; *Halifax Evening Courier*, 3rd Dec. 1918.

but arrive it did.[1] Higham, however, was a craggy independent who cared nothing for 'coupons'. Asked if he would go to the House as a supporter of the Coalition or as a Liberal, he gave an unequivocal, if impolitic, reply:

'I go to the House of Commons as a Liberal. If the Coalition bring in any measures that I, as a Liberal, approve of, I shall support them. If they bring in any measures I disapprove of I shall vote against them.'[2]

At another meeting on the same evening he readily responded to a request 'to make his position clear', saying:

'I have had a letter from the Government, but I have never used it and I don't intend to. I have come out as a Liberal candidate, and I appeal to the electors as a Liberal. I never sought that letter, and the Government never asked me to promise anything. I stand as a Liberal candidate, fighting the Liberal battle on the Liberal programme.'[3]

Brave words but not ones likely to commend Higham to the local Conservative electors, who were thus expected to vote the 'coupon' for a candidate who was going to choose exactly when he would be a Coalitionist and when a Liberal. As a leading local Conservative, J. Sutcliffe Thomas, was to complain later: Higham did not act 'fairly in this matter'—'he tried to hunt with the hare and run with the hounds'.[4] As Higham saw it, of course, he was preserving his independence and integrity as a Liberal; in any case, his action and open declaration weakened his already threatened position. For, at the eleventh hour, an unexpected rival had appeared in the lists— Major Robert Barker.

'Bob' Barker was a major in the 6th Lancs. His father was the chairman of a firm of cotton spinners and manufacturers in Todmorden and he himself had taken an active interest in the family business, so, although educated at Bedford Grammar School, he was 'a local boy'.[5] He was also a popular one: he had played rugby for the Kersal R.F.C., and for the county and had proved himself in the

---

[1] The uncertainty about his colours is perhaps reflected in *The Times*, which on 26th Nov. (preliminary list) called him 'Co. L.' but on 5th Dec. (nominations list), plain 'L'. By 9th Dec. (Election Supplement) he had reverted to his earlier status. The *Halifax Evening Courier*, 26th Nov., noting the first of these descriptions, commented: 'But up to this morning the momentous document (!) had not arrived'.

[2] *Halifax Evening Courier*, 3rd Dec. 1918.

[3] ibid.

[4] At the annual meeting of the Hebden Bridge Constitutional Club. *Halifax Daily Guardian*, 25th Jan. 1919.

[5] *Halifax Evening Courier*, 4th Dec. 1918; *Halifax Daily Guardian*, 7th and 14th Dec.

field of battle. Politically, he was described as an 'Independent',[1] and certainly he appeared as the nominee of the local branch of the National Association,[2] but there was much more in that than met the eye. His candidature was the resultant of convergent forces. The (organized) ex-servicemen themselves sought a representative different from Higham. They had expected (their president revealed) Simpson-Hinchcliffe to 'champion their cause', but when he had suddenly retired, they had 'persuaded Major Barker to step in'.[3] But already in about the third week in November (as he himself revealed), Major Barker had been invited by some 'influential gentlemen' to stand as an Independent; he had, however, declined.[4] Why, on the eve of nomination, should he decide to throw his hat in the ring?

Partly, no doubt, as he told a Midgley audience, he was responding to the call of the 'discharged soldiers'.[5] But his 'chief reason' for fighting was that 'Mr. Higham had refused the Coalition ticket', while the Conservative candidate 'had withdrawn by orders'.[6] Here we reach the heart of the matter. There can be no doubt at all that the 'influential gentlemen' who approached Barker had spoken for local Conservatives, because the local party, *at that stage*, were not going to oppose Higham as a Coalition candidate.[7] It was only when Higham refused to be bound by the questions put to him by the local Unionist Association, including a question about supporting the 'Coalition Government at all times',[8] and when, at the next party meeting, their former candidate, Simpson-Hinchcliffe, displayed a 'thrusting' attitude to his re-adoption, that the earlier decision was reversed.[9]

Imagine the disappointment, therefore, when pressure on Simpson-Hinchcliffe 'by the most high in the councils of our party'[10] compelled his withdrawal on 2nd December. What should have been a battle hymn turned into a dirge. There were only 150 people in the

---

[1] ibid.

[2] *Halifax Daily Guardian*, 30th Dec. 1918 and 2nd Jan. 1919; interview at Rochdale, 22nd June 1957.

[3] *Halifax Daily Guardian*, 30th Dec. 1918.

[4] *Halifax Evening Courier*, 10th Dec. 1918.

[5] ibid.

[6] *Halifax Daily Guardian*, 9th Dec. 1918 and 3rd Jan. 1919.

[7] *Halifax Evening Courier*, 19th Nov. 1918.

[8] ibid., 25th Nov. 1918.

[9] ibid.; also 23rd Nov. in which, after Higham's replies had been read to the E.C. of the Conservative Party, Simpson-Hinchcliffe is said to have made a 'truculent speech, expressing his view that this "opportunity" should not be let pass'.

[10] J. Sutcliffe Thomas, J.P., at the annual meeting of the Hebden Bridge Constitutional Club, *Halifax Daily Guardian*, 25th Jan. 1919.

hall and—a more bitter pill perhaps—'under half a dozen on the platform'.[1] Decline and fall without benefit of friends.

So, from the platform where fourteen years earlier he had started his political career, Simpson-Hinchcliffe 'wished them adieu and disappeared into the night'.[2] But the Conservative cause was not yet lost; a Conservative by any other name would smell as sweet. Now Barker was 'a strong Conservative. He has been active in local Conservative circles and as a member of the Manchester Constitutional Club'.[3] Everyone knew he was a Tory.[4] On the other hand, he would not be permitted to run as a Tory because that would have broken the 'coupon' arrangement, so he ran in the colours of the National Association. No one doubts that these local ex-servicemen did approach him after the Conservative candidate had withdrawn, but, in effect, and possibly in intention, it was on behalf of the Conservative party as well as of ex-servicemen.

The upshot of the campaign was that the gallant major defeated J. W. Ogden, the President of the T.U.C.,[5] by 981 votes, leaving Higham ingloriously at the bottom of the poll. *The Times* called it a 'N.F.D.D.S.S.' majority:[6] it was, in form, a N.A.D.S.S. victory (Sowerby Branch). They nominated him and he certainly spoke of himself as their 'Parliamentary representative'.[7] Doubtless, as he himself judges, he received many a vote from the men overseas,[8] as well as from discharged men in the constituency. As a 'local lad', he must have attracted many of the uncommitted and some of the nominally committed: Higham estimated that he had captured about 3,000 'sentimental' Liberal votes.[9] But also, using the local Conservative party machine,[10] he must have got the solid support of his own party. It comes as no surprise, accordingly, to find that only the Conservative *Halifax Daily Guardian* forecast his success:[11] the other

[1] *Halifax Evening Courier*, 3rd Dec. 1918; *Halifax Daily Guardian*, 3rd Dec. 1918.

[2] *Halifax Daily Guardian*, 3rd Dec. 1918.

[3] ibid., 4th Dec. His father, John Barker, was also a well-known Conservative. ibid.

[4] Interview.

[5] *Yorkshire Post*, 5th Dec. 1918.

[6] 30th Dec. 1918, El. S. vi. In fact, the Federation men were opposed to him (Interview and *Hebden Bridge Times & Calder Vale Gazette*, 10th Jan. 1919). The returns were as follows:

Major Robert H. Barker (N.A.D.S.S.)	8287
J. W. Ogden (Lab.)	7306
J. S. Higham (Co. L.)	6778

[7] *Halifax Daily Guardian*, 2nd Jan. 1919. *Hebden Bridge Times*, 14th Mar. 1919.

[8] Interview. [9] *Hebden Bridge Times*, 28th Feb. 1919.

[10] Interview. [11] 11th Dec. 1918.

newspapers thought little of his chances.[1] 'A tip from the stable', the *Guardian* called it,[2] and that phrase was perhaps even more revealing than the writer realized. Nor is it a surprise to find Sutcliffe Thomas exulting over what he had good reason to regard as 'their' success. Commenting on Major Barker's 'brilliant victory', he proclaimed:

'A seat which had been in Liberal or Radical hands since 1872, exactly forty-six years, has passed away, I hope for ever, from the Liberal Party'.

Amid the chorus of agreement he exulted:

'What a climb down it is for the old Liberals, the Asquithians, the Little Englanders and the little Navy men! '[3]

A 'little Navy' man had been knocked out by an Army man, and the ex-soldiers were naturally pleased. Barker himself was delighted at defeating a man whom he had contemptuously dismissed as 'a notorious little Englander',[4] a man, who, like Mr. Asquith, 'still kept to his Liberal principles'. 'We don't forget them, and we are not going to forgive.'[5] But if there could be said to be a single victor, it was the Conservatives. They had not simply won locally; they had also beaten the Whips of both parties, Bonar Law as well as L.G., London as well as Leeds. In a way, it was a modest success for the little men, but that is another story.

II. THE ATTEMPT TO INFLUENCE CANDIDATES

A group may try to influence Parliamentary candidates (other than their own) in two ways, which differ in degree rather than in kind. Convinced that a certain candidate is of the right quality, or at least has the right views, an association may throw itself into the battle in order to secure his election. By this method an association may hope to exercise influence at one remove. Alternatively, an association may content itself with what might be called 'challenge by questionnaire', although if that method is rationally used, the implication must always be one of contingent support or opposition.

(a) *Active Intervention.*

The process may be illustrated from the activities of ex-servicemen in Lincoln, where the Silver Badge Party threw 'the whole weight of their organization in favour of Mr. Davies', the Coalition Unionist candidate, which 'largely improved' his chances.[6] As to that, the

---

[1] *Halifax Evening Courier*, 14th Dec.; *Hebden Bridge Times*, 3rd Jan. 1919.
[2] 30th Dec. 1918.
[3] *Hebden Bridge Times*, 31st Jan. 1919; *Halifax Daily Guardian*, 25th Jan. 1919.
[4] *Halifax Daily Guardian*, 9th Dec. 1918.
[5] ibid.
[6] *The Times*, 12th Dec. 1918; *Grimsby Gazette*, 14th Dec. 1918.

only certainty is that Lincoln was one of the few places where the Silver Badgers could boast of a branch.[1] But Davies could have been confident for another, sounder reason—the National Association had a branch of 600 members there.[2] Having interviewed the candidates, they decided 'without a dissenting voice to support Mr. Davies', who had answered their questions 'straightforwardly and to the point'.[3] Such unanimity may have led to active intervention.

No doubt Federationists, too, actively intervened here and there: in Hackney, for instance, they were prepared to give a former lieutenant-colonel 'active support',[4] which in the event was not invoked because he withdrew. The Hackney Federationists were in fact most unlucky because in a neighbouring constituency they backed an ex-officer of still higher rank and apparently of much great learning (LL. D.) only to have him put out on a technical error in his nomination papers.[5]

Among the earlier associations,[6] it is probable that only the Comrades of the Great War refrained from active intervention) Perhaps one or two of their *own* M.P. leaders (such as Wilfrid Ashley. received some unpublicized assistance, but the general assumption of a positive role in the electoral process would have been out of character.[7]

In this, broadly speaking, the British Legion eventually followed the Comrades rather than the Federation or the Association. At first, bombarding candidates with questions,[8] the leaders certainly visualized 'active support' for one candidate where the other had shown himself 'unfavourable to the inquiries or declined to make any pledge'.[9] Doubtless some branches did act accordingly in 1922, perhaps too enthusiastically because the chairman, T. F. Lister, had occasion later to say:

'... despite what may be said by one or two people to the contrary I think we can take credit in steering clear of party politics. I do not say one or two branches did not go slightly off the rails ...'

But 'very few' did so, he went on, and they found 'that there are more pleasant things than going off the rails'.[10]

---

[1] See above, p. 134.
[2] *Grimsby Gazette*, 26th Oct. 1918.
[3] ibid., 14th Dec. 1918.
[4] *The Times*, 7th Dec. 1918.
[5] *Hackney and Kingsland Gazette*, 4th and 6th Dec. 1918.
[6] Neither the N.U.X. nor the Officers' Association had yet been established.
[7] However, I have not tried to work through the local newspaper files.
[8] Hist. B.L., appendix 15, for the earliest example, and appendix 1 below for the 1923 version.
[9] Hist. B.L., appendix 14, for the chairman's instructions to branches, 1922.
[10] Verb. Rep. 1923, p. 21. The Darlaston branch reported that the election circular from H.Q. had caused 'much confusion and heated discussion in many branches and was the cause of introducing party politics which is against the rules of our constitution'. Provisional Agenda 1923, resolution 7.

In any case, the instructions issued for the following General Election show a significant change of emphasis.[1] It was now explicitly ruled by the N.E.C. that in order to avoid 'overlapping or friction of any description, all action, including the addressing of questions to candidates, must be confined entirely to the constituency in which the particular branch is situated'.[2] Secondly, support or opposition should not be offered unless a candidate were 'distinctly' unfavourable,[3] where previously he need only have been 'unfavourable' or unwilling to sign the pledge. Besides, under the new dispensation, positive action (*i.e.*, support or opposition) should 'only be taken in very exceptional circumstances'.[4]

The writing was on the wall. The history of the twenties was, in this context, the history of the Legion leaders' gradual withdrawal from electoral politics. In December 1928 the N.E.C. decided not to submit a questionnaire during the next Election,[5] and the following April it 'most emphatically' impressed 'upon every Branch, that it would be entirely wrong to take action in its corporate capacity as a branch as a result of the replies received from any one or other candidate'.[6] Thus in 1929 the Legion finally withdrew from such 'positive (electoral) politics' as it had engaged in, and has shown no real sign of returning to it.

(b) *'Challenge by Questionnaire'*

Active intervention on behalf of, or in opposition to, a particular candidate was no doubt the less common technique. More commonly, ex-service associations tried to influence and if possible commit candidates to a specific policy.

With this end in view, ex-servicemen of the various associations might simply attend public meetings during the campaign, but two more ambitious techniques can be discerned: the formal interview with a candidate and the submission of a questionnaire.

At first, in the 1918 Election, there seems to have been some tendency to interview candidates in person rather than, so to speak, through the post. This might be done on some very public occasion, as in Cardiff, where the Association men interviewed several candidates before a 'large audience',[7] but private meetings would surely have been the norm. The interviewing of all three candidates in the

---

[1] Journal, Dec. 1923, p. 176. (See appendix 1 for a shortened version, dated 21st Nov. 1923, but containing the essential points.)

[2] ibid. [3] ibid.

[4] ibid. [5] 29. P.Q. 1958, 34.

[6] Circulars, 22nd April 1929. See below appendix 2.

[7] *Western Mail*, 6th Dec. 1918.

Holland Division (Spalding), again apparently by the local branch of the Association, leaving members free to vote as they pleased,[1] may have been an example of the more private meeting. In Dudley, a 'large proportion' of the local Federationists (if not the branch itself), opposed to the continuance of compulsory service, were 'pressing Sir Arthur Boscawen [Parliamentary Secretary, Ministry of Pensions] for a definite assurance on the point'.[2] As himself a member of the Federation, he is likely to have been seen in private.

On the whole, however, and certainly over the whole period here surveyed, the usual technique was the 'long range interview' by questionnaire. The most ambitious attempt of this kind, reflecting an extreme form of the radical theory of democracy, was the Silver Badge Party's in the 1918 Election. At an early stage, it had persuaded eleven candidates to sign, and another twelve to promise to sign,[3] a pledge that each would resign his seat if 'a majority of his electors decide in writing that he has not done his utmost to carry out the programme on which they elected him'.[4] The penalty was a severe one: £5,000 to charities.[5]

The Federation, too, tried to extract pledges but with a political rather than a financial sanction. Candidates were required to accept and sign the statement of Federation Policy, and perhaps in addition, to answer the 'test questions' with which branches had been supplied by headquarters.[6]

At first, the Legion continued the Federation tradition. In each of three General Elections from 1922 to 1924, questionnaires were hurled at the heads of the candidates,[7] who no doubt found it disagreeable. The chairman, T. F. Lister, told the 1924 Conference that he understood:

'... there was a growing apprehension among Members of Parliament about questionnaires and that a movement to form a Trade Union of Members of Parliament to abolish altogether these questionnaires, would receive the hearty support of the House of Commons. They were not going to subscribe to that particular Trade Union but they were going to subscribe to a Trade Union to see to it that M.P.s kept their written promises.'[8]

As the Legion discovered, it needed more than a 'trade union' to ensure that M.P.s kept such promises, although many Legionaries

---

[1] *The Times*, 12th Dec. 1918.   [2] *The Times*, 10th Dec. 1918.
[3] ibid., 14th Nov. 1918.
[4] *Liverpool Daily Post and Mercury*, 5th Dec. 1918.
[5] ibid.
[6] Letter, Secretary, South Liverpool Branch, to General Secretary, 23rd April 1920. Lister-Griffin letter, 9th May 1920. See below chapter XXIII.
[7] See below appendix 1 for an example of the way a Prime Minister answers an election questionnaire.
[8] Verb. Rep., pp. 32-3.

remained puzzled and some are still puzzled today. The Swansea delegate was speaking for many when at the 1925 Conference, reviewing the three elections, he said he could not 'understand why ex-service Members of Parliament did not stand firmly together and walk out of the House of Commons when ex-servicemen did not get a square deal'. He added that the General Secretary would be justified in 'writing to every M.P. and asking why he did not carry out his pledge when he signed the questionnaire'.[1]

Although it was quite a common practice at the time, the questionnaire method in general simply did not work, and no one who understood our political system would have been under any illusion about it from the start. In the face of the 1929 Election (as already noted) the technique was abandoned, though this was not simply a matter of cause and effect. The Legion was considered by the Palace to have been occasionally too 'involved in politics', and a strong hint was dropped that royal patronage might be withdrawn. The criticism, in so far as it was justified, no doubt related to active intervention of the kind mentioned in the previous section rather than to the submission of questionnaires as such, but in the event the document was jettisoned as well as the behaviour corrected.

The Limbless Ex-Service Men did not at first appreciate the weakness of the questionnaire method: although appearing, in its English form, some three years after the questionnaire method had been discarded by the Legion, it nevertheless used something of the kind in the 1935 Election. Its Executive Council wished to promote a Bill to take the limbless out of the labour market, and 'the only prospect' the General Secretary could then 'see available to enable this Council to launch such a Scheme' was to send a message to every candidate.[2] 1,350 messages were sent and 700 replies received: a fifth of the new Parliament, it was estimated, were in favour of such a measure.[3] But that experiment need only be recorded in passing; four years later the BLESMA Conference, discussing the prospect of an early election, considered whether 'all candidates should be canvassed for support of the Association's requests', but decided that 'only elected M.P.s should be approached'.[4] BLESMA had proved an apt pupil in the ways of the political world.

[1] ibid. 2a/19.

[2] Executive Council Mins., 19th–20th Oct. 1935, p. 3.

[3] Report of E.C. Sub-committee, 23rd Oct., p. 4; 1936 Conference Report, p. 7.

[4] 1939 Conference Report, p. 10.

XVIII

DOMESTIC AIMS:

(A) THE TECHNIQUES OF INFLUENCE (1917–39)

(2) THE HOUSE OF COMMONS (ii) AFTER THE ELECTION

'Post-Natal'

IT may now be assumed that a new Parliament has been returned, and that organized ex-servicemen face a 'given' House. Whether or not the 'ante-natal' influence has been successful, they will use one or more of three techniques: they will try to make an impact on (i) individual M.P.s; (ii) groups of M.P.s; (iii) the House as a whole. To that stimulus M.P.s, in their turn, may be expected, individually or collectively, to respond by way of the various 'parliamentary routines'.[1] Thus this chapter falls naturally into two parts: (i) the methods of approach to M.P.s as such, and (ii) what M.P.s do in consequence.

I. METHODS OF APPROACHING M.P.S

(i) Individual M.P.s

Naturally, the approach to individual M.P.s should have been easiest where 'ante-natal' influence of one kind—that achieved by sponsorship—was greatest, but the truth of this proposition was never put to the test, since, as we have just seen, sponsorship was an almost complete failure. The exceptional success—Major Barker's—proved nothing because the headquarters of the National Association had no claim upon him.

Lacking a sponsored M.P. or two, associations have to manage with an ostensible second-best that may turn out to be 'as good as the original': group representation through 'linked' M.P.s, often achieved by having them on the executive committee.[2] Such relationships have existed almost throughout the history of the ex-servicemen's movement in this country, and have already been recorded in these pages and elsewhere.[3] But to the Federation's list of 'linked' M.P.s one should add Captain Colin Coote's name. Currently the

---

[1] J. D. Stewart, op. cit., ch. V.   [2] ibid., p. 152.
[3] Hist. B.L., pp. 3–4, and above, esp. chs. XII and XV.

editor of the *Daily Telegraph*, he was in 1919 the President of the Eastern Divisional Council of the Federation and a champion of their cause.

Throughout its history the Legion has always been represented in the House by at least one member of its N.E.C. At the beginning it 'inherited' Major (later Sir) Brunel Cohen, who, a member of the House from 1918, had come on to the N.E.C. from the Officers' Association; eighteen months or so after the formation of the Legion, he was joined by ex-Sergeant-Major Douglas Pielou and Captain J. E. Rogerson. The Captain disappeared in Baldwin's 'tariff mandate' election in 1923, but for most of that year the Legion had had three M.P.s in the House.

From that election until May 1929, the Legion had two M.P.s 'of its own', Smedley Crooke replacing Pielou in 1927. Smedley Crooke fell out of favour in 1929 and so Brunel Cohen again held the fort alone until 1931, when Smedley Crooke returned but Cohen himself did not seek re-election. Smedley Crooke survived until 1945. Thus, in the inter-war years (as indeed in the whole period covered by this work) the Legion was never without direct representation.

It is, however, a mistake to suppose that it 'sought' representation in the usual sense of that term.[1] Greatness was thrust upon it rather than achieved. Brunel Cohen it inherited; Pielou was certainly a member of the N.E.C. before his election to Parliament but he had established himself locally by his activity in the movement since his discharge in 1916, and Earl Haig wisely refused to lift a finger to help him when asked to support his candidature.[2] The West Midlands Area of the Legion may have helped Pielou unofficially but that is another matter. Rogerson, too, was a member of the N.E.C. before his election, but the 'gap' was a narrow one of about four months, and he, too, had his local distinction, though this was of quite another (Master-of-Foxhounds) kind. Smedley Crooke had been as prominent in the Comrades and then in the British Legion Unity Committee as Pielou had been in the Federation, and, as treasurer of the West Midlands Area, was Pielou's natural successor on the N.E.C.[3] Sir Ian Fraser had had a distinguished and varied career and was already, for the second time, an M.P. when he became national vice-chairman in 1943. He could have been chairman, but his presidency in 1947 was actually won against the grain of the Legion leadership, who sponsored Admiral of the Fleet, Lord Tovey.[4]

[1] John H. Millett, 9 West P.Q., Dec. 1956, 917.

[2] Hist. B.L., p. 109.

[3] N.E.C. Mins. and Annual Reports, passim, for these details.

[4] Hist. B.L., p. 284. Although these events fall outside the period here reviewed, it is convenient to mention them at this stage because it was Ian Fraser who kept up the 'functional' representation after 1945.

Doubtless, the Legion generally (though not universally) was glad to have some of its leaders in the House but it did not really 'seek' representation.

Where an organization has no 'claims', it falls back on the 'ordinary' interested M.P. He may be interested simply because he is the local member: Philip Snowden, for a while, gave the Blackburn (later the National) Association,[1] some assistance. Others may be drawn in through a combination of local connexions and an interest in the cause: Sir Joseph Nall in his work for BLESMA, then essentially a Manchester organization,[2] was an example.[3] Again, a member may take an interest simply because it is partly his 'subject': Hogge of the Federation used to be known as the 'King of Pensions'. Associations such as BLESMA have never found any difficulty in attracting the services of M.P.s: of its original nine patrons, for instance, seven were in the Commons and one in the Lords.[4]

(*ii*) *Sub-groups*

There is at Westminster a division of labour that goes unrecorded in *Erskine May*: it is, of course, primarily of a party kind (1922 Committee, the P.L.P. and their offshoots) but has all-party manifestations as well (*e.g.*, the Glass Manufacturers Group, to which some success has been attributed).[5]

Party Groups

There seems to be no evidence that organized ex-servicemen have ever approached any of the party groups as such in the House of Commons (or Lords). That an informal approach or two might have been made, especially before the formation of the Legion, should not be completely ruled out, but if so all trace of it has been lost or covered over. But the odds are against such connexions. Since 1921, the ex-servicemen generally have been neutral as between the parties: even active intervention during general elections would not confer party advantage over the country *as a whole*. That neutrality might have been less easy to maintain had it not found institutional expression in the House of Commons Branch of the Legion, founded in 1922. Since then it has always been possible to use an all-party chan-

---

[1] See above, p. 95.

[2] In the late 1950's it found the pull of the metropolis irresistible.

[3] General Secretary's Report for 1942, para. 4.

[4] 1936 Conference Report, p. 10. They were: Sir Patrick Hannon, Col. Sir E. Ruggles-Brise, Bt., the Hon. Harold Nicolson, Lt.-Col. Sir W. A. Wayland, Major H. A. Procter, Col. A. W. Goodman, Sir Robert Young; Lord Strabolgi (Commander Kenworthy). The other patron chosen was Lady Bailey.

[5] Political and Economic Planning, *Industrial Trade Associations*, 1957, p. 88.

nel, making an approach to party groups ostensibly unnecessary even if not undesirable on other grounds. The contrast with the National Farmers' Union (since 1944) is striking.[1]

All-Party Groups

(a) Probably the first of these was the committee of all 'Service' Members of the House of Commons set up early in the life of the 1918 Parliament.[2] While it would not be surprising to find that some of its members had served on the Unionist War Committee, which had had both service and non-service members,[3] its immediate origin obviously lay in the influx of ex-service members from Lloyd George's 'khaki' election. This was reflected in the composition of the Executive Committee. The chairman was Lt.-Col. Martin Archer-Lee (Unionist), who had been elected to Parliament in 1910, but almost all the other members of the Committee, including the secretary, Major Ralph Glyn, had come in on the 1918 wave.[4]

(b) From such a committee to a branch of the Legion is no great step, for all the formal difference in status. Some members took it in 1922, when the branch was founded as part of the N.E.C's membership campaign.[5] The branch survived until March 1955, when it reverted to a 'Legion Parliamentary Group', thus turning the wheel three-quarters circle. In the years between, the Legion had an official (if yet to Mr. Speaker *as such* and the Lord Great Chamberlain, a quite unofficial) foothold in the Palace of Westminster.

Of course, the House of Commons Branch of the Legion was ever a branch in a special sense, even more so than many Legionaries realized. It was not exactly 'a Legion "Branch" in title only':[6] it was a 'house' branch (*i.e.*, based on the place of work), a kind sufficiently common to provoke complaint at the 1922 Conference,[7] and it embraced not only M.P.s but also the professional staff of the Commons.[8] It was allocated to the Metropolitan Area for administrative purposes and its members paid affiliation fees—when the appropriate official succeeded in extracting the money from them. Some members paid regularly and willingly; others showed reluctance

---

[1] Stewart, p. 159.

[2] *Bulletin*, 22nd May 1919.

[3] *The Times*, 21st Dec. 1916. Most of the recorded office-bearers seem to have been 'Unionist' or 'Conservative Unionist', *e.g.* apart from those mentioned in the text: Viscount Curzon, Admiral Sir (William) Reginald Hall. Commander Kenworthy's was a Liberal voice on the E.C. But the list is probably incomplete.

[4] *Bulletin*, ibid., and 24th Aug. 1919.

[5] Press hand-out 25th May 1922 in Circulars 1922; Journal, May 1922, 253, for the inaugural meeting.

[6] John H. Millett, 9 West. P.Q., Dec. 1956, 919.

[7] Journal, July 1922, 12.   [8] Journal, May 1922, 253.

and took successful evasive action, claiming, no doubt correctly, that they had already paid 'at home' (*i.e.* in their own 'territorial' branch or branches). But certainly it was no ordinary branch.

As with the Legion itself, Earl Haig, coaxed 'upstairs' by Major Brunel Cohen, undertook the launching ceremony.[1] He persuaded those present that a Legion branch in the House would be an 'immense advantage' and a 'great moral encouragement to the various branches in the country'.[2] A branch was formed on the spot and officers appointed, and it was soon claimed that 'a large number of members and officials' had joined its ranks.[3] Certainly by the autumn the membership had grown to ninety-nine, which was reduced to seventy-six by the 'Carlton Club' election. The losses, however, were soon made good. At a general meeting on 5th December 1922, Brunel Cohen (the real driving force) became chairman, with another Legion N.E.C. member—Douglas Pielou— as secretary. The treasureship went to Labour: J. J. Lawson, destined to become a Privy Councillor and a peer of the realm. The large executive committee included officials of the House as well as members.[4]

Meetings of the branch were never frequent: M.P.s obviously have other interests and calls on their time. The predictable meeting was the (presumably) annual one to elect the officers and committee; otherwise they would come together only as some special occasion demanded. Thus in 1930 the branch was convened as part of the campaign to abolish the seven years' time limit on applications for war pensions.[5] About fifty of the invited hundred 'favourable' M.P.s put in an appearance.

The Legion's approach to the Branch was of two main kinds, the first leading from the N.E.C. to one or more of the Branch officers, usually (taking the period as a whole) the chairman, *i.e.*, the device of 'dual roles' or interlocking leadership. Brunel Cohen, Smedley Crooke and Ian Fraser were the principal 'role players'. But in order to play their parts it would not have been necessary or useful to summon many meetings: membership of the House affords so many opportunities for informal discussion. On the other hand, meetings were called by them to give other Legion leaders (usually the full-time specialists) an opportunity for exposition, argument and persuasion. This was the second 'influence-route'. An early example (March 1923) was Colonel E. C. Heath's talk, as General Secretary, on various subjects such as T.B. ex-servicemen and the time limit on applications for widows' pensions.

---

[1] Journal, May 1922, 253.   [2] ibid.
[3] ibid.
[4] ibid., Jan. 1923, 166.   [5] Hist. B.L., p. 131.

(*iii*) *The whole House*

Strictly speaking, associations cannot make direct contact with the whole House. Even the public petition to 'the Honourable Commons of Great Britain and Northern Ireland in Parliament assembled' has to be presented by a member and perhaps carried by some unfortunate doorkeeper. But petitioning, lobbying and some other techniques may perhaps be regarded in this light.

Written Communications

Writing to M.P.s (in intention, *all* M.P.s) was normal Federation policy. It was at times undertaken from headquarters: a circular letter to all M.P.s went out in 1921, for instance, arguing for a higher rate of disability pension, and hoping it would be possible 'for you personally to raise this question in the House of Commons at an opportune moment'.[1] But most of the writing was intended to be done by the branches, for obvious—and sound—reasons. 'Pestering' M.P.s with resolutions was the form it took. A characteristic example of the intention and style was the N.E.C's request to branches in 1920 to communicate with their local M.P.s 'demanding the withdrawal' of certain clauses in a War Pensions Bill that had recently had its second reading.[2] The following month all branches were asked to pass resolutions 'demanding the continuance of the out-of-work donation scheme so far as ex-service men are concerned', and to send copies to local M.P.s (as well as to the Prime Minister and the Minister of Labour).[3]

The other early associations seem to have done little of this kind, but once again the Legion carried on where the Federation left off. Thus, in April 1923, headquarters circularized all M.P.s about a Bill amending a War Pensions Act, urging support for the second reading even though certain safeguards might have to be inserted at the Committee stage.[4] Nor was the approach through the branches neglected: a few weeks later branches were informed of this action and asked to send reminders to their local M.P.s.[5] As with the Federation, the branch approach to M.P.s was indeed emphasized again and again: 'It is their strength and pressure in their own localities that is the best way of helping forward a fighting policy', the chairman told Conference in 1923.[6] Power and influence do not rest on activity at headquarters but on the 'strength and determination of the individual branches throughout the country'.[7] Another

---

[1] Circulars, 19th Feb. 1921.

[2] ibid., 1st June 1920. [3] ibid., July 1920.

[4] Circulars, 12th April 1923. [5] ibid., 30th April 1923.

[6] Verb. Rep., p. 146. [7] ibid., p. 21.

attempt to mobilize that strength was made in 1924 in favour of the Bill for the Employment of Disabled Men.[1]

None the less, headquarters was responsible over the years for the dispatch of a vast quantity of paper in the general direction of M.P.s. BLESMA, too, tried its hand at this 'writing business': in January 1939, timed to coincide with the re-assembly of Parliament after the Christmas recess, memoranda were dispatched from headquarters to all M.P.s on the question of the employment of the limbless.[2]

Other 'Communications'

Intervention in a by-election will, of course, be noted in the Lobby as well as in the Cabinet Room; and the backwash of a demonstration will be felt there too. Indeed, some demonstrations, although mounted to impress the Cabinet, had the House of Commons as the immediate physical objective. It was during a march on the House that the Federation clashed with the police in May 1919.[3] But this technique may be mentioned here for completeness only to be promptly dismissed.

The Petition

Nor need the Parliamentary petition detain us. Tried, I believe, only once in the whole history of the ex-service movement, it is recognized as a curious survival from a very different age. The circumstances in which the Legion tried this now desperate throw have already been briefly described.[4] 'Ordinary' pressure having failed to remedy some war pensions grievances, the Legion, chiefly through Brunel Cohen, argued for a Select Committee. This the Government refused, and the Legion's response was a petition bearing 824,000 signatures. What it achieved other than bad feeling at the Ministry is uncertain.

Lobbying

Thus, at last, we reach the main technique for attempts at influencing the whole House: lobbying. The term, of course, has a deceptive simplicity. As a noun, it has been used by S. E. Finer in the hope of dislodging both the old term 'pressure group' and the perhaps newer one, 'interest group'.[5] As a gerund, it has, in J. D. Stewart's hands, been taken to mean 'any approaches made to M.P.s on a large scale

---

[1] See appendix 4 below. For a summary of the Bill, see Hist. B.L., app. 17.

[2] 1939 Conference Report, p. 8.

[3] See above, p. 125.

[4] Hist. B.L., pp. 78–82 and p. 87. See also p. 162 below.

[5] *Anonymous Empire:* A Study of the Lobby in Great Britain, 1958, p. 3.

by outside organizations', not necessarily within the precincts of Parliament.[1] This is a wider interpretation than is usual[2] but I accept it. On the other hand, Stewart includes within his definition the dispatch of those written communications[3] that I have thought useful to keep distinct from face-to-face approaches.

Lobbying at Westminster

Stewart has discerned two forms of the lobbying that is practised at Westminster: 'the mass assault and the steady trickle'.[4] It is curious that neither of these variations has commended itself to organized ex-servicemen (with the exception of BLESMA in the post-1945 period) despite their possession of what might be called a Mother-of-Parliament fixation. But for one reason or another they were induced to behave in a different, though obviously not unrelated, way.

The 'mass assault' has been rarely mounted. It is, of course, true that the distinction between an organized demonstration and mass lobbying begins to break down the moment the procession turns from Hyde Park towards Parliament Square. The Federation's demonstration in May 1919 illustrates the transformation that may occur. But in general the early societies cared nothing for swarming around the Lobby, which was never favoured by the Legion either.

Nor has a 'steady trickle' flowed. Occasionally a Legion branch, (*e.g.* a Government Department 'house' branch) has been known to burst its bonds and to undertake a little lobbying on its own account in order to remedy some special grievance, but that is all. In general, ex-servicemen have shown good sense in directing their attention to the constituencies.

Lobbying in the constituencies

No society knew better than the Federation the value of 'local' lobbying. Thus in 1920 the leadership was urging the branches to press their M.P.s about the out-of-work donation[5] and the unemployment problem as it affected ex-servicemen. At the very first meeting of the Legion's N.E.C., it was decided to ask branches to approach local M.P.s about amending the War Pensions Bill of that period.[6] Early in its history, BLESMA, too, was suggesting to branches that local M.P.s should be asked to put down a question for

---

[1] Stewart, op. cit., p. 207. [2] ibid., n. 1.
[3] p. 209. [4] p. 207.
[5] Circulars, Aug. 1920.
[6] N.E.C. Mins., 24th July 1921, Min. 29.

answer by the Minister of Labour,[1] but as BLESMA had only fourteen branches at the time, this effort (in so far as it was made) was obviously not on the same scale as that made by either the Federation or the Legion.

II. THE ACTION OF M.P.S

So far we have been considering the various ways in which ex-servicemen's associations tried to activate the House of Commons, conceived of in three permutations. It is now necessary to observe the consequential action of M.P.s.

(i) Individual M.P.s

The member who is linked or simply well-disposed to an association may serve it in various ways. He will certainly ask questions in the House for the purpose of extracting information that the group has found it difficult to obtain from the Department as well as in a more direct attempt to exert some influence. A member may privately urge some policy on the Minister or his colleagues: in 1923 Brunel Cohen went, accompanied by two senior Legion officials, to see the Minister, his Parliamentary Secretary and some leading civil servants.[2] A member may be able to arrange a debate: T. J. Macnamara, a former Minister of Labour, having been approached by J. R. Griffin the previous month, may have been instrumental in having the Estimates of the Ministry of Pensions chosen for the 'supply day' debate on 5th June 1923.[3] Another such debate was arranged on 26th May 1925, in order to voice various pensions grievances, and especially to force the appointment of a Select Committee.[4] A debate having been initiated, the really 'interested' member may then reveal the depth of his commitment by threatening to go into the Division Lobby against his party. Brunel Cohen so declared himself in the June 1923 debate; in the event, because the Minister gave way, such heroism was not necessary, but on the May 1925 occasion, Brunel Cohen did find himself voting with his political opponents, and so did Douglas Pielou and Smedley Crooke.[5] Again, a member may collect signatures from other members in the hope of impressing the Cabinet: the 250 signatures to a petition to the Prime Minister in 1925[6] constitute an example.

Occasionally a member tried to initiate legislation, or, more

[1] 1939 Conference Report, p. 9.
[2] Lister-Griffin, 15th May 1923. See below p. 164.
[3] ibid. [4] Hist. B.L., p. 80.
[5] ibid.
[6] Circulars, 1925: Notes on some recent work.

commonly, to amend the Government's. Sir Patrick Hannon, a BLESMA patron at the time (and prominent in the Comrades of the Great War from its inception) was willing to assist with a Bill to take the severely war disabled out of the labour market, but he was unable to report progress.[1] Douglas Pielou, lucky in the ballot, introduced a bill in 1924, drawn up by A. G. Webb in Legion headquarters, to secure the compulsory employment of disabled men: it received a second reading but nothing else.[2] In 1931 Brunel Cohen scored a personal triumph when introducing a Legion Bill to remove the seven years' time limit on applications for pensions.[3] But the Government fell, he himself retired and the bill disappeared from sight.

This disappointing record is, of course, exactly what one would expect: the success of A. P. Herbert and some others are the exceptions to a familiar modern rule. The use of members to secure amendments to the Government's own legislation, on the other hand, may be quite rewarding. In 1921 the Legion was perturbed at its lack of direct representation on the various local war pensions committees set up under the Bill then before Parliament.[4] The Executive Council discussed the matter at its meeting in July, when it was resolved to write to the Prime Minister, to publish the letter in the Press and send a copy to all branches with instructions to bring their influence to bear on their local M.P.s.[5] In the House, Brunel Cohen wrestled manfully with the Minister, who, however, resisted 'the amendments which would give the British Legion power to nominate the ex-servicemen's representatives'[6] on the local committees. On the other hand, the Minister 'did say most definitely that he would request the advice and assistance of ex-servicemen's organizations in existence in the various areas concerned'.[7] Thus the amendment forced a decision and yielded an assurance that virtually gave the Legion what it wanted. Later (though falling outside the period here surveyed), the most important example of what can be achieved by way of amendment is probably the 1943–44 battle to amend the Disabled Persons (Employment) Bill so as to give ex-servicemen (and women) preference within the quota. But this episode has already been recorded.[8]

The use of M.P.s to secure amendments to Government Bills (or compensating assurances) has, then, been of appreciable importance

---

[1] 1936 Conference Report, pp. 10 and 7.

[2] Hist. B.L., pp. 68–9 and appendix 17. See also appendix 4 below.

[3] Hist. B.L., pp. 132–3.

[4] War Pensions Act, 1921 (11 and 12 Geo. 5. Ch. 49), para. 3.

[5] Mins. 24th July 1921, Min. 29.

[6] Journal, Sept. 1921, 66.　　　　　　　[7] ibid.

[8] Hist. B.L., pp. 270–1.

for ex-servicemen, but what of the thinking behind such Bills and indeed behind Government policy in whatever form? The impact of well-briefed and 'committed' members was most in evidence during the last war,[1] when Smedley Crooke and especially Sir Ian Fraser (mentioning here only Legion leaders in the House) helped to formulate Government policy. But, although impossible to prove, individual members connected with the movement must, even in the years of peace, have played a not inconsiderable part in 'conditioning' Government thought. Hamar Greenwood of the Comrades was one such member. His warning to Winston Churchill in 1919 about the Empire Services League[2] may well have influenced the Secretary of State's thinking, and so, ultimately, the Cabinet's on the future control of the canteen funds.[3] This is not a good example because by this time Greenwood had become a junior minister, but it is suggestive. On the other hand, there are those Parliamentary party occasions when the voices of members may be raised in advocacy, explanation or defence: Wilfrid Ashley (Comrades) with the four (main) Legion M.P.s and the four or five of BLESMA's on the Conservative side; F. J. Bellenger (Legion) with Leslie Lever and James Simmons (BLESMA), most obviously, among the Parliamentary Labour Party. All these at various times must have contributed to that formulation of ideas before policy has crystallized which is perhaps all the more effective for being hidden from the public gaze.

(ii) Sub-groups

Fundamentally, the response of the House of Commons Branch of the Legion as such to the stimulus of the national leadership was to send a deputation to the erring or reluctant Minister. A pre-war illustration has been provided elsewhere:[4] the convening of a Branch meeting in 1930 as part of the campaign to remove the seven years' time limit, the appointment of an all-party committee of nine to work out a compromise, and their visit 'as a body' to the Minister of Pensions to urge the compromise upon him.[5] But he was just as resistant to their blandishments as he had been to earlier Legion representations. Generally the Branch was an ornament and not an instrument for exerting influence on decisions; it was left to BLESMA after the war to show how an all-party committee[6] could be really effective.

---

[1] Hist. B.L., pp. 262–5, esp. p. 264.

[2] See above, p. 92.

[3] The Ashley Papers, Greenwood to Ashley, 10th March 1919.

[4] Hist. B.L., p. 131, based on N.E.C. Mins. 7th June 1930, Min. 11.

[5] ibid.   [6] See below ch. XXV.

(iii) *The whole House*

What action did M.P.s take in response to attempts to influence the whole House? As it is extremely difficult to discover tangible advantages, perhaps one should proceed by way of elimination. The response to most written communications was no doubt decisive: these would have been dropped into the waste-paper basket. Few M.P.s would have replied or even bothered to send an acknowledgement. Of course, an ostensibly personal letter from an address within the member's constituency would have been an entirely different matter, but the routine circular from whatever source cut no ice. 'Communications' in the other sense (by-elections and demonstrations) were likewise unproductive, as was the petition.

Thus one comes to consider the technique of lobbying, primarily, over the whole period, lobbying in the constituencies. For this there is really nothing to show, but it is none the less probable that members were in turn stimulated to 'have a word with the Whips', to buttonhole the Minister and perhaps even ambush the Chancellor. And there can be no doubt that members raised their voices in the Parliamentary party meetings. In short, local lobbying is likely to have influenced that grass-roots formulation of opinion among back-benchers which is one important factor in the crystallization of Cabinet policy.

XIX

DOMESTIC AIMS:

(A) THE TECHNIQUES OF INFLUENCE (1917-39)

(3) THE MINISTRIES

SOME of the techniques used to influence the Ministries have already been mentioned obliquely in the two preceding chapters and need not detain us. Obviously, the Ministries will be targets for many a written communication. The Federationists fired from three parapets. Branches sent in resolutions; so did the Divisional Councils and the national headquarters.[1] The Comrades seem to have done little of the kind, but in general most associations have used this simple technique and one need not take up space for further specification.

Attempts to win over the Ministries flowed along two main channels: the deputation and the advisory committee. Naturally, as a technique, the deputation appeared first. It was never true that 'the four organizations which consolidated to form the Legion in the first place utilized the formal deputation frequently—sometimes once a week during a period of intense activity'.[2] The Officers' Association hardly used it at all.[3] The National Association certainly made representations, though the method is not clear;[4] doubtless, by means of deputations occasionally, but it was far less powerful than the Federation and Comrades, and so was accorded 'access' far less readily.[5] Besides, the very fact of its location in Blackburn for about four-fifths of its existence (combined with its obvious poverty)[6] militated against frequent deputations to Departments located over two hundred miles away.

The Comrades may well have made more use of the deputation as

---

[1] *Bulletin*, 27th Nov. 1919, 4th Mar. and 8th Jan. 1920.

[2] John H. Millett, 72 P.S.Q. 1957, 74. Millett apparently relied on some informant's faulty memory.

[3] Interviews with writer.

[4] Annual Conference, 1918, Secretary's Report, p. 5.

[5] *The Bayonet*, September 1920, 3.

[6] *e.g.* the issue of its official journal just referred to in note 5 was its first one, whereas the Comrades began publishing in Nov. 1918 and the Federation in March 1919.

a technique than the Association did. In 1918, it made 'urgent representation' to the Ministry of Pensions, though by what channel is unrecorded; in 1919, the organization, 'latterly', of three deputations was reported; in 1920, none.[1] Even if there were others that went unreported, the total would scarcely justify the term 'frequent'.

As one would expect, the Federationists were the great exponents of the deputation technique, but even in relation to them, it is misleading to speak of 'sometimes once a week'. There were hardly enough 'subjects' (or Ministers and civil servants) for that even in 1919. In May of that year there was indeed *one* breathless week in which four deputations waited on Ministers or civil servants,[2] and there was a 'follow-up' (to the Ministry of Labour again) twelve days later.[3] That was the period of most intense activity, and needless to say it was exceptional.

The Federation seems to have used the deputation from a very early stage: to the Minister of Labour and National Service, for instance, in April 1918, followed by at least two others before the Armistice.[4] After the Armistice, as we muddled on, the number of deputations naturally increased, reaching a climax, though not coming to an end, early in 1920. These were not merely to the Minister of Pensions, as one tends to expect, but also to the Minister of Agriculture and Fisheries (twice in 1920), the Minister of Food, the Minister of Labour and the Secretary of State for War,[5] indicating the wide range of problems encountered. How far these comings and goings produced results will be discussed presently, but the chairman, T. F. Lister, was surely right to say that the deputation was 'probably the most important' of the 'various methods adopted by organized ex-servicemen to make their views vocal'.[6] Certainly that was true about his own group, for when the sound and fury of the demon-

---

[1] Annual Reports, 1918 (p. 14), 1919 (p. 20) and 1920.

[2] 12th May (Minister of Pensions); 13th May (Ministry of Labour); 14th May (a.m.) (Ministry of Labour); 14th May (p.m.) (War Office: junior Minister). This flurry was due to the fact that the chairman, T. F. Lister, had to travel from Liverpool, and had to fit in many meetings at one 'go'. On the evening of 14th May he addressed the Service members of the House; on 15th May he gave evidence before the Select Committee on Pensions!

[3] *Bulletin*, 5th June 1919. Also T. F. Lister's letter to me, 1st Dec. 1957. The 'follow up' deputation leader, F. W. Jackson (General Secretary) complained that this was the third deputation within a fortnight but they still had not seen the Minister. But they had 'gone up one': this time they were received by the Parliamentary Secretary.

[4] N.E.C. Mins. 10th–11th April, 4th June, 25th Aug., 2nd Nov.

[5] N.F.D.D.S.S., Sundry Papers, pp. 1–9; Circulars Aug. 1920, G.P.C. Mins., 6th–7th Mar. 1920, Min. 15.

[6] *Bulletin*, 4th Mar. 1920.

stration had died away, someone had to meet a Minister face to face and argue. In the last resort, reason had to be brought to bear (if not prevail). As Sir Frederick (then Mr.) Lister recalls: '. . . on all the deputations I had anything to do with, we tried to be specific and have our case based on reason'.[1]

In their formal approaches, the Comrades ranged less widely (*e.g.*, the War Office and the India Office in 1919),[2] but the Legion, of course, used the technique both intensively and extensively.[3] There would be little virtue in a catalogue. The range was fairly wide: (Pensions, the Service Departments, the Treasury, Health and Labour).[4] It was quite frequently used in the twenties: thus, for instance, a flurry of activity followed the change of Government in 1924. Four deputations in quick succession waited on Ministers (Labour, Pensions, Health and Admiralty)[5] in the vain hope of persuading them to do what had been refused by their predecessors. The Legion had to learn the hard way that although Ministers come and go, their advisers remain.

The post-Legion societies scarcely fall for consideration here because they did not in this period enjoy access to Government Departments. Ministers and civil servants would have been as likely to receive a deputation from the L.L.X. as from a trade union of burglars. The Comrades of the R.A.F. was too small to be taken seriously even if it had exhibited ambitions of the relevant kind. The Limbless Ex-Service Men, on the other hand, certainly set out to be a pressure group but tended to be officially regarded as rather small and unrepresentative.

Of the impact on the Ministries through the advisory committee channel, it is difficult to speak with confidence, so well wrapped are its proceedings in the cocoon of 'confidentiality'. But some comments can be made, first of all in rebuttal. It was certainly not in the Central Advisory Committee on War Pensions that 'the major provisions of the pensions programme for ex-servicemen of World War I were worked out—one might say, bargained for'.[6] Those major provisions were, of course, enacted in a series of measures between 1915 and 1921, the last of which (the War Pensions Act, 1921) created the very Advisory Committee we are discussing. And had there been any bargaining through 'advisory' channels, its locus would have been the Standing Joint Committee for Ex-Service Questions, which in all probability was the (relatively) important advisory committee of the period, *i.e.*, basically, the 1920's, for at the beginning of the

---

[1] Letter to writer, 21st Feb. 1957.
[2] Annual Report, 1919, p. 20.
[3] Hist. B.L., passim.   [4] ibid.
[5] Circulars, Mar. 1924.   [6] Millett, op. cit., p. 73.

following decade, these channels ceased to be used. The nature of the evidence will emerge as we proceed.

Up to 1920, no 'regular' relations between the authorities and the organized ex-servicemen had been established. It was all *ad hoc*, or catch-as-catch-can. The turning point came on 6th February 1920, the day of the Federation deputation to the Prime Minister, when L.G. also received representatives of the Comrades and the Association.[1] It was they (doubtless the Comrades men made the running) who put up the idea for some standing committee to link the Departments to the movement,[2] and the Prime Minister agreed. It was soon announced that the Government had decided to hold 'regular conferences between ex-servicemen and Government Departments'.[3]

But would all ex-servicemen join in? The Federation took strong exception to a paragraph in the proposed scheme that would have canalized their deputations into the new committee.[4] Understandably, the leaders refused to surrender their right to send deputations direct to the Government; without them the scheme could not work, and so the original memorandum was withdrawn, 'such withdrawal meaning that the right of the Federation to send independent deputations to Government Departments at any time was not interfered with'.[5]

The Committee was composed of nine Government and fifteen ex-servicemen's representatives.[6] The 'Big Three' each sent three men to speak for the rank and file, and one each to represent the ex-officers among their own members. Additionally, the Officers' Association had separate representation.[7] The Government side of the committee embraced all interested departments: doubtless, the Ministries of Pensions and Labour were predominant. The committee worked through two panels (for officers and 'other ranks'), the Parliamentary Secretaries to the Ministries of Pensions and of Labour alternating as chairmen, and, perhaps, the Minister of Pensions himself presiding over the main committee meetings.[8] These virtual sub-committees each met on nine occasions from April 1920–March 1921, while there were ten meetings of the main committee.[9] Thereafter the meetings became less frequent: six of the main committee in

---

[1] *Comrades' Journal*, Mar. 1920, 11 and 2.

[2] ibid., June 1920, 2; Griffin-Lister, 15th Mar. 1920.

[3] *The Times*, 2nd Mar. 1920.

[4] N.E.C. Mins., 20–21 Mar. 1920, Min. 9.

[5] G.P.C., Mins., 17th April 1920, Min. 10.

[6] 4th Annual Report, Ministry of Pensions, para. 51.

[7] *The Bayonet*, Sept. 1920, 3. This source gives two from the O.A., making a total of fourteen. Presumably there were in fact three of them as well, matching the official total of fifteen.

[8] *Comrades' Journal*, Oct. 1920, 17; Nov. 1920, 17; and Feb. 1921, 21.

[9] 4th Annual Report, Ministry of Pensions, para. 51.

each of the two succeeding (financial) years, then a sharp decline until in the period 1926–30 they became just an annual event.[1] The last meeting seems to have been held in the year 1931–32.[2]

Official records are reticent about the scope of the committee, merely asserting that a large number of important matters were discussed,[3] though they do reveal that as late as 1928–29, over seven years after the establishment of the Central Advisory Committee, the Standing Joint Committee discussed pensions (*i.e.*, the accumulation by the Ministry of part of a disabled man's pension).[4] The precise dividing line between the two committees is thus obscure, but the range of topics discussed in the earlier committee in the 1920–21 period extended from pensions for disabled regular officers, grants to start up businesses and training allowances, on the one hand, to widows' pensions, the employment problem and V.C. annuities.[5] Under the Legion régime, the topics included, in 1921–22, pensions for certain widows of men who had died in earlier wars; widows' re-marriage gratuities; procedure at Pensions Appeal Tribunals and the payment of treatment allowances.[6]

The Standing Joint Committee of 1920 was, on its 'public' side, a committee of representative ex-servicemen: the Central Advisory Committee of 1921 was a broadly-based committee,[7] comprising not only such ex-servicemen but also representatives of the local pensions committees, which included widows, local councillors, trade unionists, industrialists and members of associations here called 'societies *for*', as well as local ex-servicemen.[8] In the mid-twenties it was composed of four representatives of the Ministry, with an equal number (nine) drawn from the War Pensions Committees (doubtless the chairmen) and from the ranks of ex-servicemen.[9] These ex-servicemen were both organized and unorganized: there were four to speak for the Legion (compared with what the chairman called 'a big representation on the Standing Joint Committee').[10] Meetings were probably infrequent: in 1922–3, 'from time to time', supplemented

---

[1] Annual Reports, Ministry of Pensions, passim.

[2] 15th Annual Report, para. 22. There was no meeting in 1930–31.

[3] 4th Annual Report, para. 51.

[4] 12th Annual Report, para. 39.

[5] *Comrades' Journal*, June 1920, 22; Nov. 1920, 17; Feb. 1921, 21.

[6] Journal, August 1922, 35.

[7] War Pensions Act, 1921, para. 3.

[8] ibid., para. 1 (3).

[9] 9th Annual Report, para. 52. Cf. 193 H. C. Deb., c. 567–9.

[10] Conference 1923, Verb. Rep., p. 128. The Legion presumably inherited the fifteen ex-service places, or at least twelve of them (omitting the seats that had been allocated to the O.A.). 193 H. C. Deb., c. 569, 18th Mar. 1926.

by 'correspondence', and in 1923–4, the same formula was used.[1] From perhaps the summer of 1923 to December 1924, there were no meetings, certainly a gap of over twelve months. On the other hand, when a Legion deputation met the new Labour Pensions Minister, F. O. Roberts, in February 1924, to discuss a whole series of questions, he concluded with the usual expression of sympathy, adding that 'most' of the points would 'be discussed in detail with the Legion representatives on the Government Standing Joint Committee'. The last official meeting of the C.A.C. occurred in 1927–8, although informal meetings at provincial centres continued until 1930–31.[2]

As for the scope of the C.A.C., the topics, almost by definition, were much more circumscribed than those that could be raised on the S.J.C. In 1922–3, the regulations governing the procedure at meetings of the War Pensions Committees were discussed in the C.A.C.; in June 1923, the important issue of a time limit on applications for widows' pensions was on the agenda (put there by the House of Commons), and the Minister professed to find the advice of the Committee of 'great assistance'.[3] Besides, in the C.A.C., ex-servicemen did not have the initiative. The C.A.C.'s function was to 'consider such matters as may be put before them by the Minister for their advice'.[4] Thus the Minister was made master of the agenda, and master he remains to this day.

Thus the S.J.C. began earlier than the C.A.C., lasted longer, met oftener, was wider in scope, was homogeneous in a representative sense as the C.A.C. never has been, and had powers of initiative denied to members of the C.A.C. Had there been any 'bargaining' through the 'advisory' channel in the twenties, it would surely have been through the S.J.C. and not through the C.A.C.[5]

Was there any bargaining through the S.J.C.? It is impossible to be sure but there can have been very little of it. After only nine months even the Comrades turned on their own creation. By February 1921, they were characterizing the S.J.C. as a 'one-sided debating society', and they did not mean their *own* side.[6] So far as the 'big questions' were concerned:

'It is clear that the Government representatives on the Committee are tied hand and foot by decisions of the Cabinet. The monthly meetings, therefore, have . . . become, to a considerable extent, futile. It is merely a

[1] 6th and 7th Annual Reports, paras. 54 and 57 respectively.

[2] 12th, 13th and 14th Annual Reports, paras. 37, 37 and 29 respectively; Journal, March 1924, 272; 177 H.C. Deb., c. 710, 9th Oct. 1924.

[3] 7th Annual Report, para. 57.

[4] War Pensions Act, 1921, para. 3.

[5] Here too Millett seems to have been relying on someone's imperfect recollections of long ago. Cf. ch. XXIV, n. 2.

[6] *Comrades' Journal*, Feb. 1921, 4.

case of attending in order to hear a stereotyped formula, which, for all practical purposes, might just as well be emitted by a gramophone.'[1]

The Federationists must have been similarly frustrated.[2]

On the other hand, the Comrades claimed success on many a 'small question';[3] and later the Legion followed suit,[4] so the possibility of bargaining on this Committee should not be ruled out. Yet here too disillusionment set in later. By 1925 Legion H.Q. was telling branches that, having failed to gain concessions on either the time limit or the final awards question[5] through the S.J.C., C.A.C., or any other channel, it proposed 'as a last resource' a national public petition.[6] As, employment apart, these were the two main policy questions, it seems that such bargaining as occurred through the S.J.C. was limited.

There is even less to show for the efforts canalized through the C.A.C. The one important possibility to be considered concerns the issue of the time limit on claims for widows' pensions. Already, in January 1923, the Minister had been authorized by the Cabinet to use his discretion in applying the rule, but the Legion stood out for complete abolition in the form of an amendment to the Royal Warrant,[7] and for a right of appeal. This matter was discussed by the C.A.C. on 26th June 1923;[8] in October, the Minister put it up to the Cabinet; in January, the required decision was announced.[9] Was this the result of bargaining in the C.A.C.? The Press announcement on 5th January certainly mentioned consultations with the C.A.C. *but* also with M.P.s and the headquarters of the British Legion.[10] Moreover, the discussion would not have been opened in the C.A.C. in June had it not been for sustained pressure from all sides in the House of Commons exactly three weeks earlier.[11] The Minister had already met the C.A.C. the previous February; it was only the general criticism in the debate on the Ministry Vote on 5th June, including the threat of supporters like Brunel Cohen and Gerald Hohler to go into the division lobby against the Government, that persuaded the Minister to refer the matter to the C.A.C. As Emanuel Shinwell remarked, there was 'in some measure, a revolt against the Government'[12] amongst its own supporters. This, as we

[1] ibid. [2] Circulars, Nov. 1920.

[3] ibid., p. 5.

[4] 1st Annual Report, p. 11; Journal, August 1922, 35.

[5] Hist. B.L., pp. 78–80. [6] Circulars, 1925.

[7] Journal, Feb. 1924, 247; 164 H.C. Deb., c. 2020–21, 2124, 5th June 1923.

[8] 165 H.C. Deb., c. 1668–9. [9] Journal, Feb. 1924, 247.

[10] ibid.

[11] 164 H.C. Deb., c. 2009–2128, 5th June 1923.

[12] ibid., c. 2115.

shall soon see, was by no means the end of the story, but it does shed light upon the role of the C.A.C.

The course of the discussion so far may be summarized as follows: although one cannot be sure, the C.A.C. in the twenties seems to have been a weak reed, and the S.J.C. a not very much stronger one. It is surely significant that T. F. Lister, Legion chairman from 1921–7, 'was never a member of either committee, and would have been if important matters were raised—even though I might not have been able to attend all the meetings'.[1] On the other hand, judged by the constitution and working of the two bodies and by the claims of success made by the associations themselves, any bargaining there was is likely to have been accomplished through the S.J.C. rather than the C.A.C.

It is now natural to ask: was there *any* bargaining, then, through *any* channel? Bargains were occasionally attempted. In June 1920 J. R. Griffin had an unofficial interview with the Treasury, where he received an impression 'that an offer will be made to us in the shape of a bargain for a change in our attitude towards the Territorial Forces'. This 'offer' was about war-service gratuities, which the Federation wanted to have increased, and this 'attitude' was their reluctance to recruit men for the 'Terriers'. It was an accurate forecast, despite the Federation's later denial. On 12th July, a large Federation deputation waited on Winston Churchill at the War Office. He is reported to have said that the country at the moment could not afford such an increase in war gratuities, but 'that he would represent our case as an individual member of the Cabinet'.[2] Further, the Secretary of State is said to have discussed 'the majority of the points in the Federation's programme', and to have given the men 'a definite promise that he would do his best to voice the views of the Federation on these particular questions in his capacity of Cabinet Minister'.[3] But the leadership denied that in return for increased war gratuities they would assist in recruiting. If so, then the Secretary of State had been unusually and needlessly pliant. I believe that the Press 'leak' on 12th July suggesting the possibility of some such bargain was substantially true,[4] but true or not, this episode has its interest as an example of the kind of arrangement that may be attempted.

Bargaining moves of a sort, if not an actual bargain, occurred in 1923 in relation to an issue just discussed, the time limit on claims for widows' pensions. The formal pattern of the moves has already been outlined, but that was superimposed upon an informal pattern. Early in May, J. R. Griffin, as Assistant Secretary, met the Minister; a few

---

[1] Lister to writer, 1st Dec. 1957.
[2] Circulars, August 1920.   [3] ibid.
[4] *Liverpool Echo*, 12th July, p. 8; Lister–Griffin, 12th July 1920.

days later he talked to T. J. Macnamara, a former Minister of Labour and a good friend of the Legion, as well as some other members of the House. From these informal discussions he formed the view that the complete abolition of the seven years' time limit was unlikely to be achieved. Even Macnamara, he judged, was not going the whole way on abolition. He therefore suggested a compromise: extend the time limit from seven to ten years, and amend the Warrant so as to give the widow a definite right of appeal. Even to get such a compromise would call for a week or ten days' (personal) lobbying in the House. Lister, however, was reluctant to compromise, unless 'we have to admit that replies from 430 M.P.s are not worth the paper they are written on'.[1] But in August, *i.e.* after the C.A.C. meeting on 26th June, negotiations for a compromise gathered momentum; Brunel Cohen, J. R. Griffin and A. G. Webb had a private meeting with the Minister, his Parliamentary Secretary and two civil servants. The visiting contingent reaffirmed Legion policy but offered to consider instalments of it, only to be told that the Cabinet had set its face against complete abolition. What then should they do, faced with this blank wall? They told the Minister that if he would give them a definite statement of the maximum concessions he was prepared to put up to the Cabinet and Treasury, they would put that statement before the N.E.C. So it came about that Webb found himself at the Ministry helping to draft a memorandum in which the maximum concessions that the Minister was prepared to recommend to the Cabinet were carefully interpreted.

Before the Minister would approach the Treasury, he wished to be assured of the Legion's agreement. Accordingly, in September, the N.E.C. studied a paper setting out the concessions that were thought to be obtainable from the Ministry in this matter, and then resolved to accept the concessions on the understanding that such a settlement would not debar the Legion from raising questions relating to the revised Warrant if in practice hardships were disclosed.[2] Then, as we know, the Minister put the matter up to the Cabinet in October, having no doubt been to the Treasury meanwhile, and in January the concession was announced.

There was a concession but was there a bargain? The *quid pro quo* is not obvious. It does not seem to have been anything 'positive', such as assistance with army recruiting. It may have amounted to no more than a gentleman's agreement to relax this particular pressure. Certainly in the September–October campaign that followed, the

---

[1] Lister–Griffin, 15th May 1923. These were the M.P.s who had replied favourably to the relevant question in the 1922 Election questionnaire. Hist. B.L., pp. 61–62.

[2] N.E.C. Mins., 18th Sept. 1923, Min. 19.

plan was to concentrate on 'a few outstanding subjects';[1] all but one of these subjects (T.B. ex-servicemen) reflected the theme of employment. On the other hand, the time limit issue was soon put back on the agenda, though the word 'abolition' was no longer used, by being included in the questionnaire to candidates[2] in the November Election. This is not necessarily inconsistent, however, with the interpretation offered. The Cabinet, apparently, had yet to take a decision, and the N.E.C. might well have seen the Election, with its prospect of a new Government, as a contingent threat to the whole arrangement (if such there was). Whatever the correct interpretation should prove to be, this episode is interesting as an illustration of the 'inner working' of our political system. It is to the side door of the Ministry that we should often be looking, not to the main entrance.

To mention the side (*not* the back) door is at once to raise the question of informal approaches of a more routine kind than those recorded in the previous section. From the very beginning informal relations have been maintained with the Departments, notably with the Ministry of Pensions. As a 1950 Report correctly put it, 'in the matter of pensions, contact between the British Legion and the Ministry of Pensions runs from top to bottom on both sides . . .'[3] Certainly this was true of the inter-war years, too, and the relationship between A. G. Webb, as head of the Legion's Pensions Department, and various senior civil servants was a close one. How far did these day-to-day contacts create a climate of opinion favourable to the stretching of the regulations?[4]

It is important here to distinguish between individual case-work (*e.g.* whether this or that applicant is entitled to a pension) and those matters of policy which govern the case-work and form the substance of this inquiry. With individual case-work as such we have no concern. On the other hand, individual case-work would come within the scope of this study if it could be shown that the regulations were so far stretched as to be productive, in cumulative effect, of a new or modified policy.[5]

During the inter-war years, the close, informal relationship with the Ministry of Pensions (which is easily the strongest 'test case') was not productive of 'stretched' decisions on such a scale as to be tantamount to a change of policy. It is true that applications were considered 'out of time' and that the so-called 'final awards' were in

---

[1] Circulars, 27th Sept. 1923.

[2] See below appendix 1.

[3] Cmd. 7904 (1950), Report of the Committee on Intermediaries, para. 128.

[4] Samuel H. Beer, 50 A.P.S.R. 1956, 7.

[5] Cf. John Millett, op. cit., p. 75.

fact varied by administrative action. In that sense the regulations were indeed stretched, but that was due not to cordial personal relations and 'dropping in' but to sustained pressure of the familiar kind. Virtually nothing was granted until the 'principle' of stretching had itself been fought for and won, as is illustrated by J. R. Griffin's personal lobbying in the issue cited above.

Why were close personal contacts not more fertile in the inter-war years? Generally, one cannot help wondering to what extent *any* association derived real advantage from the close, personal relations that its officials may have had with their 'opposite numbers' in the Ministry. No walls in Whitehall collapse at the sound of a telephone bell, and personal charm, even combined with technical and topographical knowledge (of Whitehall), is hardly enough. One suspects that just as the 'contact man' theory of politics is put about chiefly by contact men, so the 'let official speak to official' version of pressure-group influence is derived from the officials themselves. From a temporary 'observatory' in the Cabinet Office and some other Departments in the early fifties, I, at least, formed the view that *the normally-recruited*[1] senior civil servants, casting themselves for the role of Platonic guardians, are clad in shirts of mail and not of silk.

It is plain, however, that I am in no position to speak of other associations, and in any case one can imagine that, for some of these, a 'simple' stretching of the regulations here and there might well be achievable and worth achieving even if it were not one particle in a policy decision 'by accretion'. The safest ground to stand on, undoubtedly, is the statement that the opportunity for stretching in the inter-war years was less in the Ministry of Pensions than in the other (relevant) Departments. Why?

The first reason is that the general shift of power from the Cabinet to the Departments had gone less far in the Pensions Ministry than in other (relevant) Departments. It seems obvious that the Pensions Ministry was a less 'autonomous' group than, say, the Board of Trade. At the simplest level, the Board of Trade must have administered many more regulations than the Pensions Ministry had dreamt of; correspondingly, opportunity for stretching must have been greater.

This certainly held good in another sense. The pensions regulations are embodied in a Royal Warrant, which is scarcely a plastic document, especially when the onus of proof is on the claimant, as it was until 1943. In any case, no formal code of whatever degree of plasticity seems to have governed the relations between, say, a trade

[1] War-time recruits may be guardians of the industry they were recruited from, as in the notorious case of the Ministry of Agriculture for about a decade and a half after the outbreak of the Second World War.

association and a 'production Department' in Whitehall. It is one thing to stretch regulations in general: quite another to stretch a Royal Warrant. It seems, in fact, that stretching may have the importance attributed to it only (other things being equal) where no formal code exists.

Of course, other things are not always equal: one of the variables is evidently the sympathy of the officials administering the regulations in whatever form. In the inter-war years, the civil servants within the Pensions Ministry had, in ex-servicemen's circles, the reputation of being unsympathetic.[1] The explanation commonly offered is twofold. On the one hand, the new Ministry had had to draw its staff from the existing Departments, including the Treasury, and accordingly its tradition from the start tended to be one of Gladstonian parsimony, rather than that of a Department administering a kind of social service. On the other hand, the staff were, at the levels that mattered, not ex-servicemen but 'civilians', *i.e.* men who had not served in the Armed Forces. In the early years the associations liked to draw attention to this no doubt inevitable, but for them objectionable, feature.[2] Whether this was good tactics is another matter; the point is that this fact is often held to explain in part why the atmosphere in the Ministry was, in the inter-war years, perhaps not conducive to stretching the regulations.

By contrast, the senior civil servants of the post-1945 period (having more of a 'social service' outlook and being themselves ex-servicemen of the First World War) are said to have been highly sympathetic, and ready to interpret the Royal Warrant as liberally as its nature allowed. But in the inter-war period, with which we are here concerned, I doubt whether the routine relationship was productive of much more than the Royal Warrant intended.

To say that is to raise once again, but as a general issue rather than as part of a narrative, the question of that bargaining which authorities such as S. H. Beer have observed in our pressure-group politics.[3] For stretching the regulations *may* be the 'supply side' of the bargaining equation. Presumably some stretching at least is part of a bargain. What, then, constitutes the 'demand side'?

Before attempting to answer that question, it is necessary to recall one feature of the 'supply position'. If the Ministry of Pensions has been less 'autonomous' than the other (relevant) Departments, it must have afforded fewer bargaining opportunities. It is true that a bargain may be struck with a Minister in return for his going to the

[1] Journal, April 1926, 282 (Editor).

[2] ibid., pp. 282 and 288.

[3] American Academy of Political and Social Science, *Annals*, Sept. 1958, pp. 135–6.

Cabinet; some apparent examples have in fact already been tentatively put forward.[1] But, other things being equal, the greater the autonomy of the Department, the greater the stimulus to bargaining. So for this 'supply' reason alone one would expect bargaining to be less important for organized ex-servicemen than it might well be for some other associations.

Taking now the 'supply side' as given, one sees at once that the 'demand function' must comprise a bargaining asset and a propensity to bargain. Have organized ex-servicemen had anything to bargain *with*? If they have had nothing tangible to offer such as increased exports or an efficient agriculture, their advice, knowledge and co-operation have been needed by the official groups almost from the beginning. The Cabinet and Parliamentarians generally needed to learn what the millions of returned soldiers and sailors were thinking and demanding, and found it useful to look to the associations even though these could never speak for all the veterans, and even though there were other methods available (the use of the politicians' 'sensitive antennae'). The need of the Ministries was more concrete: specific information in half a dozen fields and on a hundred and one particular items, especially in the unprecedented period of the First World War and after; specific information of a more formal kind, as in evidence before this or that official committee; co-operation in the administrative system, especially in the field of war pensions, where the associations have always performed a valuable function not only by virtually selecting members for official committees, central and local, but also by building up a fund of knowledge and experience, by acting as a sieve for applications, separating the relatively straightforward cases from the awkward, the difficult and the obscure, and perhaps providing skilled representation when the difficult case has been rejected by the Ministry and gone to appeal, which is of course as convenient for the Ministry as it is for the appellant himself. At every stage of the proceedings the associations play a valuable part (with no increase to the Ministry Vote), and so one is tempted to say that if the associations, notably the Legion, had not existed, it would have been necessary to invent them.

Nor was this true only of the Ministry of Pensions: other Departments, notably the Service Departments, needed the co-operation of organized ex-servicemen, which underlies the whole episode of the Empire Services League and the United Services Fund.[2] The War Office in particular would never have gone to such lengths to satisfy the associations' leaders, and have shown, given its traditions, such

[1] See above pp. 163–4.

[2] See above chapter XI.

patience in negotiation if the need for securing the ex-servicemen's co-operation had not been regarded as paramount.

Of course, it requires a bargaining spirit as well as a bargaining asset to produce a bargaining relationship. In varying degrees, all the early associations showed a marked propensity to bargain. In particular, the Federation would have bargained with the highest and mightiest in the land; even the Comrades, so much an offshoot of the 'Establishment', did not let itself be inhibited by its origin. At times, as in the case of the Empire Services League, it could strike a vigorous bargaining attitude. Less brash than the Federation and more a respecter of persons, it still had a bargaining 'style'.

Something of the spirit of these early associations passed over into the Legion: it showed itself in the 1923 moves noted above. But gradually the propensity to bargain weakened. The decisions required were fewer in number and somewhat less urgent. The leaders who sought these decisions lost something of their zest and drive. They were older, and in addition to their war experiences (generally, though not invariably, extensive), they had not spared themselves in what was for most of them a leisure-time activity.

The propensity to bargain may be weakened in more subtle, if quite unintended, ways. If an association enjoys prestige, then sooner or later its leaders' names will begin to appear in the Honours Lists. It is at least not easy for recipients of honours to make 'a damned nuisance of themselves', which is what bargaining may at times require; and if, as the years roll by, some people are attracted into the association precisely by the prospect of an honour (which is *one* of the incentives our voluntary system relies upon), then it may be awkward for them ever to be really 'difficult'.

The general point is illustrated, although it is *not* an actual example, by the dispute within the Legion in the early thirties, which resulted in the dismissal of the *Journal* editor.[1] The fight was taken to Fleet Street, the *Sunday Dispatch* for 6th May 1934, carrying this comment:

'It is significant that following recent deputations to the Prime Minister and Minister of Pensions, made by leaders of the Legion after strong pressure from the branches, the following two things happened. First the Chairman of the Legion received a knighthood. Then both the Prime Minister and the Minister of Pensions replied in the negative to the requests of the deputations.'[2]

Now, the channel then used was the deputation and not an informal approach; and in any case, the charge was grossly unfair to the then chairman, John Brown. But that it touches upon a genuine problem, which springs from the nature of our voluntary system, there can be no doubt. The withdrawal of a recommendation for a (well-deserved)

[1] Hist. B.L. chapters XXI and XXII.   [2] ibid., p. 162.

knighthood on a Legion leader of the twenties, because the Legion was deemed to be 'too political', is an illustration of the kind of sanction that is implicit in our honours system.

But, it may be objected, do these observations not apply with equal force to other associations, where, it has been already conceded, bargaining may be an important activity? It would be an interesting exercise to compare the distribution of honours over the years to (in effect) unofficial groups, but in any case one can see that for the other associations there are strong countervailing forces at work. An obvious inference to be drawn from the considerations so far adduced, both 'supply' and 'demand', is that bargaining is very likely to be much more important for other associations than for ex-servicemen. Besides, in this particular context of the propensity to bargain, the distinction between economic interest groups (which is what the 'other associations' we have in mind are likely to be), and 'voluntary bodies' in the special sense becomes significant. For almost by definition an economic interest group has a greater propensity to bargain, and even if its leaders tended, in time, to sag, the hot breath of its members would soon scorch their cheeks and singe their beards. This contrast is no doubt made less sharp by the 'Michelsian' tendency to oligarchy but nevertheless it still stands.

Thus, ex-servicemen's associations have special features to account for a comparatively low propensity to bargain. A low propensity to bargain means, of course, that one's bargaining assets are not fully utilized. But, in any event, there are to be found on the 'supply side' obstacles to bargaining which other associations, apparently, have not had to surmount. In total, these reasons may explain why ex-servicemen generally have not 'bargained' to any significant extent.

If the Ministry of Pensions is hardly an 'autonomous' Department, what is the purpose of sending deputations to the Minister or indeed of making any other approaches? These, of course, are attempts to use the Minister 'instrumentally', *i.e.*, to persuade him to go to the Cabinet. A remark made by Winston Churchill, as Chancellor of the Exchequer, in 1926 illustrates the true position. The issue was whether the rate of (war) pensions, linked to the cost of living in 1919, ought not to follow the cost of living downwards. The Legion policy, naturally, was stabilization of the rates, which the Cabinet eventually decided not to reduce. Referring to this decision, the Chancellor said it was something for which the Minister (G. C. Tryon) 'had so earnestly pressed, and which he so ardently desired'.[1] In going to see the Minister, then, ex-servicemen hope to imbue him with their own ardent spirits, so that he will 'earnestly' press both Treasury and Cabinet.

[1] 193 H.C. Deb., c. 285, 16th Mar. 1926.

Aims and Methods (1945-57)

BROAD AIMS : CHAPTER XX

METHODS : CHAPTERS XXI–XXII

XX

DOMESTIC AIMS

Introduction

IN the period since the Second World War, only four associations are germane to this inquiry, and examination soon shows that two of these need be mentioned only for the sake of completeness. The Comrades of the R.A.F., which had organized the earlier generation, came of age as the R.A.F. Association, while, during the 1950's, the Ex-Service Movement for Peace came on the scene, inducing echoes of the Labour League of Ex-Servicemen of 1927–29. For completely different reasons,[1] neither of these bodies requires much attention. On the other hand BLESMA, which like R.A.F.A. grew to full stature only in this period, has been lively and effective as an interest group, while the Legion, recruiting the new generation as well as the old, reached a (paying) membership never before achieved in this country.

BROAD AIMS 1945–57

The broad aims of this period may be readily presented as a series of contrasts with the inter-war years. These contrasts are three in number: the absence of 'external' aims after 1945; the concentration on pensions, to the exclusion of employment, policy; and the change in the nature of the pensions claims themselves.

In the first place, the ex-servicemen's movement proper articulated no external aims. The only conceivable exception would be that of the Ex-Service Movement for Peace, *provided* it were taken at its face value. Its aim was apparently indicated by its title, which seems unobjectionable, until one recalls that, since the Cold War, 'peace' has become 'political'. In origin it seems to have been an offshoot of the British Peace Committee, which, founded in 1948, was itself a branch of the World Peace Council; later, the Movement was characterized by the Admiralty as 'an activity on behalf of the Communist Party.'[2] The evidence on which this identification is based has not been published, but when, to satisfy myself, I visited the Movement's office in May 1957 I found that it formed part of a

---

[1] See Part Two above.
[2] *The Times*, 24th March 1952.

173

building occupied by an enterprise specializing in trips to Eastern Europe, and its side door had a wooden holder containing copies of the *Daily Worker*.[1] This visit of course 'proved' nothing but it at least suggested that the authorities were not hopelessly wrong in their assessment.

In any case, whether or not the Ex-Service Movement for Peace was a Communist 'front' is of little importance for my thesis. If it was not a 'front', it was certainly a 'paper' organization of *some* kind. The 'office' was not open except in the evenings and the establishment had a spurious air. Although Edgar Young claimed that 'the Movement had many allies, including some in the United States',[2] it is impossible to believe that it ever enjoyed more than a nominal *ex-service* membership.

Thus, despite a second world war, there was no reversal of the settlement reached after the first. The aims continued to have that 'domesticated' status which they attained in 1921, and to which the activities of the L.L.X. in the late 1920's were scarcely a real exception. The aims have remained comfortably inward-looking, representing no challenge to the socio-economic 'framework'.

Why, in this post-1945 period, were the associations' aims solely of this 'domesticated' kind? The answer is to be found in the circumstances and in the political culture. Full employment was maintained throughout the period. From the moment when the war was resumed in 1939, a pensions system was not only on the statute book but in working order. Perhaps above all, the community, including the official groups, had attained a high level of consensus. For within it were large numbers whose services in the Armed Forces had ceased only a quarter of a century earlier; they knew and they remembered, and they formed a sort of outer group giving strength and succour to the new generation of soldiers (and of veterans). The community as a whole had reached universal suffrage, and had had some twenty-five more years in which to move further along the collectivist path: two Labour Governments, Conservative or Coalition Governments that kept moving in the same direction, and then in 1945 another Labour Government in power as well as in office. The organization of the Second War itself, with its great mobilizations, its far-reaching control of the economy and its systematized welfare arrangements had carried the country to a still higher plane of collectivist endeavour: and when peace returned the demobilization was orderly and fair.

Within the official groups, the decision-makers of today were the

[1] This was at 100 Rochester Row, London, S.W.1. By chance, I have also met (at a Summer School) a former Communist Party member who claimed to have played a part in the Movement.

[2] *The Times*, ibid.

ex-servicemen of yesterday; they, too, knew and remembered, and the bitter complaints expressed in the earlier period of a lack of sympathy in high places (*e.g.*, in the Ministry of Pensions) were not heard again. Within the unofficial realm, ex-servicemen did not have to wait until the middle of the war before becoming organized. For the disabled limbless, for the returning airmen, above all for ex-servicemen without distinction of service or injury, the organizations already existed, and these, in particular the British Legion, were able not only to defend their interests *during* hostilities but also to anticipate difficulties and to make constructive suggestions. In short, history in this later period had accorded ex-servicemen's associations a creative, and not merely a largely defensive, role. As for the relations between the official and the unofficial, twenty years of access, consultation and discussion lay behind them in 1939, and over a quarter of a century of it when peace returned to the land in 1945. The easy revival of the Central Advisory Committee in 1939 tells its own tale: in the earlier period, systematic access had had to wait until long after the fighting had ceased. The absence of external aims, then, is no surprise; and it is significant that the one conceivable exception (the Ex-Service Movement for Peace) reflected an international conflict and not a conflict at home. This time there were no rifts in the political culture.

Of the domestic aims, little need be said here since a catalogue is unilluminating and in any case the main items in it have to be specified in the two following Parts. It is sufficient to state that the main conditioning factors shaping these aims were the ones suggested in the foregoing paragraphs. Of the general circumstances, the existence of full employment and of a pensions system accepted in broad terms by all concerned removed at one fell swoop most of the inter-war claims.

For BLESMA, the most important single aim was an increase in the basic rate of pension, but the one pursued most persistently, was an 'age allowance' in addition to pension for the first generation of limbless disabled. The progress and fate of this claim is the subject of chapter XXV.

The two principal objectives of the Legion also fell within the field of pensions. One was the attempt to save the Ministry of Pensions as an independent entity. This is the subject of chapter XXIV. The other, by far the main, preoccupation of the Legion throughout the post-war period, concerned the rate of pension. The details emerge in Part Six; here we need remark only that its essence was a claim for a doubling of the basic rate of pension, and that in reality the claim was never conceded, although a substantial gain was registered. Such an objective was itself something entirely new in the history of the

Legion; in the inter-war years the real value of pensions increased as the price-level fell, and so the obvious policy was to prevent the level of pensions from following the price-level. This meant a policy of stabilization, which was finally achieved in 1928. In the post-1945 inflation, the obvious policy was to have the rates of pension raised.

Here was one striking contrast. Another lay in the narrow range of pensions objectives pursued by the British Legion. In the post-war period there were no long-drawn-out conflicts over final awards, the time limit within which claims could be made and all the other issues that made a morass in which official group and petitioning group had been partly submerged in the inter-war years. The Legion was free to concentrate on one or two issues; indeed, for most of the period, it was one issue and that a quite straightforward matter in principle.

Thus, the post-1945 aims were narrow in every sense: domestic rather than external, pensions policy as against other issues, and a very restricted range even within the field of pensions.

XXI

(A) TECHNIQUES OF INFLUENCE (1945-57)

ECHNIQUES of influence as well as aims may be contrasted. For reasons that will become apparent in the following chapter on strategy, attempts to influence the Cabinet through the person of the Prime Minister or a senior deputy were almost absent from the post-war scene. On rare occasions the Prime Minister received a written communication, as when in 1953 Sir Ian (now Lord) Fraser sent him a copy of a resolution passed by Conference condemning the proposed merger of the Ministries of Pensions and National Insurance. The very high level deputation was rarely used or sought. In 1953, and on the same issue, the Prime Minister (Sir Winston) refused a Legion request that he should receive a deputation, and instead nominated Lord Woolton. The only occasion when a Prime Minister (Harold Macmillan) received such a deputation was in 1957, and this was not from the Legion only but from a group representing twenty-two ex-service societies. Besides, that was not an occasion for persuasion: it was an open secret that the decision to increase war pensions had already been taken by the Cabinet. The occasion was one for rejoicing, good cheer—and public relations.

Nor did the Legion revive the demonstration as a technique. Here however the fairly sharp contrast with the early inter-war years ceases to hold good, for BLESMA's methods included two campaigns (1951 and 1955) that were strongly reminiscent of the Federation's demonstrations, even to the marshalling of the very badly wounded as in London and Sheffield in 1919–20.[1] But after 1955 a number of BLESMA's main demands were met, and in any case there is reason to believe that the implied criticism in *The Times* has had some deterrent effect on the leadership.[2] Such campaigns, therefore, are unlikely to be repeated.

The relations between organized ex-servicemen and the House of Commons again afford sharp contrasts with the early inter-war years. Thinking in terms of Elections, one perceives not only that there was no sponsorship and no intervention in favour of a particular candidate, but also that both the Legion and BLESMA would recoil in horror from the very notion of such behaviour. All that remained

[1] *Bulletin*, 28th Aug. 1919, and 29th April 1920 (quoting the *Daily Mail*).
[2] Interviews with writer.

for a part of the period, and even so in an attenuated form, was the use of the questionnaire. In 1950 the Legion returned momentarily to the use of a questionnaire but on so modest a scale that the same term hardly suffices.[1] Only four main questions were raised and everyone knew that sanctions were inconceivable. Thus the poisoned dart of the early twenties became the blunt pin of the early fifties. Since a pin-prick serves only to annoy, the leadership was surely right to reverse that new-old policy the following year. A circular to branches simply stated that 'it is undesirable to send questionnaires to candidates', and that the purpose of approaching a candidate was not to obtain 'his views in detail, which may run the risk of being interpreted as a threat'. What then *is* the purpose of approaching a candidate? It is to ensure that he is 'aware of our case',[2] *i.e.* the Legion's policy at that moment (*e.g.* in 1951, 'The Case on Disability Pensions'). Such was the Legion's technique as practised in the 1945, 1951 and 1955 Elections: an unassertive statement of policy, with no shots fired in anger.

BLESMA, too, did not repeat its 1935 use of the questionnaire, so what one sees in this period by comparison with the years immediately after the 1914–18 War is a marked unwillingness to participate in the *electoral* process. But, as one would expect, there was no withdrawal of relations with the House of Commons once it was elected. Despite Smedley Crooke's disappearance from the Westminster scene in 1945, direct representation was maintained by Sir Ian (now Lord) Fraser, and even strengthened by him in that he took the presidency in 1947. Thus for the whole period covered by this study the Legion has never been without direct representation in the House. Apart from direct representation, the Legion had the backing of other M.P.s such as F. J. Bellenger (Labour). BLESMA spoke through many M.P.s, notably Sir Robert Cary, Bt., and Richard Wood (Conservative), and Leslie Lever and James Simmons (Labour), to mention only the exceptionally active and prominent.

Relations with all-party groups in the House provide a curious study in fluctuating fortunes. For the Legion, the basic modification was the change in the status of its House of Commons Branch, which in March 1955 became a mere 'Legion Parliamentary Group'. Already the use to which the Legion had been able to put the Branch had declined markedly compared with the inter-war years, and even with the years 1939–45. The device of inter-locking leadership, *i.e.*, Sir Ian Fraser's role in the Branch and on the N.E.C. of the Legion, did not work well after the Conservatives returned to power in 1951, for the 90s. basic pension campaign was an obvious embarrassment

---

[1] See below appendix 3.

[2] Special Circular No. 15, Oct. 1951.

to him, and in any case the issue was so big as to be certain to split the Branch down the middle. Thus one of the two main approach roads from Legion to Branch was blocked for most of this period. As for the other road, the then general secretary, J. R. Griffin, addressed the members from time to time, as did the chairman in 1952; while throughout the whole period of its existence the then head of the pensions department, A. G. Webb, either appeared on stage or hovered in the wings. In the late fifties, such comings and going were rare. Membership was of the same order of magnitude as in 1922, but meetings became ritualistic. If it did not 'wither away', then (to adapt another famous Victorian phrase) it went 'into a decline'. It is symbolic that its change of title in 1955 passed almost unnoticed in Legion circles.

As the Legion was about to retreat (in this sense) from Parliament, BLESMA was preparing to advance upon it. In 1951, at a meeting in the House, a small all-party committee was set up to seek interviews with Ministers on BLESMA's behalf.[1] This has grown into a permanent body (so far as there is permanence in the world of politics); officered chiefly by Labour and Conservative M.P.s, but embracing distinguished Liberals such as Roderick Bowen, it has already done notable work.

The link between BLESMA and the all-party committee in the House has not been as direct as the corresponding Legion connexion once was (though it has been more effective). Here the trail led not from the executive council as such but from the advisory committee (of well-wishers) to the House of Commons, and so, at one remove, to the all-party committee. Richard Wood was the link from 1950–55; he was then succeeded by another Conservative, W. R. Rees-Davies. As with the Legion, of course, officials made a 'personal appearance' from time to time: the 'indefatigable' George Chandley, for instance, as general secretary. (Later his successor, C. W. Dunham, played the same role).

Of the attempts to influence the whole House, only lobbying remained in use in this period as a significant form. As we know, lobbying at Westminster may be usefully separated into 'the mass assault and the steady trickle'.[2] The trickle still failed to appeal to organized ex-servicemen. True to its traditional techniques, the Legion also steered clear of the mass assault. How far BLESMA's demonstrations in 1951 and 1955 should be regarded as forms of mass lobbying is debatable. The elements of a 1919-type demonstration are clear enough: the procession from the Cenotaph to Church House, for instance. But then, as in 1955, about a hundred delegates made their way slowly to the House of Commons, holding

---

[1] *Blesmag*, Jan. 1952, 4–5.   [2] See above, p. 151.

up the traffic at a peak time, and descended on the Lobby.[1] To *The Times* this looked, understandably, like mass lobbying,[2] but if its essence is a 'forced personal interview',[3] then the term is not entirely apt because *by prior arrangement* they crowded into Committee Room No. 14 with some two hundred M.P.s.[4] This, therefore, was an *un*forced collective 'interview', which was also true of the 1951 occasion.[5] But, it must be admitted, another hundred and fifty delegates assembled in the Lobby, and there were indeed other occasions when BLESMA men congregated there.[6]

In so far as these activities constituted mass lobbying, BLESMA did not undertake them to the detriment of the constituency approach. In 1951, for instance, the branches were said to have 'played their part magnificently' in 'enlisting the interest and support of their local M.P.s'[7] But in the constituencies the most ambitious effort without doubt was the Legion's so-called Day of Demand in 1952.[8] On a day in March, some two and a half weeks after a Budget in which the basic pension rate had been increased by 10s., every branch was expected to button-hole its M.P. in the constituency in order to impress upon him that the increase was insufficient.[9] How far branches fulfilled this expectation is uncertain: it was officially claimed that 'a majority' had done so and with good effect.[10] There probably was a good turn-out, though even if it had been on a really massive scale, it would not have justified 'Peterborough's' wild comment in the *Daily Telegraph* that it was 'certainly one of the most concentrated exercises in political pressure ever organized by a national institution. Whether it was an equally good exercise for democratic methods is more questionable.' He added ominously: 'In America pressure groups have reached the point of threatening stability'.[11]

So much for the approaches: what did the approached do in consequence? Individual M.P.s asked questions in the House, of course. Thus Sir Ian Fraser's 1952 question about ex-servicemen in the Civil Service came from the Legion's Employment Committee

[1] *Blesmag*, Jan. 9 1956,.

[2] 30th Nov. 1955: 'Mass Lobbying Increasing.'

[3] Stewart, p. 209.   [4] *Blesmag*, Jan. 1956, 9.

[5] ibid., Jan. 1952, 4.

[6] *The Times*, 30th Nov. 1955. The 'It must be admitted' is relevant to the aptness of the terminology. I cannot regard mass lobbying as improper, although it may well be unwise.

[7] *Blesmag*, Jan. 1956, 8.

[8] Journal, May 1952, 2; *Daily Telegraph*, 24th Mar. 1952.

[9] Journal, May 1952, 2.   [10] ibid.

[11] *Daily Telegraph*, 24th Mar. 1952, p. 4, c. 5.

via the N.E.C., to whom he later reported the Minister's reply.[1] For BLESMA James Simmons was a constant questioner on many subjects. But of amendments to bills there were none, a sign that ex-servicemen entered this period with the 'framework' more or less prepared and accepted.

The all-party groups, themselves stimulated, tried to stimulate a Minister or Ministers, usually the Chancellor of the Exchequer or the Minister of Pensions. Thus in 1954 the Legion's House of Commons Branch nominated a deputation of four (led by its chairman, the National Liberal-Conservative member, David Renton) to see the Chancellor about 'the possibility of some increase in the war disability pension'.[2] They saw him but came empty away.

At least one post-war approach of this kind gave rise to controversy. On 19th February 1952, the Speaker presided over a meeting of the Branch when Sir Richard Howard-Vyse argued the case for doubling the basic rate of pension.[3] The Branch decided to ask the Chancellor to receive an all-party deputation. The following day, Clement (now Lord) Attlee, as Leader of the Opposition, asked whether the Speaker's presence did not make him 'a party to actions by that body in urging increases of pensions on the Government and in sending a deputation to the Government'.[4] The Speaker defended himself by saying that he had taken no part in the discussions, and that he had 'expressed no opinion of any kind, confining myself strictly to the calling of members and putting the questions proposed'.[5] Attlee returned to the attack, but the Speaker still maintained his position, saying that there was 'nothing very dreadful'[6] in sending a deputation.

BLESMA's experience of an all-party committee has been happier. With Sir Arnold (now Lord) Gridley as the first chairman and Leslie Lever as its energetic secretary, it followed the pattern of deputations to the Minister (to J. A. Boyd-Carpenter as Financial Secretary to the Treasury, 1951; to the Minister of Pensions as well as the Financial Secretary in 1955),[7] using, on the latter occasion, Sir Robert Cary, Bt., the new chairman, to hurry things along by direct intervention with the Chancellor. Yet the Committee has never been content with the obvious. Knowing the limits of what can be achieved by routine Parliamentary methods, and perhaps stimulated and

---

[1] N.E.C. Mins., 25th Oct. 1952, Min. 3; 509 H.C. Deb., c. 193. (written answers); N.E.C. Mins., 10th Jan. 1953, Min. 3 (a).

[2] *Journal*, April 1954, p. 3. The others on the deputation were: James Simmons, Lord Malcolm Douglas-Hamilton (C) and Frank Beswick (Lab.).

[3] *The Times*, 20th Feb. 1952.

[4] 496 H.C. Deb., c. 235.   [5] c. 235–6.

[6] c. 236.

[7] *Blesmag*, Jan. 1952, 4–5; ibid., Jan. 1956, 10.

sustained by feelings of compassion, they carried on the battle outside the Chamber and even outside Whitehall.[1] Ironically enough, the experience of the Legion and BLESMA is that all-party committees in the House have been really useful only when they have surmounted the Parliamentary routines.

As for the impact on the whole House by lobbying, it is, as with the inter-war years, impossible to demonstrate what M.P.s did in consequence of being so approached. There are those high in the Legion's counsels since the war who think that it produced nothing of any real value, and that the 'services' of M.P.s could accordingly be dispensed with. It is doubtful whether BLESMA's efforts yielded very much. Local M.P.s may have passed on to their leaders the views that local Legion branches expressed during the 'Day of Demand' in 1952, but if so the effect is hardly traceable. The 'mass assault' is not improper, as *The Times* would have us believe, but it may well be unproductive.

As techniques for approaching the Ministries, the deputation and the advisory committee continued to be used in the post-war period but with their relative importance very much changed. The deputation became an annual event with both the Legion and BLESMA, and now has something of a routine, almost ritualistic, air about it. For some years the Legion sent its team along early in the year in anticipation of the Budget and BLESMA showed some disposition to follow suit, although its important meeting was usually held in July. But two new features are worthy of note: the two-wave attack and the combined attack.

In December 1951 BLESMA's deputation of two (president and general secretary) was admitted to the Minister's sanctum immediately after he (the Pensions Minister and his Parliamentary Secretary) had been closeted with BLESMA's all-party committee.[2] This two-wave attack of an all-party delegation from the House followed by the group's representatives was an innovation in the methods devised by ex-servicemen, and perhaps deserved a better reward (a 'nil return') than it in fact received. Unhappily for BLESMA, the Departments have strong foundations: they cannot withstand earthquakes but they are resistant to slight tremors even in quick succession.

So far, following the pattern established in earlier chapters, associations have, where necessary, been mentioned individually. The most significant post-war development (in this context) is that, towards the end of the period under review, separate treatment ceases to be adequate. In March 1957, eighteen ex-service societies

[1] Part Five.
[2] *Blesmag*, Jan. 1952, 5.

joined in a combined deputation to the Minister of Pensions;[1] and since then, thorough discussion prior to action as well as a joint approach have become commonplaces of ex-service pressure-group activity. This has not been at the expense of the individual approach, such as it is, but the development is worth noting both for its significance now and for what it portends. It means that even the Legion can in fact no longer 'go it alone' on a really major issue: it foreshadows more and more joint action as the years go by.

While the deputation as a technique has somewhat declined in importance, the advisory committee has been more fully utilized. The Central Advisory Committee to the Ministry of Pensions has met often, much more frequently in fact than in the corresponding period after the first war: between 1939 and 1957 over seventy meetings were held, well over half of them in the post-war period. Useful work seems to have been done, such as in the sixteen meetings up to early June 1940 when the details of the new Royal Warrant were fully discussed. But Whitehall reticence being what it is, one's knowledge is scanty and insufficient to permit sound generalizations.

Thus one brings to a close this summary account of the techniques of influence used in the post-1945 period. Added to the outline given in chapters XVI to XIX, these are 'the facts' about specific methods of achieving aims, but what do 'the facts' *mean*? The answer to this question takes up the succeeding chapter.

[1] 29 P.Q. 1958, 36.

XXII

(B) THE STRATEGY OF INFLUENCE (1917-57)

BY using the five chapters (XVI–XIX and XXI) as 'building blocks' and then re-arranging the material into chronological order, one can now reconstruct in outline the strategy that organized ex-servicemen employed at various stages in the period under review, and suggest the conditions that governed it. The warning offered against 'intellectualism', however, should be borne in mind throughout.

'Strategy' was earlier[1] defined as the general design of a pressure-group's approach to the appropriate official group for the purpose of securing some desired decision. Thus the strategic appreciation must indicate the distribution of power among official groups. But in order to secure a decision, unofficial groups, too, may be 'activated', so the disposition of unofficial power also comes into the reckoning, including the situation of the petitioning group itself. Both patterns of power, finally, have to be viewed in the light of the prevailing political culture and circumstances of the day.

No neat chronological division of the period into phases does justice to the complexity of the subject, and indeed some alternative classifications are conceivable, but on balance it seems most useful and accurate to distinguish three periods: 1917–June 1921; July 1921–1929; 1929–1957. (1st July, 1921 marks the official birthday of the British Legion.)

Phase 1: 1917–June 1921

The outstanding feature of the early strategy was its (relative) directness. It was direct in two senses: within the complex of official power but also as between that and the structure of unofficial power. Directness in the first sense may be seen in the ex-servicemen's 'communications' to the Cabinet (in the person of the P.M.), in their waiting upon the P.M. in deputations, in the monster demonstrations staged partly to intimidate that august body. Parliament was not neglected; on the contrary, it was in this period that an appreciable effort was made to change its composition in favour of organized ex-servicemen, and to extract pledges from the other candidates.

[1] p. 123.

Nor were the Ministries overlooked, but the approaches to them were at first haphazard, and there was undoubtedly a feeling, long since lost, of striving towards the heart of things, to the immediate location of decision-making power.

The strategy was also, and much more markedly, direct as between the official and the unofficial. Certainly, from, say, the Armistice onwards, the 'public' was not neglected. The ex-servicemen's leaders were mindful of the value of publicity. The Federation leaders in particular were always aware of the need to reach out to the Cabinet indirectly as well as directly. From February to June 1918 they negotiated with Elias and Palmer representing Horatio Bottomley of *John Bull*,[1] to which the Federation seemed to be indebted to the extent of at least £275.[2] In return for an annual subvention of 'up to £2,000', for the honorary treasureship *and* 'some place . . . for Mr. Bottomley', *John Bull* was to 'give the Federation weekly publicity'.[3] Although almost all of the (current) Executive Council were willing to make room for Bottomley (as Patron) and to proceed generally,[4] the deal somehow fell through, a happy outcome, for the (potential) Huey Long of England might have done the movement untold harm.

Obviously, in this instance, the Federation leaders were hoping for financial support, but in part they may be presumed to have been searching for a popular weekly platform. Later that year, they took steps to produce a platform of their own. In late October or early November, James Hogge and H. E. Phillips, a member of the Executive Council and himself a Fleet Street journalist, discussed the launching of such a paper with the former managing editor of the Liberal *Daily Chronicle*.[5] After permission for a supply of paper had been obtained early in 1919,[6] the Federation brought out its fortnightly *Bulletin*, of, at first, a modest 4–8, then an ambitious 12–16 pages. By May the editor was claiming a circulation of 20,000 and looking forward to 50,000.[7]

Thanks to its 'Establishment' connexions, the Comrades received permission for a supply of paper even before the war ended; and thanks also to its wealth it got away to a very good start, easily

[1] Federation N.E.C. Mins., 5th March 1918, unnumbered.

[2] ibid., 19th July 1918, Min. 15; 25th Aug. 1918, Min. 8; 28th Sept. 1918, Min. 4; 5th March 1918, unnumbered.

[3] 6th March, Min. 1; 10th 11th April, Min. 18; 4th May 1918, Min. 5. T. F. Lister and J. R. Griffin, later so prominent in the Federation and Legion, were not yet on the Executive Council.

[4] ibid.

[5] Federation N.E.C. Mins., 2nd Nov. 1918, Min. 5.

[6] ibid., 12th Jan. 1919.

[7] *Bulletin*, 22nd May 1919, 15.

disposing of its 5,000 copies.[1] Within three months the circulation had trebled, and special issues sold even better.[2] Wilfrid Ashley knew how to get 'names': in October 1918 he had asked Beaverbrook (then Minister of Information) for an article: the Beaver said he was too busy and refused,[3] but many a famous name decorated the pages of the *Journal*. Ashley and his colleagues knew the value of publicity in general. They set up a Publicity Department, which 'not only prepared much propaganda literature in the shape of leaflets, progress reports, etc., and many articles and interviews of topical interest concerning the "Comrades" movement for the Press, but has developed, as a means of securing perpetual publicity of the most fruitful kind, an extensive Information Bureau'.[4] As part of that policy, 'a permanent feature (which of course means permanent publicity)' was started in the *People*, which put 'two or three columns per week' at the disposal of the Comrades.[5] In January 1919, this medium was yielding over a thousand letters a week.[6]

Of the other societies, the O.A. did not aspire to journalism, the N.U.X. could not afford it, though they managed to secure space in *The New World*, 'the Soldiers' and Sailors' Own Paper' that was published in Glasgow from about March 1919 onwards. Very late in the day (September 1920), the Association launched *The Bayonet*, which soon 'folded'.

Even the two big associations encountered heavy weather quite soon. The *Comrades' Journal* became self-supporting in 1920[7] but it was still an uphill struggle to make the Comrades itself self-supporting (in the strict sense of the term);[8] in June 1920, the Federation's general secretary was warning branches that unless they rallied to its support, the 'paper must cease to exist'.[9] At the end of the year it was losing heavily on each issue, and never recovered. As for other kinds of publicity, the Federation tried hard to make use of Fleet Street, and with some success, but its resources were really slender; indeed, after 1919, as an association (the *Bulletin* being legally a separate entity), it was itself financially embarrassed.

Thus, although publicity-minded, the appeal that the ex-servicemen's leaders were in practice able to make was desultory and

---

[1] 3rd Annual Report, 1920, p. 13; *Comrades' Journal*, Dec. 1918, 3.

[2] Annual Report, 1920, pp. 13–14.

[3] The Ashley Papers, 11th Oct. 1918.

[4] 1st Annual Report, 1918, p. 16. This Department also prepared Parliamentary questions.

[5] ibid.

[6] 2nd Annual Report, 1919, p. 19.

[7] 3rd Annual Report, 1920, p. 14.

[8] See above p. 102.

[9] Circulars, 1st June 1920.

haphazard. They can hardly be said to have run P.R. (or public relations) campaigns; they certainly did not reach the heights of a consistent P.R. policy. Nor in general did they attempt to win over particular groups as instruments of their cause. Parallel to their approach within the official boundaries, there was a distinct sense of going to the centre of things, where power resides, and of going it alone. How is the directness of this early strategy to be explained?

In order to answer this question it is first necessary to recall that the contemporary political culture already tended towards strong political leadership. An aristocratic conception of authority, related to that social deference which Bagehot observed in society generally, both perhaps reflecting our slow change from one social system to another,[1] had made possible the pre-eminence of the Government, and within it, of the Cabinet. This cultural element had been reinforced by the unintended consequences of two inter-connected developments: the extensions of the franchise, and the acceleration of what Dicey called 'collectivism'. The extensions of the franchise produced the parties to organize the electors and canalize their demands, to which collectivism has been in substantial measure the response. Hence the aggrandizement of the Cabinet and of the Departments. Thus even before the First World War it had ceased to be 'a political axiom that the Commons alone determined the fate of ministries, and the policy of the state'.[2] Already, the Commons had ceased to be 'the centre of political power'.[3]

The circumstances of a world war and the policy decisions then taken tilted the balance of power still more towards the Cabinet and Departments at the expense of the Commons. New Ministries were created, old ones strengthened: the new bureaucracy (and so the world of Max Weber's imagination) had arrived. In a sense the tiny War Cabinet epitomized the new age.

Thus when ex-servicemen appeared on the scene in 1916–17, the decision-making range with which they were confronted comprised the Cabinet and Ministries, with Parliament but a pale shadow of its nineteenth-century self. But what determined the *particular* official group at which they should set their caps? At the very beginning there was little choice. The general political culture prescribed 'voluntaryism': until the end of 1916, *their* Ministry did not exist, and it could not begin work until February 1917.[4] The regulations

---

[1] K. B. Smellie, *A Hundred Years of English Government*; H. Eckstein, in Beer, Ulam, etc., op. cit., Part 2, esp. ch. 8.

[2] *Encyclopaedia Britannica*, Vol. XVIII (1885) of 9th edition, 1875–89. reprinted 1898, article 'Parliament'.

[3] ibid.

[4] Cmd. 14 (1919), p. 3; Report of the Comptroller and Auditor General on the Appropriation Act, 1916–17, paras. 4 and 5.

laying down the rates and conditions under which pensions would be granted were operative from the following April.[1] But when 'choice' had been established, it was the needs and aims of ex-servicemen, and, correspondingly, the nature of the decisions they sought, that determined what the 'choice' should be. Demands, and therefore decisions, may be called 'first-order' or 'second-order' according to the magnitude of their implications for the community generally (the 'public interest'). First-order decisions are taken by the Cabinet (though this, under collectivism, may tend to be a formality). Such decisions may be invoked at any time but especially when the political culture shows fissiparous tendencies and when the political and economic situation is unprecedented; as these were features of the First World War, it is not surprising that ex-servicemen's demands were of the first-order kind. 'Justice, not charity'; abandonment or modification of the Review of Exceptions Act; claims for democratic representation and control; exemption of disability pensions from income tax liability; independent appeal on entitlement to and assessment of pension—all necessitated Cabinet decisions. Thus the nature of 'consumer demand' in relation to the given structure of official power served to select the Cabinet as '*the*' relevant group for ex-servicemen. And so the strategical 'picture' almost drew itself:

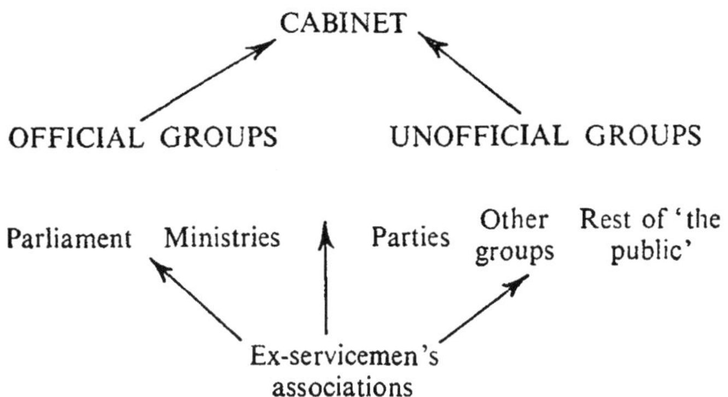

But if the 'destination' was thus determined, what determined the 'route'? In other words, what determined the strategy?

The urgency of the required decisions, the political culture, the official and the unofficial power structures (including the petitioning group's own 'situation') were the determinants of strategy. The decisions were urgently needed: modification of the Review of Exceptions Act *now*; independent appeal while it was worth having;

[1] ibid.

an increase in war gratuities before it was too late. Accordingly, ex-servicemen made direct application to those who could decide.

The 'political culture' is, in this context, really a 'sub-culture', *i.e.* the values, beliefs and emotions of the returned soldiers in general and of the organized ex-servicemen in particular. Some of their values and beliefs about the objects and modes of government implied a direct strategy. Thus many of them held that the Prime Minister was and ought to be the 'servant of the people'; by extension, the Cabinet were and ought to be the servants of the people. Correspondingly they believed that such decision-makers *could* be kept 'up to the mark', especially by meeting them face to face. They therefore thought it natural to go direct to the Prime Minister and to mount demonstrations in order to impress (or even to 'put the wind up') him and his Cabinet colleagues.

Of course, the notion of a direct approach to the Prime Minister was not confined to ex-servicemen: witness the famous pursuit of Lloyd George by the mayors of the London boroughs. Hence this may have been in part a more general cultural factor, though obviously Lloyd George's uniquely powerful position is highly relevant. But ex-servicemen gave to these values and beliefs a greater emotional 'charge'; their experiences in the trenches, their isolation, their conviction that they, at least, had 'done their bit' and saved the country—all tended to prescribe a direct approach to the centre of power. 'They' (the Government) had had it all their own way; now it was to be the ex-servicemen's turn.

The structure of official power also tended to induce a direct strategy. At the beginning of the movement (1916–18), Parliament, generally denied new blood by the electoral truce and for the moment not quite as sharply divided into 'sides', was a rather flabby group even for 'instrumental' use; and although the 1918 Election restored one feature of normal political life, the Coalition survived. More importantly, the Ministry most relevent to ex-servicemen's needs not only took some time to become a going concern but also failed to come into rapport with the men until as late as 1921. 'Consultation' of any 'regular' kind had started only the year before.

In order to account for directness in the other sense, one has to advance boldly into the field of unofficial power. Our political culture has perhaps not always been quite so favourable to 'corporatism' as some writers have supposed.[1] Discussing 'the bi-coloured legislator', Sidney Low in 1904 perceived 'a divided duty' when a member 'sees a chance of assisting the particular interest to which he is pledged at the cost of voting against his leaders and the allies with whom he

---

[1] *e.g.* Harry Eckstein in Beer, Ulam, etc., op. cit., p. 161 and passim.

usually acts'.[1] The passage is not free from ambiguity, but Low was in no doubt that the dilemma should be resolved at the interested group's expense, which by extension we may apply to our purposes here. And as late as 1930, Ramsay Muir could speak of 'control by organized interests *outside of* the constitution';[2] attempts by these interests to put pressure on the Government, whether privately or publicly, he considered 'exceedingly dangerous'.[3]

Nor, in the period 1900–14, do there seem to have been many politically significant pressure groups. Some of the 'household words' of today had already emerged, but in general they were rather unrepresentative, and individually they may have played no great part in the political process. The 1914–18 War seems to have been the turning-point. Total war meant the total mobilization of our productive resources and the centralized allocation of the gross national product, and hence stimulated the growth of trade associations in general and of the N.U.M. and F.B.I. in particular. Full employment gave the trade unions a shot in the arm; their membership reached undreamt-of heights. Politically, the tilting of the balance of power towards the Ministries (part of the same process) contributed to the same result, *i.e.*, to the stimulus of 'groupism', while the electoral truce must have meant that demands which would have been canalized through the parties had to find another way.

Yet, although the barometer pointed unerringly to 'groupist' weather, the tendency had not advanced very far by the time ex-servicemen were organizing themselves for battle. In general it seems safe to suggest that ex-servicemen were 'out on their own': they had no natural enemies among unofficial groups (except, to some extent, each other),[4] and since relatively few groups had been fully articulated, they did not think in terms of alliances.

Except in the eyes of the N.U.X., alliances with the party machines did not find favour. The connexions with the (Parliamentary) parties had been established at the beginning, and a series of clear-cut alignments, such as emerged later in France, was not inconceivable. But first of all in the Association, then in the Federation and even, in a sense, in the Comrades, the returned soldiers squeezed out the politicians and in so doing rejected alignment. The N.U.X. kept up its alignment with the Labour Party but not its place in the ex-service movement; the Legion made its non-party position perfectly plain.

---

[1] *The Governance of England*, p. 122.

[2] *How we are governed*, 2nd ed. 1930, ch. VIII. Emphasis added.

[3] ibid.

[4] *i.e.*, of course, no enemies in their *pressure-group roles*. There was serious friction with the trade unions after the Armistice, but that is another matter.

Finally, what of the electorate? Although not a group, it has relevance to the theme of 'directness' and 'roundaboutness'. At the beginning of the movement, it was, of course, still small, and even two years later, after it had been swollen by the 1918 Act, it was not yet the force it was to become. So in this respect, too, ex-servicemen had less need than today for a systematic public relations policy. Thus ex-servicemen had little inducement to 'look outside themselves' in preparing their approaches to the decision-makers, *i.e.*, they tended to go straight across the meadow and not to enter or even really examine the neighbouring fields of unofficial power.

So much for the 'external' conditions of strategy, but naturally there were conditioning factors inherent in the ex-servicemen's own situation. The organizations they created were at first quite small, and even when, in 1918–1919, they built up large memberships, they were still deeply divided, and became even more divided during 1919 by the secession of the strongly left-wing N.U.X. from the ranks of the Federation. And for all their numbers, they were, with the exception of the Comrades, not wealthy bodies; in 1920, even the Comrades was beginning to feel the pinch. In brief, they generally had no money for a sustained public relations policy. Here, then, were 'internal' reasons for directness as between the official and the unofficial groups.

Phase 2: July 1921–1929

By the opening of this period, it will be recalled, four of the earlier societies had merged into the British Legion, leaving the N.U.X. to travel its self-chosen path into oblivion. What were the main features of the structure of official power that confronted it? Cabinet and Ministry, of course, still comprised the effective decision-making range, from which the Legionaries virtually (by the nature of the claims they put forward, *e.g.*, the retention of the Pensions Ministry; stabilization of the rates of pension; removal of the time limit on claims) selected the Cabinet as their 'adversary'. But what of the approach to the Cabinet?

This approach was, on balance, much less direct than it had been. Some paper missiles were still hurled at the Cabinet (in the person of the P.M.); the Legion conducted a public argument with Bonar Law;[1] a deputation might even wait on another Prime Minister, as in 1929 (when the Election was only some five weeks away). On the other hand, the demonstration was unceremoniously cast aside and buried. Parliament was used intensively, the Legion even trying to shape it beforehand to its own views. The path to the Ministries became a well-trodden one. Meanwhile in relation to the unofficial

[1] See below chapter XXIV.

191

realm, the Legion paid more and more attention to influencing the public.

At the very first meeting the N.E.C. discussed an approach to certain Sunday papers for a British Legion column,[1] and resolved to write up its new programme as a leaflet 'to be distributed as propaganda'.[2] It also agreed to draw up a poster for the use of branches. From the start, as one would expect, Legionaries had their own journal. At the 1922 Conference, Earl Haig himself thought it 'vitally important' to 'enlighten the public', adding:

'Propaganda is necessary to tell them what we are really doing and to enable us to make known what our real objects are—that we want to make the country better not only for the ex-serviceman but for the whole of the community. We are only trying to teach and practice the lessons of good fellowship and honest service which most of us learned during the war'.[3]

These actions and quotations merely indicate an attitude; but the practical use of publicity techniques soon followed. In November 1921 the N.E.C. decided to hold a short membership campaign the following spring: 'The week should show an increase of one million new members'.[4] Launched by Haig from the Central Hall, Westminster, it was to be sustained by meetings throughout all Areas and in all branches. Lapsed members were to be reached by 'a special message' informing them of the campaign and urging them to come back and 'receive instructions for the special work expected of' them.[5] Lapsed and potential members were to be appealed to through lantern slides at cinemas, 'Join the Legion' posters in buses and trams, propaganda literature[6] and streamers across the street.[7] The Press, too, was to be brought into play: the N.E.C. approached the national Press but branches were also asked to 'keep local newspapers well supplied with full reports of their doings'.[8] An attempt was also made to influence ex-servicemen through other groups: through employers, councillors, trade unions and, above all, the churches.[9] Haig himself addressed the church leaders but branches were also asked to send each local minister a copy of the Legion Constitution and Programme.[10]

Even these efforts do not illustrate the tactical use of publicity, for, intentionally, the recipients of it were ex-servicemen and not decision-makers, but a campaign the following year may be taken into account.

---

[1] N.E.C. Mins., 24th July 1921, Min. 31.
[2] ibid., Min. 48.
[3] Verb. Rep., p. 4, but reconverted to direct speech to avoid confusion.
[4] Special circular, 15th Feb. 1922.
[5] ibid.   [6] ibid.
[7] Special circular, 24th March 1922.
[8] ibid.   [9] ibid., and 15th Feb.
[10] ibid.

This was the employment drive of the autumn of 1923,[1] designed to bring in more members (the better 'to obtain the concessions from the Government and from public and other bodies . . . for which we are pressing'), but also to 'focus public opinion on the questions raised by the Legion and on the main points of policy'.[2] Faced with mass unemployment and on the threshold of another grim winter, the Legion naturally took as its theme the 'Army of *No* Occupation', which was first elaborated in September from a public platform in Chatham in accordance with its plan to win over public opinion. In the middle of October, the Legion's 'Manifesto'[3] embodying its views was dispatched to all M.P.s, asking 'whether the policy outlined therein meets your approval and has your support'.[4] Three days later copies of it went out to branches with a circular asking them to call a special meeting and to pass appropriate resolutions of support, copies of which should be sent to the P.M., the local M.P. and Mayor as well as to the local newspapers. For the local Press a copy of the 'Manifesto' was to be enclosed.

The new emphasis in these methods on reaching the Prime Minister through public opinion is plain enough, but the boldest stroke was yet to come. On 26th October Baldwin was to speak at Plymouth,[5] and the Legion decided to carry the battle there. At 8.15 p.m. on the 24th, the Legion Area Organizer, H. J. Trevillyan, descended on Plymouth, having planned his campaign in the train from Paddington. Posters ordered that morning followed him by passenger train that night and were delivered direct to the bill-posting firm commissioned to put them up in the town. On the following two days, twelve sandwichmen and two 'advertising' lorries circulated the Legion's message, while six men spent their time distributing the 'Manifestos'. 10,000 of these are said to have been distributed in two days. Meanwhile letters and leaflets had gone to the local M.P.s asking them to ensure that the P.M. had a copy of the 'Manifesto' before his speech.[6]

When the hour struck, Baldwin made his famous announcement that to him 'this unemployment problem is the most critical problem of our country', and that for him 'the only way of fighting' it was 'by protecting the home market'.[7] No doubt the occasion had been carefully chosen and the speech prepared well in advance, but the Legion's intervention nevertheless has its interest as an example of that (relatively) 'roundabout' approach to the Cabinet which was to

---

[1] Hist. B.L., p. 64.

[2] Special circular, 29th Sept. 1923.

[3] Hist. B.L., appendix 16.   [4] Circulars, Nov. 1923.

[5] G. M. Young *Stanley Baldwin*, pp. 65–6.

[6] Circulars, Nov. 1923.   [7] Young, p. 66.

become more and more relied upon as the years went by. The direct approach, as, for instance, the dispatch of 'many resolutions' from Legion branches to the P.M., as his secretary C. P. Duff acknowledged,[1] was still retained. But the 'appeal' to public opinion was growing: the launching meeting, the use of the Press, whose reception of the 'Manifesto' the Legion considered 'remarkable',[2] combined with the Thomas Lipton methods in Plymouth, were the signs of it.

From 1923 onwards the Legion turned more and more to the mass media of communication. In November the Willesden Branch put up to the N.E.C. a suggestion that a Legion speech should be broadcast, and the leaders decided to make inquiries.[3] Representations were made to the B.B.C.,[4] and, presumably in consequence, when the Legion launched another employment drive in September 1924, Haig inaugurated it with a broadcast from 2LO.[5] Later, in 1927, the N.E.C. appointed a full-time publicity man at a salary that showed a determination to find someone good.[6]

What factors governed the Legion's strategy in this obviously transitional phase?

Important claims were still made, but, especially after the 1919 reforms and the measures that culminated in the War Pensions Act of 1921, were far less urgent. The men's values and beliefs had changed. It is doubtful if they thought any longer of the Prime Minister as a servant of the people. Certainly they no longer believed in the efficacy of merely bearding a Prime Minister in his den. Most of them no longer thought it right to mount demonstrations, even little ones, as a technique of influence. What was left of their original values and beliefs had a smaller emotional 'charge'. Accordingly, it was natural to turn rather more consistently towards Parliament especially as at least two of the Legion's N.E.C. were in the Commons, but another strand in the web of ex-servicemen's beliefs pointed in the same direction: the belief, held by many, that Parliament could be used 'autonomously'. Hence, in part, the House of Commons *Branch* of the Legion; the attempt to commit Parliamentary candidates to particular policies during election campaigns; the various Parliamentary techniques, including the attempts to initiate legislation. The extent to which the Legion concentrated its fire on Parliament in this period illustrates the confusion of many members about the place of Parliament in the contemporary political order: to some degree it fell into the trap of trying to use the House as a decision-

---

[1] Circulars, Nov. 1923.   [2] Circulars, Nov. 1923.
[3] N.E.C. Mins., 17th Nov. 1923, Min. 23.
[4] ibid., 2nd Feb. 1924, Min. 2 (c).
[5] Hist. B.L., p. 69.
[6] N.E.C. Mins., 10th Dec. 1927, Min. 8 (b).

making centre 'in its own right', and consequently suffered much frustration, some of which survives to this day. Once again, this may have reflected a more general cultural characteristic (witness the general popularity of the Election questionnaire), but ex-servicemen were perhaps more confused than most groups.

Of course, these attitudes were nourished in a soil that, between 1922 and 1929, produced four General Elections, so the 'structural' and the 'cultural' were intertwined. Another important structural factor was the use made of the system of consultation established in 1920–21. Why should this *in itself* affect the directness of approaches to the Cabinet? It cannot be that, in dealing with a Ministry:

> '. . . fool'd with hope, men favour the deceit;
> Trust on, and think tomorrow will repay . . .'

because one knows (and generally ex-servicemen knew) that the decisions they sought were not in the Minister's gift. Yet tomorrow might repay if the Minister would become one's advocate in or at the Cabinet. From the point of view of the Cabinet, it is obviously convenient to canalize demands in such a way that the details can be settled and the issues crystallized. In time, too, consultation adds a new dimension to the political culture—it becomes not simply convenient but right and proper to see the under-gardener before approaching the Head Gardener. Thus, consultation has the consequence of 'deflecting' a group 'off course' in its voyage towards the Cabinet.

As between the official and unofficial power structures, other pressure groups were becoming important and beginning to impinge on the ex-servicemen's consciousness, and the electorate was increasing, for natural reasons as well as by formal extension (as in 1928). In general, the growing importance of the organized publics as well as of the unorganized public made 'the people' more and more a factor in the Legion's calculations. At the same time, the unity that the Legion embodied, its own increase in numbers and the strengthening of its finances made possible a more systematic cultivation of them.

Phase 3: 1929–57

In this period of about a generation the pattern was complicated not only by the Second World War itself but also by the growth of some other ex-servicemen's associations, yet on the whole what Liddell Hart was to call the 'strategy of the indirect approach' became more and more apparent. With the decline of the L.L.X. in 1929 went its form of the demonstration; in the same year, despite the flare-up at the National Conference, the Legion finally washed its hands of the technique in any form, though BLESMA briefly revived it in the early fifties. The year 1929 also marks a profound change in the Legion's attitude to General Elections: candidates received not a questionnaire but a statement of policy. The Legion was virtually contracting-out of the electoral process.

Meanwhile, the minds of the Legion leaders were turning more and more to the cultivation of public opinion. The 1931 decision to appoint a professional journalist to the editorship of the *Journal*, a post previously held by the general secretary, was a portent.[1] Two years later, the N.E.C., long interested in film as a propaganda medium, authorized the making of one, subject to a maximum cost of £5,000.[2] Yet although the N.E.C. deemed it wise to try to create for itself a favourable climate of opinion, it was not yet fully committed to a consistent public relations policy. What some Legion leaders had in mind in the late thirties was indicated by the setting up of a small committee to examine the collating of news and the issue of information to the Press.[3] Under T. F. Lister's chairmanship, this committee reported, in January 1939, that the publicity obtained by the Legion was 'very considerable' as well as 'satisfactory', and that they were 'well satisfied' with the services of the official responsible for providing it.[4] The N.E.C. adopted that report[5] but the minority who wanted a public relations department returned to the attack the following year.[6] They were defeated then and again in March 1941,[7] but at the end of the year they gained some ground[8] and about eighteen months later they got their way. In June 1943 the *Journal* and Publicity sections were merged into a Public Relations Department, to be responsible, under the P.R. Committee, for 'publicizing the work and policy of the Legion'.[9]

One of the first tasks of the new committee was to seek the advice of Fleetwood Pritchard, Director of Public Relations at the Ministry of War Transport and in normal times head of a famous firm of publicity consultants and agents. He advised the appointment of a Public Relations Officer to prepare the ground, otherwise advertising on an extensive scale would be a sheer waste of money.[10] The immediate context was the question of how to create a desire on the part of men and women then serving to join the Legion when they left the Services,[11] but Sir Frederick Maurice revealed the mind of the

[1] ibid., 12th Dec. 1931 and 24th Sept. 1932.
[2] ibid., 9th Dec. 1933, Min. 19.
[3] ibid., 29th Oct. 1938, Min. 10.
[4] ibid., 14th Jan. 1939, Min. 6.
[5] ibid. [6] ibid., 15th June 1940.
[7] ibid., 8th March 1941. [8] ibid., 13th Dec. 1941.
[9] ibid., 12th June 1943.
[10] Journal, Sept. 1943, 168. [11] ibid.

leadership when he said that after the war they would have to adopt the same method as had recently brought success with pensions, *i.e.*, arouse public interest in the Legion case through the Press and their friends in the House of Commons.[1] It was only a short step to the pronouncement made in a circular to branches in 1945: 'We must have Public Opinion with us.'[2]

The N.E.C. did not then appoint a P.R.O.; instead it retained Current Affairs Limited to undertake special propaganda and publicity for the Legion at a cost of between £6,500 and £7,000 a year.[3] The intentions were to attract members on demobilization; to retain public confidence; to project the views of the ex-service community. 'Stunts' were not to be used; the essence of the method was to be a steady placing of accurate information about Legion activities and views. About twelve statements a month began to be issued to the Press on subjects such as pensions and housing, and many papers used them; about six features a month were issued to national and provincial newspapers; there were articles in women's journals and occasional 'mentions' on the B.B.C. (such as a message by the President to the Merchant Navy).[4] It was specially noteworthy that articles appeared in papers and periodicals that had not previously published Legion material.[5] In 1944–45 about a quarter of the *Journal*'s circulation of 100,000 was being distributed to the Forces at home and overseas.[6] Two films were produced and distributed,[7] and a publicity van equipped with a public-address system toured the country.[8]

The arrangement with Current Affairs Limited came to an end in 1945, and the following year the Legion appointed its own Director of the Press and Publicity Department (as the P.R. Department was re-named). By 1947–48, the Legion was claiming that its 'stories' had been used to the extent of over 5,000 lines in the national Press and over 61,000 lines in the provincial Press.[9] By 1950, Press hand-outs at the rate of one a week were being distributed and 'used by a considerable section of the Press or Journal to which it was specially directed'.[10] At the end of the period under review, the Department, under R. L. Pennells, a former weekly newspaper editor and Press Gallery man, was arranging Independent Television News coverage of Legion events; B.B.C. Television put out the Legion's Poppy Day film (*Where does the money go?*) two years in succession; the *Radio*

---

[1] ibid., Oct. 1943, 182.

[2] Circulars, January 1945, Special Circular No. 3.

[3] N.E.C. Mins., 25th Sept. 1943, Min. 7; Journal, Oct. 1943, 182.

[4] Journal, April 1944, 73.　　　　　[5] ibid., Oct. 1944, 199.

[6] Annual Report, 1944–45, p. 10.

[7] ibid.　　　　　[8] ibid., 1947–48, p. 12.

[9] ibid.　　　　　[10] ibid., 1950–51, p. 11.

Times, with a readership of perhaps thirty millions, carried a special article on the first page by J. R. Griffin. Another special article (by Sir Ian Fraser) appeared in the *News of the World*, readership perhaps twenty millions, while the pensions campaign was helped along by the *News Chronicle* columnist, Alan Wood. In a way most significant of all, the *Daily Express*, not always well-disposed towards the Legion in the past, printed a 'Poppy Day' leader and a news story appealing for support.[1]

Of BLESMA and R.A.F.A. one can speak with less confidence; before the war they made little impact on the political process and so there is hardly any basis for comparison. Certainly BLESMA's two demonstrations in the early fifties bear the hall-marks of a direct strategy, which can be accounted for by a sense of urgency, a high proportion of its members being men of the 1914–18 War to whom any decisions would have to apply soon if ever. On the other hand, BLESMA took care to arrange that the newsreel cameras should be on hand in 1951; and both demonstrations show a flair for publicity. R.A.F.A., too, had an arrangement with Polygon Publicity Services until 1955, when that firm was superseded by a Fleet Street journalist who became the honorary adviser on public relations and publicity. Thus the trend towards an indirect appeal seems to be sustained by these smaller associations; if their effort is on a smaller scale, it is because they *are* smaller and have fewer resources.

For the Legion, the conditions prescribing indirectness may be readily summarized. For them the strategical map remained much as it had been throughout. The decisions they sought were still first-order decisions, *i.e.*, in the hands of the Cabinet. This may be surprising in the light of the tendency, after 1939 and especially 1945, for the balance of official power to tilt away from the Cabinet and towards the Departments. But, as suggested in the discussion of bargaining,[2] the Ministry of Pensions (always the strongest 'test case') was in the inter-war years a less 'autonomous' group than the other (relevant) Departments; and this remained true after 1945. In other Departments, collectivism and the welfare state extensions no doubt increased the range and number of second-order decisions, which the appropriate pressure groups (*e.g.* the trade associations) could hope to influence. Legislation such as the Agriculture Act of 1947 might even give rise to a first-order decision (*e.g.* the grand total of subsidies) that the Cabinet still takes in form but hardly in fact. For after the months of haggling in the Annual Price Review, what *can* the Cabinet do except grumble (unless it wishes to review the whole policy fundamentally)? But in the period under review ex-servicemen still sought first-order decisions of a kind still 'really'

[1] ibid., 1956–57, pp. 20–21.   [2] Chapter XIX.

taken by the Cabinet rather than the Department: the transfer of the onus of proof in pensions cases from the appellant to the Ministry; the doubling of the basic rate of pension; the retention of the Ministry itself; an 'age allowance' for the limbless. So, as before, the nature of 'consumer demand' in relation to the structure of official power contrived to maintain the same strategical picture. But what of the change of 'route' to this same 'destination'?

The decisions were less urgent. Despite inflation, the doubling of the basic rate of pension cannot be regarded in the same light as the many critical issues after 1918. When a sense of urgency was felt, there was some return to directness, as when in 1953 the Legion sought out the Prime Minister to prevent the merger of the Ministries of Pensions and National Insurance. (He passed them over to Lord Woolton, who listened patiently). Some apparent signs of urgency were nothing of the sort: when in 1957 another Prime Minister (Harold Macmillan) undertook what Sir Winston had refused, the decision apparently sought (an increase in the basic rate) had already been taken by the Cabinet. The occasion was a thanksgiving, not a supplication—with photographers and reporters summoned to the scene. Even in the mid-thirties the issues were largely exhausted, while the falling price-level continued to increase the real value of the pensions.

The political sub-culture, as indeed the whole culture, had changed. Except as a rather desperate move in a critical situation (1953) or as a piece of stage-management (1957), Legionaries believed even less than their predecessors of 1921–29 in the efficacy of a direct approach to a Prime Minister, still less again that he was the servant of the people. Demonstrations came to be abhorred, not merely disapproved of. That Parliament is no longer an 'autonomous' group was slowly borne in upon Legionaries, who in any case came to feel that the less they were 'involved' the better, certainly in terms of Elections.

Within the structure of official power, the main factor making for indirectness was the revival of the C.A.C. in 1939. The seventy or so meetings between 1939 and 1957, and especially the forty-four or so from 1946 to 1957, are testimony to the wholly changed situation compared with the years after 1918. Energy was induced to flow along this channel from the very beginning.

Within the realm of unofficial power, two general trends sustained and then increased the indirectness of the Legion's strategy. With the growth of the electorate and of the polls, public opinion came (or seemed to come) into its rightful inheritance, a Queen to be wooed if not worshipped. More certainly, there was the growth of particular publics, stimulated in part no doubt by post-1945 collectivism and the welfare state policies, as with the N.F.U. and B.M.A., but emerging already out of the structure of our complex society. Thus, unlike the earlier period, ex-servicemen now operated in a world of highly-articulated and vocal groups, as thrusting and resourceful as they had ever been in their 'youth'. Not one of these stood out as a counter to the Legion; every one was potentially a rival for the favours of the official groups. In an increasingly pluralistic society, Legionaries felt driven to raising their own voices in order to make themselves heard (for which purpose they happened to have more resources than ever before).

That they '*felt* driven' is a historical fact, but were they 'objectively' right? It is true that even in a pluralistic society there are other, perhaps more usual, ways of addressing the decision-makers: lowered voices in the Minister's office, for instance. Even in these cases it is easy to overlook the P.R. groundwork that may serve the group's cause but is kindly undertaken, consciously or unconsciously, by other hands. Thus, the 'town mouse and country mouse' advertisements put on by the fertilizer and agricultural machinery manufacturers to create (or maintain) a favourable public opinion towards agriculture[1] should have helped the N.F.U., which must also be a beneficiary of the B.B.C. sound radio programme, 'The Archers'. (Can it be a coincidence that Dan Archer has been known to complain about the unprofitability of farming and to be ready to try some other career at the very time when the Annual Price Review is about to begin?) But in general, of course, everything depends upon the strategic situation in which the group finds itself. For the Legion, a systematic P.R. policy for the purpose of image-building and image-sustaining and for publicizing some of its claims was not absurd. Doubtless when it comes to the point of decision-making, a Minister will not go to the Cabinet unless he has good arguments to put forward. This is the role of reason in pressure-group politics. But Cabinet Ministers are not so hypnotized by their overflowing 'In' trays that they fail to form an opinion about public opinion, and P.R. may help that 'opinion about...' to take shape. This is possibly the role of myth in pressure-group politics. To suppose that by a steady P.R. output one can create (or maintain) a climate of opinion favourable to decisions may be one of the great chimeras of the age. Here one moves in a dimly lit world where strange shadows dance and leap and the only certainty is uncertainty. Yet in a society in which groups not only overlap in membership but are 'encircled' by potential groups ready, on specific issues, to be roused and mobilized, it is not absurd to act on the unproved assumption that a P.R. policy[2] is not only useful but essential (in a certain strategic situation).

[1] George Allen, *Contemporary Review*, May 1959, 258.
[2] See appendix 6 for an example of one kind of appeal to the public.

PART FIVE

Aims and Methods Illustrated

XXIII

FEDERATION: THE STATUTORY RIGHT TO (WAR) PENSIONS (1918-19)

Introduction

THE choice of illustrative material would have been embarrassingly wide even if there had been room for more than the three examples that are given in this and the two succeeding chapters. These examples can do no more than illustrate some aspects of the aims and methods already analysed. The principles of selection were threefold: the 'influence-work' of at least the Federation, Legion and BLESMA should be illustrated; examples should be drawn from the earlier and the more recent periods; failure should be recorded as well as success. Applying these principles to the unavoidable restriction of the examples to three, we have these cases: the Federation's campaign (1918–19) to provide a statutory basis for pensions claims; the Legion's pressure in 1922 and 1953 to retain the Ministry of Pensions; BLESMA's campaign (1948–56) for an age allowance for the severely war disabled.

1. The Statutory Right to Pensions

7th August 1919, Clause 7 (Statutory Right to Pensions)

'Every officer or man suffering from a disability attributable to or aggravated by naval, military or air force service during the present war, and not to his serious negligence or misconduct, shall be entitled to receive such pension, gratuity, or allowance as shall be awarded under any Warrant or Order in Council in respect of such disability, and for the payment whereof money shall have been provided by Parliament; but the award of any such pension, gratuity or allowance shall be subject to the conditions contained in the Warrant or Order in Council.

Amendment made: After the word 'awarded' ['shall be awarded'], insert the words 'by the Ministry of Pensions'.

Clause, as amended, ordered to stand part of the Bill.[1] The Cabinet conceded the clause; many others helped to persuade them, but the real author of it was the Federation.

The claim for a statutory right to pensions first appears as one of two dozen points in a programme published in the autumn of 1918

[1] 119 H.C. Deb., c. 732-3.

and no doubt drafted just before the war ended.[1] Closely connected with it in their minds, though separated in the programme, was the setting up of a 'genuine Board of Appeal', by which they meant one that was independent of the Ministry of Pensions itself. Judge Parry, the County Court Judge who had presided over the first Appeal Court, was genuine enough and too independent for the Ministry's liking but, as he well knew, the Minister really had the last word.

The Federation's opportunity to prosecute its policy came with the General Election that was announced three days after the Armistice, and in its most important constituency—Ashton-under-Lyne—the two related demands were linked together to become the first plank in the appeal made to the electors by T. F. Lister, Hogge's successor as President.[2] Elsewhere the Federation's candidates fought on the basis of the official programme in which this claim to a statutory right was one of the major features. They must have made some impact, if only by committing a successful opponent, as happened in South-West Hull.[3]

In Ashton, Lister elaborated the argument in a speech on 20th November. He said:

'No man got a pension as a right. It was not like a man who was injured in industry, and who received his compensation as a right. Under the Workmen's Compensation Act he could claim his right. If he was dissatisfied he had the right to go from the County Court to the Court of Appeal, and to the House of Lords.

'The man who was disabled in war did not receive his pension as a right. The people who decided were the Minister of Pensions or his agents. If a man or a woman was dissatisfied there were no means in existence of getting a trial independent of the Pensions Ministry ... Nobody, he thought, would suggest that they should treat the disabled in war worse than they treated the man disabled in industry, so far as his rights were concerned'.[4]

Lister's opponent was no less a person than Sir Albert Stanley, who had been Lloyd George's President of the Board of Trade, but Lister, as *The Times* Special Correspondent reported, gave him a hard fight. In fact *The Times* correspondent had earlier sounded a note of alarm. In Lister, he wrote, Stanley 'has an opponent whose strength must not be underrated', and he went on to report that Stanley 'would be

---

[1] The 1917 Constitution set out nine objects but the claim to a statutory right was not among them. Constitution, n.d., pp. 3–4. It is possible but unlikely that there was an intervening programme which has not been discovered. For the 1918 programme, see Leaflet No. 5, n.d.

[2] See appendix 4 of my thesis.

[3] *Eastern Morning News*, 4th Dec. 1918. See below p. 209 note 7 and text.

[4] *Ashton-under-Lyne Reporter*, 23rd Nov. 1918.

the last man to pretend that his prospects are "safe".'[1] Stanley, in short, was 'supposed to be in difficulties'.[2]

Stanley had reason to be alarmed. Ashton, as a cotton spinning and finishing centre, had Liberal traditions, and the local Liberals had advertised what *The Times* considered 'a curious resolution', which they had unanimously passed, protesting against 'a forced election' and the virtual disfranchisement of soldiers.[3] As they had also refused to endorse Stanley's candidature, there was really more than 'a suspicion that Mr. Lister will receive a good many Liberal votes'[4]. The electorate generally was an unknown quantity, of course: some 25,000 instead of the approximate 9,000 on the old register. Of these over 4,800 were absent naval and military voters, three-quarters located in the proxy areas and therefore able to receive voting papers.[5] Their support could be expected to go to the ex-soldier.

Hence, although Lord Beaverbrook cannot now recall the circumstances of his visit, and search of his voluminous archives has failed to discover any relevant material,[6] there can be little doubt that his sudden descent on Ashton on the eve of the poll was intended as a rescue operation on behalf of his friend Stanley, for whom he had made way in that very constituency two years earlier.[7] 'Despite his weakness, consequent upon a long and trying illness, Lord Beaverbrook felt it imperative he should make the journey to Ashton in support of Sir Albert, who is a personal friend'.[8]

As Lord Beaverbrook stepped on the platform he received 'a roar of welcome'. Although he was (as he said) now 'something of an independent', he was a supporter of the Government for this election. That morning he had gone to Downing Street to see the Prime Minister who had told him:

'I am glad you are going to speak for Stanley. I want you to give a message to the people of Ashton for me. Tell the people of Ashton to send me Stanley. I want him at the Board of Trade'.[9]

Lord Beaverbrook was already a considerable political figure. The question posed by the *National Review*[10] the previous year—'Who is

---

[1] *The Times*, 6th Dec. 1918.   [2] ibid., 30th Dec. 1918.

[3] ibid., 6th Dec. 1918.   [4] ibid.

[5] *Reporter*, 4th Jan. 1919. Precisely, 25,715 and 9,352; 4,857 absent voters, 3,890 being in proxy areas and supposed to receive papers. 1,444 papers were returned, of which 35 were rejected, so 1,409 (or 36 per cent) were in the count. Lister earlier reported that in the Near and Far East, men had been making bonfires of their papers. ibid., 30th Nov.

[6] Letters to writer, 26th April and 11th July 1957.

[7] Lord Beaverbrook had been M.P. for Ashton until his '*relegation* to the peerage in 1916', when Lloyd George wanted his seat for Sir Albert Stanley, the new President of the Board of Trade. *Men and Power*, pp. XII and 243.

[8] *Ashton-under-Lyne Herald*, 21st Dec. 1918.

[9] ibid.   [10] Jan. 1917, 607.

this Sir Maxwell Aitken "anyway" '—was even then out of date. His journey at that stage of the campaign, despite only just recovering from a very serious illness, and his prior interview with Lloyd George himself must have given significance to the pledges that he proceeded to make; among these was one obviously designed to counter Lister's campaign:

'We pledge everything that is in us to see to the maimed and the broken in this war. For my part I am perfectly sure that the Government of Mr. Lloyd George and Sir Albert Stanley will give a statutory right to every sailor and soldier disabled in this war to his pension. He shall not be dependent upon the whim of a Minister. He shall have the same right of appeal that exists under the Employers' Liability Act.'[1]

This statement was greeted with cheers and cries of 'Bravo', and should probably be regarded as tantamount to a Government pledge, even though Lord Beaverbrook looked 'upon the policy of the Government from the outside. I have had my term of office and I will tell you a secret tonight. I never mean to have public office again, except in a period of war. It is a very irksome and burdensome duty'.[2] As he himself judges: 'If I made a statement then on a statutory right to pension, you can be sure I had Lloyd George's authority to do so'.[3]

How far Lord Beaverbrook's intervention saved the day cannot, of course, be decided. All we know is that after Stanley had had as keen a contest as any Minister,[4] he ran out winner by 2,927 votes on a 68 per cent poll.[5] Nevertheless the Government appeared to be pledged, and in the debate on the Address in the new Parliament, Hogge reminded the Government of it and asked for their confirmation.[6]

The new Parliamentary Secretary to the Ministry of Pensions, Col. Sir James Craig, gave him his answer. He foresaw 'a very great difference of opinion'. The statutory basis to pensions, as also the right of appeal, would 'greatly facilitate' the work of the Ministry, but the men themselves were better served under existing arrangements. Courts would mean delays, and there would be 'the risk of encouraging a certain class of soldiers' help throughout the country agitating and working on their behalf....' A statutory obligation would work against the man.[7]

It was evident that the Government did not, after all, intend to concede a statutory right to pensions. During another debate in April

---

[1] *Ashton-under-Lyne Herald*, 21st Dec. 1918. See also *The Times*, 14th Dec. 1918.

[2] ibid., 21st Dec. 1918.   [3] Letter to writer, 26th April 1957.

[4] *The Times*, Parliamentary Correspondent, 14th Dec. 1918.

[5] *Reporter*, 4th Jan. 1919.

[6] 112 H.C. Deb., c. 451.   [7] ibid., c. 476.

1919, M.P.s of all parties pressed upon the Government this policy of taking pensions 'altogether out of the realm of grace or good nature', but the Government, this time in the person of the Minister of Pensions, Sir Laming Worthington-Evans, refused to give way. Already he said, men can appeal to what is 'practically' an independent tribunal; in fact nine tribunals were already sitting and one more would operate after Easter. This was 'not only a better security for the man than the so-called statutory right, but it is infinitely quicker' than the alternative procedure of starting in County Court and then working upwards through higher courts. This informal appeal system was, he claimed, far better than a statutory right.[1]

No observers of this debate were more keen-eyed than the Federationists—or more critical. 'The outstanding feature of it,' Lister commented, 'was the desire of each speaker to emphasize the fact that they supported the motion to fulfil promises given at the last General Election.' One speaker remarked: 'Well, I have fulfilled my promise: it is now up to the Government.' Such a lethargic way could not be countenanced. Every M.P. must be made to realize his responsibilities.[2] But how? Lister urged all branches 'to pester their Members of Parliament' with resolutions in preparation for a visit to the Minister by representatives of the International Executive Council.[3] M.P.s should also be urged to attend the House during pensions debates, since 'there were so few members present' at that April debate. Pressure was also kept up by 'innumerable' public meetings.[4]

The Federationists had a marathon session (three hours) with the Minister of Pensions (Worthington-Evans) on 12th May. But Lister's appearance three days later before the Select Committee on Pensions was of greater significance. Under the impact of his evidence, they admitted that although the constitutional question whether the payment of army pensions should depend on Royal Warrant and be expressed as a matter of bounty or whether it should be based, as with naval pensions, on an Act of Parliament might 'seem a small point and one of sentiment', nevertheless evidence showed that the present method was 'really felt as a grievance'. They therefore recommended legislation declaring the soldier (as well as the airman and sailor) to be 'legally entitled' to his pension. The scales and administrative machinery of pensions should not be embodied in legislation but left

[1] 114 H.C. Deb., c. 2823, 2825, 2835, 2814, 2842, 2855–8.

[2] *Bulletin*, 24th April 1919. He was referring, no doubt, to a remark by Charles Edwards.

[3] ibid., The International Executive linked up the four countries.

[4] ibid., 14th Aug. 1919.

to Regulation or Order in Council or 'similar executive machinery', though the ultimate authority should still be the Act itself.[1]

The recommendations of the Select Committee, published in July, were considered immediately by the Government in two meetings[2] and a debate in the House followed within a few days. Worthington-Evans announced the Government's policy: they were ready to accept independent appeal on entitlement but not a statutory right to pension as such. In fact Worthington-Evans rather poured scorn on the suggestion that the words 'legally entitled' should be inserted in an Act of Parliament. He did not believe that this would give any man more security than he would have under the proposed scheme of independent appeal, though he was 'perfectly willing to consider any form of words which would strengthen the statutory right to pension'.[3]

His announcement aroused much criticism. The Chairman of the Select Committee, Sir Montague Barlow, was first in the field. Like other members of the Select Committee, he was 'delighted and grateful' that most of the recommendations had been accepted by the Government 'without any reservations', but he remained dissatisfied on the question of the statutory right. He went on:

> 'You may say that in the result it makes uncommonly little difference, but we have had a great deal of evidence that, in fact, though the grievance is a sentimental one, it is a real one, and if you can remove a grievance which is really felt to be so, without either upsetting the whole machinery of Government or imposing an enormous burden on the taxpayer, and this would do neither, then I cannot see why it should not be done.'

He continued by quoting the unanswerable precedent of the Naval Act of 1865 and 'strongly' urged the Government to make 'this small change'.[4] Captain Douglas Hacking supported his appeal, as did Major Cyril Entwistle, (a member of the Committee) and G. W. H. Jones, who suggested that Worthington-Evans had not been 'properly coached'.[5]

Replying to the debate, the Minister singled out the question of the statutory right as one of the two main points upon which the discussion had turned. He repeated his view that by conceding a statutory right to appeal and by setting up a statutory court, the Government would be doing everything 'in the way of recognizing that the men are legally entitled to a pension that you would do if you put the words "legally entitled" into an Act of Parliament, . . .' However he was 'quite prepared' to consider any words which would strengthen

[1] H.C. 247, 1st Special Report, Select Committee on Pensions, printed |23rd Dec. 1919, p. IV, para. 6 (I).
[2] 118 H.C. Deb., c. 2341. [3] ibid., c. 2344.
[4] ibid., c. 2360–1. [5] ibid., c. 2371–2; 2384–5; 2405–6.

that position. 'I do not care whether it is sentiment or what it is, but if men think that they can get something which is not a bounty or charity but which is something which they have earned, then I want to put those words into the Act so that they may have no false shame about it but may take that to which they are entitled. I will consider any words that can be suggested.'[1]

That consideration turned out to be very fruitful. The War Pensions (Administrative Provisions) Act conceded an unambiguous statutory right to pensions granted by the Ministry of Pensions, subject of course to the conditions of award contained in the Royal Warrant or Order in Council.[2] Clause 8 of the Act also provided for independent appeal on entitlement.[3] The Bill received the Royal Assent on 19th August 1919, about three weeks after the publication of the Select Committee's Report.[4]

It is clear from this description that the Federationists deserve most of the credit for this reform—certainly among ex-servicemen's associations. The Comrades cared little for the principle, which was no part of their 'Fourteen Points' or of their evidence to the Select Committee;[5] nor did they even claim it among the successes of the year (a more surprising omission).[6] Obviously, the Federationists did not achieve it without friends. But they were the ones who had made an issue of it originally; it was they who had extracted something resembling a Government pledge, who by their election efforts had influenced some other M.P.s,[7] and who had kept up the pressure when the pledge was honoured in the breach. It was their evidence that counted before the Select Committee. In short, this is an example of successful pressure.

The strategical elements in it may be quickly summarized. The decision the Federationists sought was urgent: the dignity of discharged men was involved[8] as well as their pocket. By the end of 1918, over one and three quarter million pensions and allowances had been granted: in February these were being added to at the rate of 15–20,000 a week, apart from the renewal of temporary pensions.[9]

---

[1] ibid., c. 2414–15. [2] See above p. 203, note 1 and text.

[3] 119 H.C. Deb., c. 733. [4] ibid., c. 2132.

[5] *Comrades' Journal*, June 1919, 6.

[6] 2nd Annual Report, 31st Dec. 1919, p. 15.

[7] Entwistle, a member of the Select Committee, had faced, among others, a Federation candidate in South-West Hull, and had expressed himself in favour of the statutory right. See above p. 204 note 3 and text. Generally, see 118 H.C. Deb., c. 2384; 114 H.C. Deb., c. 2828, 2833, 2836, 2838, 2839; and 112 H.C. Deb., c. 101, 103, 446, 453, 469.

[8] See ch. X above.

[9] 112 H.C. Deb., c. 481–2.

Urgency prescribes directness, and the most convenient form of it at the time was participation in the General Election: the sensible policy afterwards was to pursue the matter in the new Parliament. The Federationists' political culture permitted such intervention, even encouraged it since they generally subscribed to a mandate theory of democracy. 'Consultation' lay in the future; other groups were unimportant compared with today, though there was an attempt to reach the general public through 'innumerable' meetings. Neither time nor resources really permitted of a more ambitious appeal to the public when the Federation was fighting for so many other policies.

XXIV

THE LEGION: RETAINING THE MINISTRY OF PENSIONS (1922 AND 1953)

THE Legion's efforts to retain the Ministry of Pensions in 1922 against the intentions of the Cabinet have already been remarked upon.[1] The essence of the situation was that, three weeks after the Prime Minister, Bonar Law, made his Glasgow speech foreshadowing the disappearance of the Ministry of Pensions as a separate Department, electors would be going to the poll. If one of the leading themes of the campaign was 'tranquillity', Legionaries were far from displaying it. They erupted immediately and wrote to the Prime Minister at No. 10, expressing 'profound regret' at his willingness to 'throw this enormous task on to some other Department or Ministry', which 'would tend thoroughly to wreck the work which has already been done, and would undoubtedly mean that these three-and-a-half millions of people, by becoming no one's children, would find themselves and their problems regarded as of only secondary importance'. By implication, too, they reproached him with failure to make use of the Standing Joint Committee machinery.[2] On the following day in *The Times*, the chairman, T. F. Lister, made the charge of 'no consultation' an explicit one. Expressing astonishment at the news, he said 'it would have been courteous, and would have given confidence, if the Premier had endeavoured first to ascertain the views of ex-servicemen on the project'. He stressed the size of the Ministry's staff (22,000) and the number of people in receipt of pensions (some 3,000,000 including the widows and children). The care of the disabled, were the proposal 'confirmed by the electorate', would be reduced 'to a secondary position', which would 'mean a much more autocratic treatment of the men, women and children, who deserve the best consideration of the country'.[3]

When Bonar Law replied the next day, 1st November, he repeated his assurances but stood his ground.[4] The Legion's response was to

---

[1] Hist. B.L., pp. 56–57. The Prime Minister was presumably announcing Cabinet policy.

[2] Journal, Dec. 1922, 137. It should be noted that the Central Advisory Committee on War Pensions was not mentioned. See ch. XIX above.

[3] *The Times*, 31st Oct. 1922.

[4] See appendix 30 of my thesis for this correspondence.

threaten sanctions: if the proposal were not abandoned it would have to 'organize opposition',[1] which could only mean during the course of the election campaign. A suitable addition to their election questionnaire to candidates had already shown that they meant business. Copies went to 'each of the leaders of the four principal parties'; and the Assistant Secretary, J. R. Griffin, was set the task of pursuing the P.M. for his reply.[2]

Was the threat of sanctions a serious one? The Legion was still very small if measured by the standards of the post-1945 period, but its 116,000 members (together with the 6,500 in the Women's Section) would have been considerable when compared with contemporary unofficial groups. Besides, these were spread all over the country in some 2,000 branches,[3] so there would have been one or more branches in almost every constituency. At that period many of the branches would have been ready to play the part expected of them by headquarters, which showed every intention of actively intervening in the election quite apart from this particular issue. Bluff probably plays a part in all pressure-group activity, but the leaders had made such careful arrangements for bringing their influence to bear through the branches that the local organization must be credited with sufficient enterprise and responsiveness to make it possible that Bonar Law really could have been hurt.

At any rate, it seems as if he *took* the threat of sanctions seriously, whether this was objectively necessary or not. The Legion's prompt criticism may well have been as embarrassing to the Government as it itself considered.[4] Certainly some concessions to the Legion's other views were soon announced. On 8th November, the Minister of Pensions, Major G. C. Tryon, announced, on the authority of the P.M., the stabilization of pension rates for a further three years *from April 1923.*[5] The date calls for emphasis because the Cabinet need not have made its decision at that time; at least, it need not have had it broadcast then. So the announcement looks like appeasement, which in turn means that the threat of sanctions was taken seriously. So too with the statement by the Government Chief Whip, on behalf of the P.M., about the training of the disabled,[6] which may also have been in part an attempt to pacify the Legion.

As we shall see, the Premier may have had a wider 'audience' in mind, but if these *were* attempts to pacify the Legion, they did not succeed. The Legion was not pacified, but it is doubtful, on the other hand, if in the end they really did organize a punitive expedition. But

[1] Journal, Dec. 1922, 138.

[2] ibid. Polling day was 15th Nov.

[3] Hist. B.L., app. 5 and 4.

[4] Journal, Dec. 1922, 137.

[5] ibid., p. 133.

[6] ibid., p. 142.

probably the threat of one had served its purpose. For of course there were other players on the field. Sir John Simon seems to have leapt into the fray immediately, with a statement that there were 'large parts of our expenditure which could not be cut down and which it would be criminal to touch—the expenditure for old age and for the disabled, for example, . . .'[1] Only two days after Bonar Law had spoken, Lloyd George, following him at Glasgow, declared that some of the Premier's suggestions had caused 'much misgiving', such as the 'proposal to get rid of the Pensions Ministry and have it added to the overburdened Treasury'.[2] Every Department was overburdened already, and already the Ministry of Pensions was 'overwhelmed with letters calling attention to delays, to failures which are inevitable in the working of any Department'. Unless these were attended to, pensioners and their families would suffer.

There were doubters, too, as well as natural critics. Kingsley Wood, for instance, again fighting West Woolwich (which he had won for the Conservatives in 1918) told ex-servicemen in his constituency that 'he would want much more information' before he supported the abolition of the Ministry. The suggestion had been made (he went on) that the Ministry of Health should administer pensions, but that Ministry had quite enough to do, and its Minister was already overburdened. Natural supporters came to the rescue, Arthur Griffith-Boscawen and, later, Montague Barlow, two Ministers, among them. They thought that any change in the status of the Ministry could be achieved without detriment to the ex-servicemen's position.[3]

Try as he would, the Premier could not prevent his proposal, so vaguely worded, becoming an election issue, even an election rumour. On 2nd November, *The Times* Parliamentary correspondent thought that Bonar Law's letter to the Legion 'should kill the unfounded rumours that have lately been in circulation'.[4] But five days later the Premier was wryly remarking:

'You have all, I am sure, heard about my wickedness in connexion with pensions . . . Believe me, there is nothing in this cry about injustice to pensioners'.[5]

He likened it to an earlier election in which it had been said that if the Unionist Government were returned, 'they would remove old age pensions'. Balfour and others denied the rumour but 'it was repeated in every constituency, and no doubt cost us a good many votes. Perhaps the same thing will happen again, but there is nothing in it, . . .'[6]

---

[1] *The Times*, 28th Oct. 1922.   [2] ibid., 29th Oct.
[3] ibid., 29th Oct. 1922; 10th Nov. 1922.
[4] ibid., 2nd Nov.   [5] ibid., 8th Nov.
[6] ibid.

Perhaps the same thing will happen again: here we may have the clue to the whole episode. With that in mind, Tryon's announcement the following evening takes shape as part of a pattern. *The Times* Parliamentary correspondent made a revealing comment when he wrote that the announcement would 'dispose of the unfounded rumours that the economies which the government proposes to make in the Ministry of Pensions will be prejudicial to the pensioners'.[1] Two days later he was observing that 'one or two waves of feeling' had spread through the country, the greatest of which,

'... was decidly inimical to the new Government. It grew out of the baseless notion that prospective economies were to be realized at the expense of war sufferers and that a reduction of pensions was threatened'.

This misconception, he concluded, should have been completely removed by the Minister's announcement.[2]

Whether the Cabinet's concession, announced by Tryon, succeeded where the Premier's repeated assurances had failed, is hard to say. In fact, the whole episode peters out disappointingly: Bonar Law won but the Ministry survived too, though there was no formal announcement of its reprieve. Whether its (long-term) survival owed more to the chance of Bonar Law's later illness than to anything else, no outsider can tell, but it is at least clear that had it not been for the Legion's initiative, the machinery for the Ministry's destruction as a separate unit must have been set in motion as soon as the election was over. Thus the Legion exhibited at a very early stage in its history its power as a 'veto group'.[3]

The Cabinet's decision, announced in 1953, to do what Bonar Law had left undone, was also, despite thirty-three years of 'consultation', presented to ex-servicemen without the slightest prior notification. Perhaps it would have been wiser, Bonar Law mused on one occasion, 'not to have said one word or expressed one opinion, and to have said nothing at all about it until after the election'.[4] It may be that his successors took that lesson to heart. On 26th February 1953, well within a year and a half of the election that returned the Conservatives to power, the Prime Minister 'startled the ex-service community', as Sir Ian Fraser said later,[5] by announcing that the Ministry of Pensions was to be merged with the Ministry of National Insurance. The declared purpose of the proposal was, as before, to secure greater efficiency and economy. On the one hand, the work of the Ministry of Pensions was contracting; on the other hand, since that Ministry's

---

[1] ibid., 9th Nov.   [2] ibid., 11th Nov.

[3] David Riesman *et al*, *The Lonely Crowd*, Doubleday Anchor, ch. X, ii.

[4] *The Times*, 8th Nov. 1922.   [5] 517 H.C. Deb., c. 284.

foundation the Ministry of National Insurance had emerged with more than three times as many local offices as the Ministry of Pensions. The amalgamation would yield some saving and there would be economies in other directions. The war pensioner himself should also benefit by having less distance to travel to his local office. As for the medical treatment side of the Ministry of Pensions work, this would go to the Ministry of Health in England and Wales and to the Department of Health in Scotland.[1]

The reasons for the change were set out at greater length in the subsequent White Paper[2] and were repeated by Captain Crookshank, as Lord Privy Seal, in the debate in the House of Commons on 30th June. 'In a sentence, efficiency and administrative economy is the aim we have in view'.[3] The economy, when 'it has all settled down' (*i.e.* within the following two or three years), was expected to be of the order of half-a-million pounds a year out of administration costs of about £4 million a year.[4]

How far the declared purpose was the real purpose is difficult to decide. It is true, as a Labour critic, James Simmons said, and as Crookshank himself recalled, that the Conservative Government was committed to a 'searching inquiry' into the machinery of government.[5] Moreover, the Prime Minister, in announcing this merger, also announced the amalgamation of the Ministries of Transport and Civil Aviation.[6] Yet the British Legion had a strong suspicion that the purpose (or, at least, one of the main purposes) was to make it more difficult for them to pursue successfully the campaign for a basic pension of 90s. a week. By assimilating war pensions to national insurance, the Government, on this interpretation, was tending to bring the one kind of provision into line with the other, while at the same time removing the single-minded advocate within the Government of the war pensioners' cause, *i.e.*, the Minister of Pensions himself. Viscount Bridgeman, a member of the Legion, was quick to see the implications of the merger for the war pensions campaign and promptly questioned Lord Swinton, who replied that the claims would not be prejudiced one way or the other.[7] In the House of Commons, Sir Ian Fraser, another Government supporter, was at first prepared to 'wait and see', but after the Budget, when it became clear to him

[1] *The Times*, 27th Feb. 1953; 517 H.C. Deb., c. 271, 183 H.L. Deb., c. 125 (2nd July 1953).

[2] Cmd. 8842 (1953), The Ministry of Pensions: Proposed Transfer of Functions, paras. 3–7.

[3] 517 H.C. Deb., c. 271.

[4] 517 H.C. Deb., c. 271–2; Cmd. 8842, para. 33.

[5] 517 H.C. Deb., c. 332 and 267.

[6] *The Times*, 27th Feb. 1953.

[7] 183 H.L. Deb., c. 135.

that the Government had not made the desired concessions, he came round to the view that the merger 'was a way of making it more difficult for us to obtain what we wanted'.[1] These suspicions that the Government's purpose was to 'damp down the agitation which the British Legion had been making, much to the embarrassment of the Government, for better pensions', was shared by another prominent Legionary in Parliament, F. J. Bellenger, but he spoke, of course, from the Opposition benches.[2] So strongly did Sir Ian hold the view that the merger made it more difficult to win the pensions battle, that he made it the reason for voting against the Government in the subsequent debate.[3]

Whether these considerations were the ones that really weighed with the Government is impossible to say; in all probability, 'ditching the British Legion's Pensions Campaign' was seen as a happy by-product of a re-organization of government machinery that was desired for its own sake. Certainly, as Bellenger said, the decision was announced 'abruptly'.[4] Indeed, James Simmons remarked without contradiction in the presence of Crookshank that the decision had been taken without any consultation with the ex-servicemen's organizations or the voluntary workers who have special knowledge of ex-servicemen's problems and of the psychology of the war disabled.[5] The charge of failing to consult is usually regarded as a fairly serious one, but Heathcoat Amory, winding up for the Government, made no attempt to answer it. The ex-service organizations were indeed faced with a firm decision if not exactly a *fait accompli.*

The British Legion's first response came from its Chairman at the time, Major-General Sir Richard Howard-Vyse, who expressed the Legion's great anxiety and thought that the proposal tended to play down the special interests of the war disabled and so bring about a loss of status.[6] This was also Sir Ian Fraser's theme when he led a six-man deputation to the Minister on 8th May,[7] but despite these protests (and the 'strong objection' of BLESMA),[8] as well as the almost lone-wolf campaign of James Simmons to save the Ministry of which he had been Parliamentary Secretary,[9] the Order was laid before Parliament on 18th May. A week later at their Whitsun Conference the Legion kept the fight going by passing a resolution condemning the proposed merger and expressing the hope that the

---

[1] 517 H.C. Deb., c. 299.   [2] 517 H.C. Deb., c. 293.

[3] 517 H.C. Deb., c. 288. See also c. 299.

[4] 517 H.C. Deb., c. 293.   [5] 517 H.C. Deb., c. 332.

[6] Journal, April 1953, 1.   [7] Journal, June 1953, 3.

[8] 1953 Conference Reports, p. 2.

[9] *Birmingham Gazette,* 14th May 1953.

Prime Minister would receive a deputation.[1] On 27th May Sir Ian Fraser put the request to the Prime Minister.

In reality, it was all over bar the shouting, but on 12th June, Lord Woolton, deputizing for the P.M., received the second of the Legion's deputations on the subject, and devoted an hour and ten minutes of his time to the purpose.[2] Naturally, he gave nothing away, and six days later the Chairman was appealing to all members of both Houses,[3] while the General Secretary was seeking the active support of other ex-service groups. Most of these, and all the major bodies, shared the Legion's views, and some other unofficial groups, such as the Bath Trades Council, joined in the chorus of disapproval, thanks no doubt to local 'lobbying'. The Parliamentarians were less accommodating, apart from those who were in Opposition. One Government supporter, Sir Herbert Williams, was blunt in his rejection of the Legion's views, and added for good measure a sharp comment on the pensions campaign. But most of the Conservatives who answered (the *total* response was very small) combined sympathy with reasoned argument. By the time some members had replied, the Chairman had again written (29th June) to about seventy of them—those who had signed Major Legge-Bourke's motion for an increase in pensions.[4] On the same day, the Chairman again wrote to members of the Lords, enclosing a shortened version of 'the case' and informing them that Lord Carew, a member of the N.E.C., would be 'leading' for the Legion in the debate on 2nd July, when their support in the division lobby was invited.[5]

Almost all the noble lords, in effect, declined the invitation, including some who had Legion connexions. But Lord Carew, and another prominent Legionary, Lord Long of Wraxall, did all they could, supported only by the Earl of Cork and Orrery. The result of the debate was predictable, especially as the other House had already spoken. There, two days earlier, the debate had gone its certain way, unremarkable except that Sir Ian Fraser, a Conservative, was one of the 212 who were against the Order. Despite his defection (which expressed his loyalty to the Legion), the Government found a majority of fourteen.[6] Now even the shouting was over.

On both occasions the decisions were urgently required and so stimulated 'directness' (uncharacteristic of the Legion in the post-1945 period, in which the typical—virtually the only—campaign has been to win over the public and, then the decision-makers, to the

---

[1] Journal, July 1953, 3.
[2] ibid., p. 2. This was the third deputation that year.
[3] See below appendix 4.   [4] ibid.
[5] ibid.
[6] 183 H.L. Deb., c. 127–142; 517 H.C. Deb., c. 287–350.

doubling of the basic rate of pensions). In 1922, directness meant a public 'debate' with the Prime Minister and the threat to 'organize opposition' during a general election; but in 1953 the election was behind them, and in any case, the changed values of Legionaries no longer permitted the word 'sanctions' to be as much as mentioned, least of all at such a 'delicate' time but not even after the sound and fury had died away. Their political culture had been transformed. Hence 'directness' chiefly meant one 'strong' resolution to the P.M. and two decorous deputations: willing to strike (attitudes) and yet afraid to wound, as Pope might have said.

As for official power, the strength of party discipline in 1953 made resort to Parliament quite useless: the issue and whole situation was too explosive for the House of Commons Branch of the Legion even to meet, although Simmons suggested that it should be convened. The Ministry was approached—a useless ritual since even the consultative procedure had been deliberately by-passed. Within the unofficial realm, it was significant that the Legion felt the need to look 'outside' itself: more allies might have been found had time permitted, but the Cabinet had seen to it that time did not permit: just over four months elapsed between the pronouncement of the death penalty and its execution. Nor had that pronouncement been preceded by a 'public trial'. Yet it was, on the other hand, the expansion of the realm of unofficial power that proved the Legion's undoing. Its own membership six times that of 1922, extended over some 5,300 branches,[1] its prestige and financial resources vastly increased, it now found itself in a pluralistic world where it was after all only one among many. Besides, economic and social policy in the post-1945 era had created a new situation in which the integration of war pensions with other social payments made administrative sense if not necessarily distributive justice. Judged by the usual 'objective' tests, the Legion in 1953 was better placed to exercise influence than at any time in its early history, but other unofficial groups had caught up with it and some had even drawn ahead. Even so, a really vigorous counter-attack, based on that withdrawal of co-operation which doctors, lawyers, farmers and others, openly or covertly, have not hesitated to threaten, might have been successful, but that has been a method that the group norms (or at least the leaders' norms) have never permitted. And as the direct methods that *were* once permitted no longer found support in 1953, the Legion, *in this particular situation*, was impotent. Prestige can be capitalized, given time: in an immediate crisis, an association may be its prisoner. It was a changed world in 1953—in more ways than one.

[1] End 1952; 723,770 paying members (apart from 238,318 in the Women's Section) and 5,371 branches. Hist. B.L., app. 4 and 5. Cf. p. 67 above, n. 3.

XXV

BLESMA: THE 'AGE ALLOWANCE' CAMPAIGN (1948-56)

BEFORE the last war, BLESMA's main pressure was exerted in the field of employment in trying to place the very badly disabled whom industry rejected. This policy arose out of the Legion's failure to bring about the compulsory employment of disabled men.[1]

Since the War, the situation has, of course, fundamentally changed. Full employment, the Disabled Persons Act of 1944 and the 1945 Act that set up *Remploy*, have together removed the old preoccupation, so that BLESMA's post-war policy has been largely about pensions. Their main pensions objective has been an increase in the basic rate. In this respect, therefore, their policy *resembled* the main post-war objective of the British Legion. But there the resemblance comes to an end. When the Legion wanted to double the basic rate of 45s. a week (for an ex-private), BLESMA were 'refusing to be stampeded into adopting the slogan "Double the Basic Rate"'.[2] In their programme published in September 1948, BLESMA pointed out that the cost of doubling the basic rate would be about £32,000,000 a year. BLESMA's policy at this time, 'as a first step towards the general up-scaling of pensions', was that the 'rate for *all* Other Ranks should be raised to 61s. 8d. per week for 100 per cent disablement'.[3] The main reason for the divergence between BLESMA's policy and the Legion's is, obviously, that BLESMA comprises the severely disabled men; hence their emphasis that the cost of doubling the basic rate for comparatively minor disabilities (*i.e.*, the 20 per cent and 30 per cent pensioner) alone would cost about £11,000,000 a year.[4] But there is another reason: BLESMA holds the view that 'equal disablement should command equal compensation, irrespective of rank'.[5] This is the significance of the claim for 61s. 8d. for all 100 per cent disabled Other Ranks, compared with the Legion's 90s. 61s. 8d. a week was then the rate for Warrant Officers, Class 1.

Most of the history of BLESMA's pensions claims since the war

---

[1] Hist. B.L., passim.

[2] BLESMA, Annual Report for 1947, p. 5.

[3] BLESMA's 11-point Programme, Sept. 1948. Emphasis added.

[4] ibid.   [5] ibid.

consists in attempts to obtain *this* increase in the basic rate, with occasional forays, as tactics required, into the field of supplementary or special allowances. Their position immediately after the war was that the improvements made in February 1946 removed 'most' of the 'long-standing grievances' and anomalies.[1] Nevertheless it was held that grievances and anomalies still existed. What were these?

Judging by the pensions resolutions that Conference passed, there were a dozen claims, including the characteristic 'equal compensation for equal disablement' and the one into which we are now inquiring—'the up-grading of disability pensions with advancing years similar to the Canadian system', including amputation cases,[2] but this was not yet a major demand.[3]

That these demands were *ad hoc* and that the whole pensions policy had hardly been thought out in the context of the post-war world was virtually admitted at the 1947 Conference, when the General Secretary advised delegates that the 'time has come for careful stocktaking and planning of future policy'.[4] The Conference accordingly instructed the E.C. to review the whole field of pensions and allowances and to draft a policy and programme.[5] Among the resolutions referred for the leadership's considerations was the one from the previous year about 'up-grading of disability pensions with advancing years'.[6]

The Executive Council deliberated and drew up a memorandum which was circulated to branches and eventually adopted at the 1948 Conference: it became the 11-Point Programme. The main item in financial terms has already been mentioned (the increase in the basic rate to 61s. 8d. for all 100 per cent disabled Other Ranks), but amongst the various supplementaries was one asking the Minister to consider increasing pensions on a sliding scale with advancing years.

In July 1948 these policy claims were discussed at BLESMA's annual meeting with the Minister of Pensions and his principal officers.[7] BLESMA's brief for that occasion shows that the effect of amputations was to have been raised as item No. 6, under which the Ministry was to be asked to accept liability for added disability or death for various reasons, including premature degeneration of cardio-vascular tissues, which was destined to be an important issue.[8]

The Minister at this time was the former professor, Hilary Marquand. His reply in October stated that the investigation of the

[1] Annual Report for 1946, General Secretary's Report, 'Pensions and Allowances'.

[2] 1946 Conference Report, Resolutions Adopted.

[3] Annual Report for 1946, General Secretary's Report.

[4] ibid., General Secretary's Report, Pensions and Allowances.

[5] ibid., Resolutions Adopted.   [6] ibid.

[7] Annual Report for 1948: General Secretary's Report, Pensions.

[8] Brief for deputation, 7th July 1948.

effects of amputations on the individual's general health and expectation of life was being pressed forward as quickly as possible. It was hoped to issue an interim report the following year.

The 1949 Conference saw the basic rate policy unchanged but the 'advancing age' policy, although still pursued, was narrowed down. From 1946 onwards it had been so framed as to apply to all categories of pensioners; no doubt the BLESMA leaders had had the limbless chiefly in mind but in fact they had cast their net widely. In 1949 the policy was narrowed down to cases of amputation.[1]

As usual in July, Lord Willoughby de Eresby, with G. Chandley (Secretary) and C. R. Stevens (President) waited on the Minister of Pensions to discuss Conference resolutions. BLESMA again stated that they could not accept that amputations and the strains and burdens of wearing artificial equipment did not have bad effects in a large number of cases, especially where frequent breakdowns or treatment resulted in general deterioration and lower resistance to the ordinary ailments of life. In a separate but related point, they claimed that there 'can be no doubt that the burden of wearing artificial equipment increases with advancing age' and that the disability is greater.[2]

In his reply on the 24th October 1949, Marquand now took his stand on the findings of the Hancock Committee, which had come to the conclusion that it was not 'practicable or desirable to fix different assessments for different age-groups'.[3] His own medical officers supported the findings of the Committee. Accordingly, he could not undertake to increase assessments with advancing age unless the pensioner's condition had changed for the worse, because he had no authority to award or increase disablement pensions on the ground of loss of function due to old age or some other non-service factor. Of course, if the pensioner's condition deteriorated, there would be reason for reconsidering whether the assessment itself and therefore his award could be increased.

Thus BLESMA came up against the blank wall of expert medical opinion, and although the policy was reaffirmed at the 1950 Conference,[4] they suffered a further disappointment the following year when the Rock Carling Committee (on cardio-vascular disorders and mortality rates in amputees) issued its interim report.[5] This report encouraged (in the relevant sense) no one except the Ministry.

At the 1951 Conference which followed soon after, there does not seem to have been an 'age allowance' resolution. Instead, Conference

[1] 1949 Conference Report, Resolutions Adopted, Pensions and Allowances.
[2] Brief for Deputation, 7th July 1949.
[3] Cmd. 7076 (1947), para. 7.
[4] 1950 Conference Report p. 23.
[5] For the final report, see appendix 32 of my thesis.

paid most attention to the basic rate which had been steadily declining in value since 1946; delegates were by now extremely exasperated. A resolution urging a 'demonstration to gain publicity for the campaign for higher pensions' was defeated by eight votes, but the E.C. naturally had to take into account the mood of Conference. At its meeting in Manchester at the end of June, the E.C. considered two proposals designed to raise the status and influence of BLESMA, so overcoming apathy and hence removing the frustration and disappointment caused by the Government's refusal to increase pension rates. It was suggested that to raise their status and influence, royal and other recognition should be secured, and, secondly, local meetings should be held, M.P.s lobbied and a national gathering arranged in London during the summer of 1952.[1]

A month after the E.C. meeting, however, the small Advisory Committee of distinguished well-wishers, linked to the official leadership by the President and Secretary, suggested that in view of the uncertain Parliamentary situation (there were two M.P.s among them) and the strong feelings in the branches, the focus of interest in the campaign should be on pensions. Thus two alternative plans were formulated, depending on an autumn election. The first visualized questions to, and meetings with, candidates, but without asking them to pledge themselves and without their being 'blackmailed by the threat of losing votes'.[2] The second plan was part-demonstration, part-lobbying, partly an appeal to the public. The 'influence-work' was to start in the branches in October, and was to reach its climax in the Commons on a day in the week before 11th November. The demonstration was to be 'the most orderly and dignified ever witnessed, carried out in a spirit of reproach rather than remonstrance and full publicity will be gained for this aspect'.[3]

Strictly, it was this second plan that was put into operation, the choice of 7th November 1951 for the Reproach Demonstration having been made before it was known that the new Parliament would be meeting the previous day as a result of Attlee's sudden decision to dissolve. But in practice the plans were partly combined: candidates received copies of BLESMA's policy statement, and, after the results were known, copies of resolutions passed at open branch meetings,[4] but the more ambitious arrangements were also carried out as designed. Preceded by a Press Conference on 1st November, the demonstration included a protest and reproach meeting at Church House; the taking of copies of resolutions passed there to the Cabinet Office, No. 10, the Treasury and the Pensions Ministry; and a pre-

[1] Executive Council Meeting, 30th June–1st July 1951, Min. 25.
[2] Circulars, Aug. 1951.   [3] ibid.
[4] Circulars, 24th Sept. 1951.

arranged meeting in the Commons with members of all parties, attended by about a hundred of them and perhaps another hundred from BLESMA, with some lobbying by the remainder of the delegates. The cameramen from four newsreels were busy during the slow march from the Cenotaph to Church House.[1]

For our purposes the significance of this demonstration was that it gave rise to the All-Party Committee already mentioned.[2] This now became the vehicle for attempts at influencing the Ministry of Pensions. In March 1952 the Government made available £10,000,000 as 'a first contribution to your cause'.[3] This £10,000,000 made it possible to raise the basic rate from 45s. to 55s. for the 100 per cent disabled pensioner. Brigadier Smyth, the Parliamentary Secretary at the Ministry, assured BLESMA that the matter had not been 'finalized in any way' but was, on the contrary, 'a serial story to which we wish to return before the next Budget'.[4] Since it was certain that the basic rate would not be raised again for two or three years, however, BLESMA switched its emphasis from that to its claim for the ageing limbless. In bringing this policy to the forefront, E. V. Law (Vice-President) and George Chandley went to the House of Commons on 3rd April to meet the All-Party Committee, and in turn, six days later, led by Sir Arnold Gridley, nine representatives of the All-Party Committee met D. Heathcoat Amory, the Minister of Pensions, and J. A. Boyd-Carpenter, the Financial Secretary to the Treasury. On the same day a BLESMA deputation of four waited on the Minister and his Parliamentary Secretary.[5]

Both these deputations gave thanks for the recent increases, but expressed disappointment that 'the promise to give most sympathetic consideration to the special claims of the limbless had come to nought'. They made a particular plea for 'the ageing 1914–18 war men who suffered most from the burden and discomfort of amputations and artificial limbs in advancing years'. The usual 'most careful consideration' was promised them.[6]

While 'consideration' was being given, attempts were made to influence the Cabinet through the Commons. Already James Simmons (Lab.) had asked one of his many questions;[7] in November 1952, supported by Sir Ian Fraser (Con.) and Leslie Lever (Lab.), he used the half-hour adjournment debate to press home the attack.[8] But nothing came of these efforts or of the activities of the All-Party

[1] *Blesmag*, Jan. 1952, 2–5.   [2] See above Ch. XXI.
[3] Brigadier J. G. Smyth, V.C., at BLESMA's Conference. 1952 Conference Report, p. 12.
[4] ibid., p. 13.
[5] ibid., p. 10.   [6] ibid.
[7] 497 H.C. Deb., c. 193, 18th March 1952.
[8] 508 H.C. Deb., c. 444–454, 6th Nov. 1952.

Committee in 1953, when pressure was exerted on both the outgoing Minister and his successor, Osbert Peake.[1] Meanwhile, the 'indefatigable Mr. Chandley' had kept up his own fire at the Ministry, and the cumulative effect of all this pressure was a deterioration in BLESMA's relations with that Department.[2] In May 1954 Peake declined to receive a deputation from BLESMA on the ground that any improvement in war pension rates was governed by the Chancellor's Budget speech. In July, however, although unwilling to receive even the usual annual deputation, he relented to the extent of receiving representatives of the All-Party Committee to discuss the progress made by the Rock Carling Committee. Nevertheless, he took the view that the memorandum submitted before the meeting revealed no new points of substance.

At last in November the Rock Carling Committee produced its 'ultimate conclusions',[3] which, however, dashed all BLESMA's hopes by finding that the wearing of a prosthesis did not induce or aggravate cardio-vascular disorders to any significant extent, and that there was no material difference between the mortality rates of amputees, by reason of amputation, and those for pensioners generally.

Once again progress with this claim foundered on the rock of expert medical opinion. Early in the New Year, therefore, the All-Party Committee, especially Leslie Lever, its secretary, began to collect the views of the most eminent men in the medical and surgical world in order to see if the Rock Carling Committee's conclusions were in fact technically sound. A few weeks before the 1955 Conference no less a person than Sir Harry Platt, then President of the Royal College of Surgeons, appeared before the All-Party Committee and 'assured them of his agreement and support' of BLESMA's claim.[4] Professor Bryan McFarland, then President of the British Orthopaedic Association, was approached by Lever and he too came out in support of BLESMA's position. In due course Sir Russell Brain, then President of the Royal College of Physicians, also signified his support.[5]

It took many months to approach these eminent medical and surgical specialists and to gain their support. Meanwhile pressure in Parliament had been sustained. The All-Party Committee arranged for a motion to be tabled, which 324 members of all parties signed. As Leslie Lever told the Annual Conference: 'over half the House is behind the claims for limbless ex-servicemen', and a number of those in office were in agreement but of course unable to sign.[6]

[1] 1954 Conference Report, pp. 6 and 17.
[2] BLESMA files, 8th Jan. 1954.
[3] See appendix 32 of my thesis.   [4] *Blesmag*, Oct. 1955, 1.
[5] ibid.   [6] 1955 Conference Report, p. 17.

Nevertheless it became 'increasingly apparent that some special action is called for in order to move the Ministry, the Treasury and Cabinet to make a concession without further prolonged delays'. With the approval of the All-Party Committee, the Executive Council planned another meeting of Protest and Reproach to do for this claim what the previous 1951 meeting had been designed to do for the basic rate (increased, from February 1955, from 55s. to 67s. 6d. for the 100 per cent disabled man).[1] The 'sole objective' of this second meeting was to press the case for the ageing limbless.[2]

On 8th November about 250 limbless ex-servicemen assembled in London and after laying a wreath on the Cenotaph, they began their meeting at Church House, Westminster. Copies of a resolution recording the meeting's 'profound disappointment at the repeated refusals of the Minister of Pensions to concede a special allowance, additional to the fixed assessments for amputations awarded in 1919' were taken to No. 10, the Treasury and the Ministry of Pensions. That evening about 100 delegates drawn from each of the branches represented went to the House of Commons to attend a meeting of M.P.s convened by the All-Party Committee. Nearly 200 M.P.s also squeezed in. Sir Robert Cary, Bt., Chairman of the All-Party Committee, presided and gave a report of the events at the Cenotaph and at Church House. He read the resolution which had been passed and announced that copies had been conveyed to the P.M., the Chancellor and the Ministry. He also announced that they had the support of the most eminent surgeons and physicians in the country; and Sir Harry Platt, who had only just returned from the United States, came straight to the meeting in person to confirm his belief in the justice of BLESMA's claim. There was, he said, 'an overwhelming case for increased compensation for amputees in advancing years, when the ability to use artificial equipment begins to decline. The case was so obvious that it needed no argument'.[3] After further speeches by James Simmons, Richard Wood, Dr. Barnett Stross and also by the General Secretary, all the M.P.s present unanimously approved the claims for the ageing limbless and the terms of the resolutions passed by BLESMA delegates at the Church House meeting.[4]

Despite this expert support, the Government refused to budge. Soon after that meeting of Protest and Reproach, Sir Robert Cary went to see the Chancellor to impress on him BLESMA's case, and on 13th December the All-Party Committee met both the Minister of Pensions and the Financial Secretary to the Treasury. In addition the Manchester City Council sponsored a resolution, which was

[1] General Secretary's Circulars to Branch Secretaries, Sept. 1955.
[2] ibid., 31st Oct. 1955.
[3] *Blesmag*, Jan. 1956, 8–9.   [4] ibid.

unanimously adopted, stating their strong view that the Government should 'make further and better provisions' for those men of the 1914–18 War 'whose amputations and artificial limbs constituted a much greater disability in their advancing years than is reflected in their pensions assessments which have remained fixed since 1919'. Copies of this were sent to the P.M., the Chancellor and the Minister.[1]

Nevertheless BLESMA's case might never have been met had there not been a change at the Ministry of Pensions. Osbert Peake was translated to the House of Lords and replaced by John Boyd-Carpenter, who early in the New Year (1956) received a deputation from the All-Party Committee.

While taking his stand on the reports of both the Hancock Committee and the Rock Carling Committee, and while pointing out that the Ministry could not in any case deal with the limbless in isolation from the blind and the paraplegics, he nevertheless gave the impression of thinking that BLESMA's claim might have substance. He was therefore very willing to arrange for 'authoritative investigation, independent of my Ministry, of any such evidence as may be adduced'. Indeed he had already been and was still in touch with some of the eminent medical men who had been indicated as giving some support to BLESMA's claim.[2]

While Boyd-Carpenter was reconsidering the matter BLESMA continued its efforts. In March the support of Professor Sir Walter Mercer, President of the Royal College of Surgeons of Edinburgh and Chairman of the Standing Advisory Committee on Artificial Limbs, was secured.[3] In June, a motion was tabled in the House noting that 'advancing age has aggravated disabilities of the badly wounded of the 1914–18 War and calling on the Government to make provision, beyond that provided for by the basic pension assessments, to compensate them for their increased disabilities and loss of activities and amenities'. In July, the All-Party Committee met in the House of Commons with the General Secretary and had a thorough stock-taking with Sir Harry Platt;[4] the outcome of that meeting was an attempt to win support of two other eminent surgeons, Norman Capener of Exeter and Alan S. Malkin of Nottingham, who also came out in support of BLESMA's position. Sir Harry Platt also set out in writing for the first time his judgement on this 'unique problem in our society', the 'dwindling group of physically disabled individuals'.[5]

[1] ibid., 10.

[2] Boyd-Carpenter to Cary, 4th May 1956 in 1956 Conference Report, p. 16. See below appendix 5.

[3] Mercer-Chandley, 6th March 1956.

[4] Summary of Discussion, 5th July 1956.

[5] Capener–Lever, 13th July; Malkin–Lever, 25th July; Platt–Lever, 25th July 1956.

These letters were presented to the Ministry of Pensions on 31st July, but it was learned that the Department was still pursuing its own medical inquiries in an attempt to discover 'whether the prevailing opinion is substantial enough to controvert the findings of the Hancock and Rock Carling Committees'. The Minister was also considering the position of other seriously disabled pensioners, maintaining that there must be equity between them.[1] Nevertheless, the Committee felt reasonably confident that some concession would be made, though the date of its introduction depended on whether the Chancellor decided to make money available, and that decision could be 'hastened' only by constant parliamentary pressure. It was therefore arranged that if the Minister failed to give a satisfactory decision before Parliament resumed, an amendment to the Address of thanks would be tabled, and members of the Committee embracing all parties in the House would raise the matter in the debate on the Address. All branches would then have 'to bombard' their local M.P.s about the end of October 'so that they will bring pressure on their leaders to protect them by granting BLESMA's long outstanding claims'.[2]

As usual, George Chandley kept up his harassing fire, writing on 2nd August to the Prime Minister himself: one of the secretaries replied that the P.M. was indeed taking a personal interest in the matter, but the real difficulty was to get consensus among responsible medical opinion. The Minister of Pensions was still collecting the views of a number of eminent men. In the event, these men must have convinced the Minister while confounding his Ministry and the other medical experts because on 19th November Boyd-Carpenter announced the basic improvement that BLESMA had pursued so long. While not giving BLESMA all it had hoped for, the Government did provide an 'age allowance' for limbless (and other severely disabled) war pensioners at the age of 65 or over. The principle was at last conceded, at a cost, even with certain other improvements, of some £1,600,000 in a full year.[3]

On the whole, this campaign was characterized by indirectness. It had elements of directness, of course: the two demonstrations were examples of it, even though their dominant mood was one of dignified reproach, not violent denunciation. BLESMA were ready, also, to intervene in the electoral process, though without any threat of sanctions, and the foundation of the All-Party Committee was an earnest of directness of another kind. But the *successful* work of that Committee was fundamentally indirect. It is true, of course, that

---

[1] General Secretary's circular, 2nd August 1956.
[2] ibid.
[3] 560 H.C. Deb., c. 1380; 1957 Conference Report, pp. 7 and 4.

J. A. Boyd-Carpenter was persuaded by direct representations to consider that 'there might be something in it'. He was the first Minister since the issue was raised in 1948 who had not stood pat with the official Departmental 'cards'. Obviously, this was important. But it was the untiring 'activation' of other unofficial groups by the All-Party Committee, notably by Leslie Lever, that provided the material for the Minister's re-consideration of Departmental policy: without that, nothing would have been possible. And, of course, the demonstrations, well covered by Press and newsreels, were intended for the general public as well as for the decision-makers: if there were any doubt about that, recollection of the timing of the procession from Church House to the Commons for 5.30 p.m. and the inevitable dislocation of the traffic at that hour, would at once dispel it.

The conditions that governed BLESMA's strategy may be simply stated. The element of directness is attributable to the increasing sense of urgency as year after year passed by without any progress on this issue, while the potential beneficiaries were either getting older or dying off. The values of the BLESMA men ruled out some forms of directness, but, unlike Legionaries, not certain other forms, such as the demonstration. The reasons for the difference are no doubt complex, but perhaps the outstanding one is that BLESMA men have a special pride, as well they might, in being battle casualties, which was the source of their burning sense of injustice (such as Legionaries once had) and which made possible any constitutional method of pressure.

The element of directness, again, had roots within the structure of official power, for at the very time when the Legion was converting its Branch into a Group as a recognition of its uselessness, BLESMA had found friends in the House who had learned how to make the All-Party-Committee idea a reality. This can work only when the decision sought rests on a reasonable case, when the 'cost' (in whatever form) is 'marginal', and when the members are inspired to do more than go through the usual Parliamentary motions. Success has to be sweated for, not waved at.

On the other hand, in a pluralistic world, other unofficial groups have to be taken into account. BLESMA showed awareness of that in its appeals to public opinion and in its efforts to influence other groups, such as the Manchester City Council, to pass resolutions in its favour. The All-Party Committee carried the policy much further by its brilliant 'activation' of the doctors, above all, of the surgeons, through whom, in a sense, the Royal Colleges of two countries were summoned as witnesses. The Ministry's doctors and the outside specialists were good men but they were not as good as all that.

PART SIX

The Assessment of Influence

XXVI

THE BRITISH LEGION (1921-57)

Introduction

THE broad aims and methods of ex-servicemen's associations, together with some detailed illustrations of both, have now been considered. To what extent was such influence effective? There is no more difficult question in the whole pressure-group catechism. It is in the strictest sense of the term unanswerable: no one can ever be completely certain that he has isolated all the factors that lay behind a particular decision, or, even if that were possible, be completely sure of distributing credit in the right proportions. Were the Anti-Slavery movement and the movement for Catholic Emancipation *truly* successful? Did the Anti-Corn Law League *really* bring about repeal, the Anti-Saloon League make a vast country (officially) dry; was Women's Suffrage the handiwork of the Women's Social and Political Union alone or in combination with the Constitutionalists, or was it the unplanned result of the sweep through Belgium? It is hard to separate the work of Mrs. Pankhurst from Kaiser Bill's. Indeed all the answers are simple only to the single-minded people who prosecuted such causes and to over-confident authors writing about *Great Movements and Those Who Achieved Them.*[1]

If it is hard to distinguish concomitance from causation where the pressure is only 'single-purpose', how much more so is it when associations have a permanent existence and many aims to pursue? In the course of a generation, the great pressure groups will severally put forward scores of claims which both they and the official groups well know will not ever be granted in full. To ask for more than they expect to get seems to be a principle of action.

Confusion is worse confounded because some claims are likely to be advanced by several organizations. The F.B.I. and the British Employers' Confederation are likely to share certain objectives. They may even, on certain issues, coincide with the T.U.C. For most of the period here surveyed there has been more than one ex-servicemen's association in the field, which makes a further complication in the analysis of influence. In 1919 for instance, all the ex-service groups wanted a large increase in the basic rate of pensions. Such an increase was granted, but how can one distinguish the influence of the

[1] Henry J. Nicoll (John Hogg), London, 1881.

Federation from that of the Comrades, the influence of the electorate and M.P.s independently of both of them, the Cabinet's fear of Bolshevism? Similarly, since 1945, the Legion, BLESMA and many other organizations have campaigned for an increase in the basic rate of pensions, and there is no way of separating the influence of one from all the rest in the concessions actually made.

Besides, there is as yet almost no basis for a comparison of effectiveness. At the time of writing there are no other detailed studies of British pressure groups comparable to this one. Asher Tropp's history of the school teachers has a very different focus,[1] and most of our other pressure groups have yet to be examined in detail, let alone written about. A comparison with American veterans may well be a fruitful exercise in due course, but, the comparative study of pressure groups being still in its infancy, it could not fail to be 'mechanical' now.

Thus one is driven into making tentative judgements about the effectiveness of influence that have more in common with the historian's craft than the political 'scientist's'; even so, one is not out of the wood. In assessing influence, the danger is always of exaggeration, and so one ought to apply the severest test possible. Undoubtedly, the severest test is to take the complete list of demands set out in the various ex-servicemen's programmes over the years, for not only do these contain far more than the men themselves really expect to get, but also the very procedure usually fails to bring to light the veto power of groups. Yet the test is worth applying because any result that does point to the effectiveness of influence in this sense may be relied upon as an index of influence in some broader sense.

The difficulty, however, is that the test is severe on the student as well as on the ex-servicemen's associations: there are so many associations, so many programmes, so many claims, that the 'pursuit' would take far too long, and the eventual description of it would demand far too much space. Accordingly, I am obliged to confine myself to the influence of the British Legion. It may be worth while saying, however, that I believe the Federation's influence in 1918–19 (judged in these terms) to have been very considerable, as was BLESMA's in the implementation of the 11-point programme it drew up in 1948.

1. *The Inter-War Years*

The only practicable way of drawing up a provisional 'Balance Sheet' of influence is to make a selection of the outstandingly im-

---

[1] Asher Tropp, *The School Teachers*, 1957. See also S. E. Finer, 4 P.S. 1956, 61–84; and *Sociological Review*, 1955, 279–94, and 1956, 5–28.

portant claims that were advanced. Such a selection is not entirely arbitrary; often, one can see that the financial implications (as with the stabilization of pensions rates) are big even if one cannot guess at the amounts involved. Some claims are big in the sense of involving a big principle: preference for ex-servicemen on certain employment schemes. Thus one can make a rough assessment of relative importance, although some element of arbitrariness remains.

Having made a selection, the next task is simply to trace what happened, without raising the question of causation. It is important to notice that if a claim is not granted at the time, or within a reasonable period afterwards, then it is here classified as a failure, *e.g.*, the policy of the Federation and later of the Legion to make the employment of disabled men compulsory was secured a generation later in the Disabled Persons Act, 1944. That might seem to spell success but it is a strange success that has to wait a generation for its fulfilment. Thus the Federation's campaign in 1919–20 and the Legion's in 1924–25 have to be regarded as failures.

The most convenient sources for the early claims of the Legion are the three questionnaires submitted to Parliamentary candidates in the 1922, 1923 and 1924 elections.[1] A scrutiny of the first of these yields (I think) seven issues of major (domestic) policy,[2] to which may be added the national employment policy and the final awards claim from the 1923 questionnaire. Then, by 1924, the time-limit question for pensions generally as distinct from widows pensions had become an issue that was to occupy a high proportion of the Legion's attention for the next decade or so. Finally, in the period 1931–34, the Legion fought the 'Means Test' battle.

This selection is by no means unchallengeable, but that it embodies the hard core of important demands can hardly be doubted. Thus there were perhaps eleven major (domestic) policy issues in the early years of the Legion's history (*i.e.*, in, say, the first fourteen years, taking 1936 as the end of the time-limit pressure, or rather more than one-third of that part of the Legion's history here surveyed).

The first step is to say what happened to these demands. As already noted, the compulsory-employment-of-disabled-men policy cannot escape being adjudged a failure. The closely related, if somewhat ambiguous, policy of full pension if a disabled man could not get work was also a failure, and the policy of village settlement for T.B. ex-servicemen was in fact carried out by the Legion itself in its establishment of Preston Hall rather than by the Government.[3] Nor

---

[1] For the 1922 questionnaire, see Hist. B.L., app. 15; the 1923 version is reproduced below at app. 1. For 1924 consult my thesis, app. 22.

[2] Questions 1–4, 8, 10 and 13.

[3] Hist. B.L., 84–5.

did the National Employment Committee proposal commend itself to the Government.[1]

These four claims, then, were not conceded. What happened about the remainder? As we have already seen, the Ministry of Pensions was, after all, retained as a separate entity until as recently as 1953. Preference was secured: it became a condition of a grant by the Unemployment Grants Committee for any scheme submitted to them that not less than 75 per cent of the men taken on for the work should be ex-servicemen (though in approved cases that proportion could be reduced by the Committee). It was also a standing instruction of the Ministry of Labour to Employment Exchanges that, in submitting applications for vacancies, preference should be given to ex-servicemen. This meant 'that of two or more applicants for employment in a given trade who are registered at the same Local Office, and are in other respects equally suitable to fill a notified vacancy in that trade, the ex-service application is to be given preference over the applicant who is not an ex-serviceman'.[2] Attempts were made at various times in the 1920's to abolish that preference but these were successfully resisted,[3] and in the post-1945 world the question has been largely academic.

The time-limit rule for widows' applications was moderated early in 1924;[4] and the rate of pension was stabilized by a series of concessions operative from 1923, 1926 and, finally, 1929. Thus four of the Legion's aims in this early period were accomplished.

This leaves three claims to be accounted for. On the 'Means Test' issue, the Legion's policy of complete exemption for disability pensions was not conceded, but (as we shall see) the Ian Fraser compromise gave the Legion part of what it wanted and was accepted by Smedley Crooke for the N.E.C. as better than nothing. The claims in respect of final awards and the time-limit generally were rather more complicated in their outcome. Neither was granted in precisely the form that the Legion wanted. But even in 1925 after the apparent failure of the Petition to move the Cabinet, 1,100 cases of final awards were cancelled—one for every 800 signatures, Lister claimed.[5] By September 1928, 5,800 awards had been amended.[6] The Cabinet never conceded an appeals system for final awards, but to Legion influence must be attributed the evident policy of re-considering cases.

---

[1] See below appendix 1 for the replies made by the Prime Minister, Stanley Baldwin, to the Legion's 1923 questionnaire.

[2] Sir Henry Betterton, Minister of Labour, to Col. John Brown, Legion Chairman, 18th Dec. 1931. Note added to letter in Journal, Jan. 1932, 256.

[3] Hist. B.L., pp. 67 and 134–5.

[4] See above, ch. XIX.

[5] 1926 Conference, Verb. Rep. 1/20.

[6] Hist. B.L., p. 113.

By the early thirties the time-limit issue was easily the most important single claim. The clash with the Ministry of Pensions precipitated by the then Editor of the *Journal* made necessary a re-statement of policy.[1] After due consideration, the N.E.C. put forward eight demands, whose relative importance may be judged from the fact that seven of them were put forward to the Minister of Pensions and one of them—the time-limit issue—taken to the Prime Minister himself.[2]

The Prime Minister set his face against the legislative change the Legion required. Nevertheless, it would seem that, as with the final awards policy, the Legion got the substance of what it wanted by administrative action. Already in September 1930 a *Journal* editorial had acknowledged that although it was still in the Act, 'the time limit has to all intents and purposes been abolished' for first claims, which were in fact being considered. A. G. Webb, the Legion's pension expert, agreed.[3]

To sum up the outcome of the eleven major claims advanced in roughly the first third of the Legion's history, then, we may say that four claims were not conceded, four were met and three, largely so. But of course the vital question has still to be answered: to what extent were the happenings *successes*?

The Ministry of Pensions battle has already been discussed at some length in the illustrative cases. The conclusion was that the Legion took the initiative even though others took up the cudgels; without its quick response the issue would hardly have come alive in the first place. The Legion also showed sufficient strength of purpose not to let itself be deflected by other concessions. The 75 per cent preference would almost certainly not have been maintained had there not been a well-organized body of ex-servicemen ready to leap to the defence of the principle. Only five years or so after the Armistice, attempts were being made (*e.g.*, at Barnstable) to undermine the principle.

So too with pensions stabilization, one of the most important concessions ever gained by an ex-servicemen's association in this country, affecting as it did nearly one million pensioners. No one outside the Ministry can even estimate what it was worth to pensioners in the inter-war years, but the continued fall in the cost of living made it immensely valuable. Even in 1939, after prices had been rising for several years, the 40s. of twenty years earlier would have been only 29s. if the intentions of the 1919 settlement had not been thwarted by the Legion.

This crediting of the concession to the Legion's account is not, however, unchallengeable. In 1926, the Legion was about to take

<hr>

[1] ibid., p. 156.

[2] Journal, Oct. 1933, 239.   [3] Hist. B.L., p. 132.

credit in a pamphlet when Major Tryon, the Minister of Pensions, got to hear of it and was very annoyed. Sir Frederick Maurice was taken to the Ministry and shown the files to substantiate Tryon's claim that he had recommended this course to the Treasury before the Legion's Petition had been presented. He threatened a public rubuttal if the Legion persisted in its claim.

The fact that Tryon may have already put up this recommendation to the Treasury, however, is not conclusive. It is clear that the very first stabilization which took effect from April 1923 was conceded during the course of the 1922 Election in an attempt to satisfy the Legion, who were complaining about the proposal to abolish the Ministry. And A. G. Webb was surely right to suggest that if there had not been an organized body of ex-service opinion, final stabilization would not have been achieved.[1] The first two stabilizations were only temporary and by 1929 the war would have been sufficiently far off for a down-grading of pensions issues to have become politically possible. So there is not much danger in claiming this as a Legion success. The change of rule for widow's pensions claims was also, surely, a Legion success.

Of the three partial successes, there can be no doubt at all that it was Legion pressure that brought about the administrative concessions regarding final awards and the seven years' time-limit for pensions generally. Although the point is impossible to prove, it is surely plain that unless the Legion had persisted in pressing these issues, the concessions would not have been made.

To judge the 'Means Test' issue is somewhat more difficult on account of the intervention of Ian Fraser, who at that time was pursuing a policy different from the Legion's. His was the compromise that prevailed; the Legion's claim for a complete 'disregard' was a failure. But it was Legion pressure in the first instance that obtained the 'disregard' of 50 per cent in 1931, and it is probable that in the absence of Legion pressure, even that low level of exemption would not have been maintained in the subsequent legislation. Once again the very existence of the Legion may have been significant, and so here, too, we may conclude that the Legion deserves much of the credit for this result.

The attempt to abolish the time-limit marks the end of those pressures arising directly out of the 1914–18 War and the concomitant legislation. The line of demarcation may be conveniently drawn in 1936 when an attempt at the Legion's annual conference to make the N.E.C. run yet another campaign against the time-limit was given short shrift. The year 1936 is also convenient as the dividing-line because it saw the emergence of an entirely new claim, which was for

[1] *Journal*, April 1933, 349.

special legislation to help the 'prematurely aged and broken down ex-servicemen'. How an *ad hoc* committee of the Legion tried to correlate premature senility with war service, and then, failing to impress the Prime Minister, turned that into a claim for the permanently *incapacitated* ex-servicemen has been described elsewhere.[1] The result was abject failure.

By this road, then, we reach the second of the great twentieth-century conflicts. The old battles had to be fought all over again.

2. The War Years

During the earlier part of the second war, the Legion advanced six main claims, all but one of which were concerned with pensions. The new Royal Warrant of 1939 started off on the wrong foot by providing a scale of pensions lower than that granted to the men of the first war. This lower scale was justified in terms of the fall in the cost of living since the Royal Warrant of 1919 but the effect was to create a dual pensions system which it was difficult to defend.[2] No opportunity was provided for ex-servicemen to claim an 'alternative pension', *i.e.*, a claim for a higher rate of pension where pre-war earnings had been above average.[3] Once again the time-limit on claims reappeared, which was understandable because the original Act had never been repealed. The burden of proof when entitlement to pension was being considered still rested on the claimant, and there was no provision for appeal to an independent body, which represented a reversion to the pre-1919 position. In this respect, therefore, the ex-servicemen's position under the 1939 Royal Warrant had actually deteriorated.[4] As for the employment of disabled men, reliance was still placed upon the voluntary system.

What was the outcome of these six claims? By a series of adjustments in 1940, 1942 and August 1943, the 1939 scale was assimilated to the 1919 one in terms of the basic rate. 'Alternative Pensions' were not conceded; in fact 'alternative pensions' under the earlier Warrant had been granted to very few pensioners, *i.e.*, it had never assumed much importance.[5] Once again, the authorities were adamant in their opposition to the abolition of the time-limit, which survived until 1947, but the Minister was permitted to make regulations enabling out-of-time claims to be considered. The Minister of Pensions announced in the House that those regulations would not be less favourable than the regulations that had governed out-of-time claims arising from the 1914–18 War. This represented a return to the inter-war practice, and was a partial victory. The claims for independent

---

[1] Hist. B.L., pp. 208–13.
[2] ibid., p. 262. [3] Royal Warrant, 6th Dec. 1919.
[4] Hist. B.L., p. 261. [5] ibid., p. 263.

appeal on entitlement and for the removal of the burden of proof were completely successful. After a battle fought over two years, the Government, in 1943, granted a right of appeal on entitlement, with a further appeal to the High Court on points of law, which turned out after the war had ended to be a very significant addition to the pensions appeal system that had been originally established. By October 1943 the first of the Appeal Tribunals was at work in London.[1] In addition, for the first time in the history of war pensions in this country, the burden of proof was transferred, in effect, from the appellant to the State. Sir John Anderson, as he then was, enunciated the principle that was to govern pension claims in future:

'We establish the presumption that a man's condition as recorded on his admission to the Service was in fact his condition at that time; and that any subsequent deterioration in his condition was due to his service. We provide that there shall be no onus of proof on the claimant and that the benefit of any doubt should be given to the claimant.'[2]

This decision proved to be of immense importance; supplemented by High Court judgements it has come near to implementing the old Federation claim—'fit for service, fit for pension'.

The policy of the compulsory employment of disabled men was provided for in the Disabled Persons (Employment) Bill, 1943, which required employers to engage the war (and industrial) disabled on a quota basis. The original proposals did not distinguish between war disabled and civilian disabled but early the following year a preference for ex-servicemen and women of all wars was established within the statutory quota.[3]

How far was the Legion responsible for these successes? There can be little doubt that it played a major part in achieving them. The employment-of-disabled-men policy is the most ambiguous case: in the 1920's the Legion had completely failed to establish it, but it seems likely that the Legion's own proposals in 1941 had some influence on the Tomlinson Report (which led to the Bill), although it may be that the coming of a second total war would in any case have made some such provision unavoidable.[4] At least there can be no doubt that the Legion led the way in obtaining preference for ex-servicemen *within* the quota. The Minister of Labour, Ernest Bevin, had set his face against a statutory preference for ex-servicemen but the Legion turned the tables on him.[5]

The credit for putting the onus in pensions claims on the State is

[1] ibid., pp. 263–65.

[2] ibid., pp. 265–6. [3] ibid., pp. 269–70.

[4] ibid., p. 260. [5] ibid., pp. 269–70.

partly the Legion's: certainly this policy had been impressed on the Government, but many politicians played a part in this fundamental change, and it is very difficult now to separate the Legion's contribution from theirs.

In the other two matters, the Legion's hand is very much easier to discern. The assimilation of the two rates of pension was certainly the Legion's handiwork: it was they who had pressed year after year for raising the new rate to the level of the old. And while the campaign for independent appeal was helped by 'outsiders', possibly the greatest single factor was A. G. Webb's skill in obtaining the backing of the B.M.A. to the proposition that doctors *could* be provided to service the tribunals. The Government had consistently set its face against independent appeal in wartime and took its stand on the findings of the Shakespeare Committee, but Webb made it almost impossible for the authorities to resist further.[1] Certainly the prime mover was the Legion.

Thus the Legion may be said to have had a 'good war'. It failed to establish 'alternative pensions' and to abolish the time-limit, but it played *some* part in the compulsory-employment-of-the-disabled policy (and the major part in establishing preference), and in transferring the burden of proof to the State: it also played the major part in bringing together the 1919 and 1939 rates of pension as well as in establishing independent appeal on entitlement to pension.

3. *The Post-War Years*

In the post-war period the Legion has pursued four main objectives. Two of these were inherited from an earlier period and are quickly disposed of. Independent appeal on *assessment* of pensions was granted in 1946, and the time-limit on claims disappeared the following year. Thus two of the oldest problems were expeditiously solved. On the other hand, as we know, the Legion failed to retain the Ministry of Pensions as a separate entity.

The fourth major claim was entirely new and of an entirely different order. At the 1946 Conference, the enterprise of two men who had served in the second war, L. Pellowe and K. C. G. Chambers, committed the Legion to a policy of doubling the basic rate of pension. This was one of the very few occasions in the Legion's history when the rank and file carried the leadership along with it. For two years the leadership temporized, but once again, at the 1948 Conference, the rank and file insisted on their getting on with the job. As a result the leaders, if somewhat reluctantly, organized systematic campaigns between 1948 and 1957, when partial satisfaction was achieved and the campaign temporarily called off.

[1] ibid., pp. 263–5.

The full story of that campaign cannot be recounted here: it would require a substantial section of a book to itself. It is sufficient for our inquiry to say that the basic rate was raised three times in the period here dealt with.[1] The first increase in the basic rate was announced by Heathcoat Amory, the new Minister of Pensions, in March 1952, some four months after the return of the first post-war Conservative Government. The second increase was announced in February 1955, three months before the Government appealed to the country and was operative from the very month of the election. The third and greatest increase ever was made known in November 1957, payable from January/February 1958.

It is natural that each of the ex-servicemen's associations should claim these increases as victories. All unofficial groups that try to influence official groups must also try to translate concomitance as causation; that is probably a psychological necessity, if year in, year out the leaders are to find the energy and the money to proceed. Hence the claims put forward by the Legion and BLESMA, to mention no others.[2] Even *The Times* has given the seal of its approval to such a view by stating, in a special article, that the Legion's—

'brightest achievement, since 1945, has been in persuading Parliament to raise the basic rates of war pensions to 85s. a week'.[3]

How hard it is to *prove* such a claim is clear from an examination of the movement of social payments since the war. The first striking feature is that the basic rate of war pension is never raised in isolation from certain other social payments: unemployment and sickness benefits and retirement pensions. Moreover, in two cases out of three, the increases in these social insurance benefits were somewhat greater than the increases in the basic rate of war pension: 25 per cent as against 22.2 per cent in 1952; 23 per cent as opposed to 22.7 per cent in 1955. True, the 1958 adjustment rather favoured the war pensioner, the increase in whose basic rate exceeded, for instance, the increase in retirement pensions by 0.9 per cent. But the overall percentage increase, 1946–58, clearly favoured the recipient of social insurance payments by more than 3 per cent (92.3 per cent to 88.8 per cent).

Of course, no one is likely to overlook the larger base from which war pensioners started in 1946, or that, correspondingly, the percentage increase in their basic rate yielded larger amounts than the others received. In the whole period, the percentage increase gave

---

[1] This is not quite true. The third increase was paid from the beginning of 1958, but it was announced in November 1957 and to exclude it from the inquiry would be unduly rigid.

[2] See, *e.g.*, Legion Annual Report, 1957–8, pp. 5–6, and BLESMA, 1952 Conference Report, p. 2.

[3] *The Times*, 7th Nov. 1958.

war pensioners (on the basic) an extra 40s., while the 'triplets'' benefits rose by only 24s. But equally one cannot overlook the fact that 'when father turns we all turn', *i.e.*, social payments tend to move upwards at roughly the same time and at something like the same percentage increase. The crucial question therefore becomes: who is 'father'? If the successes claimed by the ex-servicemen's organizations are to be justified, it must be shown that they alone made the running, and pulled the others along with them.

Can such a hypothesis be *proved*? Hardly. This is partly because the evidence of influence is usually so very difficult to obtain, quite apart from the fundamental problem of causation. But there is also evidence pointing the other way: if the ex-service organizations had made the running, one would have expected them to gain at least the same overall percentage increase as the social insurance beneficiaries. The reverse has in fact happened; the presumed leading horse received a smaller percentage increase than the loose head.

It is also relevant that the two major political parties and the civil servants now think of social payments *as a whole*, an assimilation epitomized by the merger of the Ministry of Pensions and the Ministry of National Insurance in 1953 but inherent in the situation long before it happened. Brigadier J. G. Smyth, V.C., then Parliamentary Secretary to the Ministry of Pensions, was really speaking for both major parties when he pointed out to the BLESMA Conference delegates in 1952 that there were 'a lot of other factors' related to pensions policy, 'one of the most important' of which 'is that of the industrially injured'.[1] His view, of course, was that the war disabled deserved top priority, but the trend of post-war legislation and political thinking has been to assimilate war pensions to social insurance generally. Certainly this was the Labour Government's point of view.

The Legion itself has, of course, been perfectly well aware of the new situation. As early as 1944 the Pensions Committee was prepared to lay down 'that the Legion should not seek to obtain a higher basic rate of pension for war disablement than for disablement in industry', but the N.E.C. did not agree.[2] At the 1948 Conference Colonel Grimshaw, Chairman of the Pensions Committee, observed that 'the disability pensions are tied to the industrial disablement and *social insurance schemes*'.[3]

If, then, war pensions payments have been assimilated to social insurance, and if in an inflationary world, social insurance payments must presumably be readjusted from time to time in order to restore

---

[1] 1952 Conference Report, p. 12.

[2] N.E.C. Mins., 2nd Dec. 1944, Min. 2.

[3] Verb. Rep., p. 24. Emphasis added.

at least part of their purchasing power, does it follow that the ex-servicemen's organizations need not exert any pressure? Need they do any more than sit back and wait for purchasing power to be restored from time to time?

I think there are at least two reasons why pressure has to be exerted. In the first place, the purchasing power of *war pensions* might not be restored at all, or only partly. Already, only nine years after the war, mean voices were raised to advance just that proposition. Thus, for instance, *The Economist* could write in 1954:

'The restoration of 1946 values seems to have been less appropriate in these instances [the war and industrial casualties] than in the case of National Insurance benefits. The disabled, relatively few of whom are unemployable, are allowed to work and retain their pensions, and have consequently participated in the increase in earnings since 1946.'[1]

Whether war pensioners are in work or not is, of course, entirely irrelevant. The attempt to relate earnings to pensions was abandoned as early as March 1917 after it had proved to be entirely unworkable. Ever since then pensions have been paid for loss of function and amenities, and it is elementary justice that such payment should not be eroded by inflation.

In the absence of systematic pressure, the politicians themselves, to say nothing of all the other claimants on the national income, might well be willing to follow *The Economist*'s advice. If no one spoke up for the war pensioners as a class, they might easily be neglected. The danger is particularly acute because there is no 'contributory element' in war pensions (except the contribution of human limb or flesh), and so it would be easy for some sophist to argue that whereas there was an obligation to maintain the real value of insurance benefits, no such obligation held good for war pensioners —'after all they haven't paid in anything'.

There is a related reason. Even if there were no intention of allow-ing, by default, a cut in the real value of war pensions, pressure might have the effect of bringing forward the date of adjustment. It is true that this did not happen in the period 1946–52, when, on the contrary, ex-servicemen were unable to prevent a serious erosion in the value of their pensions. Retail prices rose steadily but the adjustment of pensions was not made until as late as the beginning of 1952. Even then the basic rate was increased by little more than 22 per cent, whereas the official index of retail prices showed an increase of 25 per cent between 1947 and 1951. The London and Cambridge Economic Service index of working-class spending showed a far greater increase.

In the event, it seems likely that pressure had the effect of com-

---

[1] *The Economist*, 4th Dec. 1954, 809.

mitting the incoming Conservative Government, which promptly raised war pensions to something approaching the 1946 level and three years later made a further adjustment that, measured by the official index, was much more generous than it need have been. Doubtless the shadow of the 1955 election lay across that decision: 'Dishing the Labour Party' was *The Economist*'s comment.[1] Even so, electoral calculation may have been bound up with sustained pressure. Thus, on balance, even though the adjustments might seem, at first glance, to have been more or less automatic, one concludes that pressure had to be exerted by the ex-servicemen's associations.

What view, then, should be taken of the Legion's influence in the post-1945 period? No one could demonstrate that the grant of independent appeal on the assessment of pensions and the abolition of the time-limit on claims constituted Legion successes; on the other hand, the Legion had argued for these policies for so many years that it is not unreasonable to give it the credit, if only provisionally. The attempt to veto the merger of the Ministry of Pensions with the Ministry of National Insurance was a complete failure. As for the doubling of the basic rate of pension, that was not in fact achieved and no one can with certainty attribute the three increases to the Legion's efforts, so that it was generous of *The Times* to claim the raising of the rate to 85s. as the Legion's 'brightest achievement'. On the other hand, reasons have been adduced for thinking that its campaign was both necessary and productive.

How, then, should one sum up the Legion's influence over the whole period, 1917–57? It is first necessary to stress the crudity of the foregoing assessment. Nothing has been *proved*. On the other hand, I may be allowed to take refuge in the reply attributed to Spooner, the Warden of New College. As a student weak in mathematics he was asked how he had fared in a geometry examination. He answered:

'I don't think I *proved* anything, but I rendered it very probable.'

Subject to the implied proviso, one may say that the Legion enjoyed over the period a substantial degree of success. In my judgement the important successes certainly *outnumbered* the important failures. But dare one take the further step of claiming that the important successes *outweighed* the important failures? I do so without hesitation but it is as well to emphasize that this requires yet another judgement. For the aims (and therefore the successes and failures) were not of equal value and ideally ought to have been assigned 'weights', but the merest glance at the list reveals that the construction of 'weights' would have been an impossible task. So in

[1] ibid.

making the transition from 'outnumber' to 'outweigh' I am in effect assigning my own values to the various claims. But I do so 'jointly' rather than 'severally', *i.e.*, on the basis of a general impression of the net result of all the influence exerted in the forty years under review. This procedure is less arbitrary than it sounds because it is derived from some years' continuous study and from interviews not only with Legionaries (and other ex-servicemen) of two generations but also with some high-ranking officials of the Ministry of Pensions. None the less I readily acknowledge that an element of arbitrariness remains.

How does the Legion's success compare with that achieved by other great associations, especially within the same culture and in the same historical period? The question can be raised but not answered, for at the time of writing there are no other comparable detailed analyses of pressure groups in this country. Until we have an assessment of the pressure-group operations of at least some of our many multi-purpose associations, it will not be possible to see the Legion's achievements in perspective. Meanwhile one has to fall back again upon an impression—a very strong one—that the Legion is entitled to quite high rank in the universe of British pressure groups.

Now that an assessment has at least been attempted, it is possible to try to make good a deficiency in the discussion of the techniques and strategy of influence, whose evaluation was usually only implicit or at most incidental. It must be said at once, however, that the attempt to evaluate techniques is bound to be unrewarding. It is not simply that the assessment of influence itself is at most no more than 'very probable'; one would need to know also the proportionate use to which each technique had been put, both in terms of its own successes and in the wider context of all techniques and all successes. Even then the successes would have to be placed in order of importance, otherwise a technique that achieved a small success fairly often would rank higher than a technique that brought about a major success once in a decade.

Were these difficulties surmountable, one would still be confronted with another obstacle which is perhaps for ex-servicemen peculiarly formidable. The possibility of obtaining decisions is no doubt never uniformly distributed throughout the complex of official groups, yet it is possible to conceive that for some unofficial groups there may be more than one decision-making centre. If so, their techniques ought to be the more productive. On the other hand, if the (relevant) decision-making powers are very largely concentrated in one group, then by definition the attempts to secure decisions from the other official groups are bound to prove very largely abortive. Of course, ex-servicemen generally did not at first realize that; for instance, they thought for a considerable time that Parliament itself was an autonomous decision-making body, amenable to direct pressure. For this reason, and because it is part of the general record for other students and part of the evidence for the chapter on strategy, the techniques for influencing Parliament were set out in detail. But we know in fact that no twentieth-century Parliament itself could, 'of its own volition', have met the ex-servicemen's demands. Nor was the Ministry of Pensions in general any better placed.

In so characterizing techniques, one is of course applying a very severe test: did this or that approach actually produce the required decision? If the test were the incidental usefulness of some move or other (*e.g.* the publicity secured when an issue is raised in Parliament), it would be another matter. And this would be true *a fortiori* when indirect influence on a decision taken elsewhere could be demonstrated. But then one would have entered the field of strategy. In fact, in the last resort, what requires evaluation is not so much techniques as strategies.

No single pattern emerges from a study of the successful strategies. The ends-means relationship was never a neat and tidy one, and in many decisions (the time limit on men's applications for pensions and the final awards issue, for instance), it is quite impossible to say where the credit lies, so long were the decisions a-coming and so many and varied were the methods used. Ignoring these difficulties (justifiable in reducing a complex matter to some sort of order), one may say that three successful influence-patterns are discernible (though not necessarily appropriate any longer).

The first successful pattern is to influence the Cabinet through Parliament, either 'ante-natally', as in a General Election (though this could of course be treated as having a direct impact on the Cabinet), or 'post-natally'. The Legion's veto on the proposal to abolish the Ministry of Pensions in 1922 was achieved during an Election. The action then taken was apparently sufficient, for the issue died an unnatural death (no more being heard of it); but on occasions influence exerted during an Election has been maintained in the early years of the new Parliament. The 1923 issue of the time limit on applications for widows' pensions is an example; so is the 1925 attempt to remedy various pensions grievances. On other occasions, again, pressure is necessarily confined to Parliament itself: the Means Test case in the thirties and the 1943 issue of preference for ex-servicemen within the quota.

In all such cases (indeed, in all strategies after 'consultation' has been established), deputations to the Ministries will be quite frequent, but most of these are bound to yield few concrete decisions, at least as far as concerns ex-servicemen's groups. But a second successful strategy entails persuasion of a Minister by way of a deputation, in the expectation that he will persuade the Cabinet. The gaining of the 75 per cent preference for ex-servicemen on all relief work may have been an example of this.[1] So was the success of the Legion deputation in 1939 in convincing the Minister that the new Royal Warrant was seriously inadequate. There are other more ambiguous cases. Certainly the Minister of Pensions went to the Cabinet in 1925 to advocate stabilization, as a successor apparently took the same path in 1956 to argue for an age allowance for the limbless. But the first event was one stage in a long-drawn-out campaign, in which it is difficult to trace the 'plan' and impossible to allocate credit. The second event was a less complicated one but still part of a substantial campaign. However, it is possible to identify one of the successful (and obvious) strategies as—association convinces Minister: Minister persuades Cabinet.

The third successful design combines influence in Parliament with the mobilization of some expert or authoritative group to destroy or weaken the opposition. Three permutations present themselves. The authoritative committee may be itself drawn from an official group: the role of the Select Committee in the securing of a statutory right to pension in 1919 springs to mind. But associations may also turn to unofficial groups. From 1941 onwards the Legion pressed hard, by way of Parliament and Ministry, for independent appeal on entitlement to pension. Pressure in the House and in some newspapers won the initial advantage, forcing the Minister to refer the matter to a sub-committee of the C.A.C., but the *coup de grâce* was given by the B.M.A., which, approached by A. G. Webb for the Legion, declared that the doctors *could* be found.

The most striking example of this pattern is to be found in the post-1945 period: BLESMA's activation of the surgeons and other specialists for the defeat of two official committees: the Hancock and Rock Carling Committees. Deputations had waited for years on successive Ministers of both major parties and two great demonstrations had been launched, without the slightest success. Here the winning sequence is evidently—association convinces All-Party Parliamentary Committee: latter enlists aid of outside experts of great eminence: association and especially All-Party Committee use experts' testimony to overcome Ministry's experts and convince Minister: Minister goes to Cabinet.

Of course, it must be re-emphasized that these patterns are far too neat and tidy; the reality was more complex. In particular, the patterns were either shot through with P.R. campaigns or at least

[1] Haig, presidential address, Verb. Rep. 1922, p. 3.

superimposed upon a steady P.R. output, but what all that achieved *in actual decisions* no one can tell. The third influence-pattern suggests, certainly, that the crucial achievement is to win over an authoritative 'public' rather than the public at large. Even so, for ex-servicemen to have dispensed with P.R. would have been a foolhardy gesture. In such a society as ours, and in their situation, especially in recent years, they could hardly *not* have resorted to it. P.R. is like a King's favourite: one suspects that she has no great influence with the King or with anyone in the Palace but one neglects her at one's peril.

PART SEVEN

Factors in Successful Influence

XXVII

TO COMMAND SUCCESS

IN so far as ex-servicemen's associations have imposed or shaped
official decisions, what factors account for their success? Here one
has in mind the associations' own qualities, characteristics and
'situation', realizing of course that these cannot in reality be
abstracted from the 'total situation', *i.e.*, the structure of official and
unofficial power, the circumstances and the political culture.

The total membership as such counts for less than one might have
supposed. Mere numbers do not explain the effectiveness of the pre-
Legion societies. The Comrades had a large membership, but its
strength came from *its* 'Establishment' connexions and from the
financial backing of industry and the City. The Federation liked to
claim a million members, but they were never present and correct
(*i.e.*, paying) at the same time. In any case the quality of the Federation's leadership was more significant, which is also true of BLESMA,
never more than 12,000 strong.

Of course, no one suggests that absolute size does not count at all.
A large association normally has considerable financial resources and
a viable structure, and carries weight with official groups, or at least
cannot be ignored. For this reason alone neither the Comrades nor
the Federation, nor, eventually, the Legion could have been left out
of official reckoning. Size commands attention.

Whether 'attention' will lead to concession obviously depends on
many other factors even within the realm of numerical strength.
Official groups naturally have an eye to the question: what proportion
of the potential membership does this or that association represent?
Judged by such bodies as the N.F.U. or F.B.I., ex-servicemen's
groups have never achieved a high 'density'. BLESMA's 12,000 is
said to have accounted for 30 per cent of its potential, which is little
enough but far more than any other ex-servicemen's association has
achieved. Of the pre-Legion societies, it is difficult to speak, so great
was the difference between the 'book' and the actual paying membership, but even the Federation's nominal million would not have
meant more than a 'density' of some 20 per cent. A decade or more
after its foundation the Legion may have achieved a 10 per cent
'density';[1] the post-1945 figures are impressive until it is recalled that

[1] Admiral Henry Bruce, chairman of the Metropolitan Area, in *The Times,*
5th Feb. 1934.

there were then two wars to recruit from. It is hard to say exactly what the potential then was, but the proportion in membership can hardly have exceeded about 15 per cent.

Low 'density', however, may be offset in at least two ways. Official groups may be persuaded or may simply think that it is higher than it really is. At the time of its foundation the Legion had a paying membership of about 18,000, but serious military commentators like Cyril Falls gave it credit for millions, and serious newspapers like *The Times* and *Daily Telegraph* actually specified a membership of between two and three millions.[1] When in 1922 the Legion vetoed the proposal to dismantle the Ministry of Pensions, it had, as paid-up members, something like 2 per cent of its potential, but doubtless the official groups gave it credit for rather more.

Low 'density' may also be offset by high 'concentration'. Even if the official groups failed to recognize the Legion's low 'density', they knew a united movement when they saw one. For whatever 'densities' the early associations may have achieved, they were in fact deeply divided among themselves, whereas from 1921 onwards the Legion could fairly claim to speak for the British ex-serviceman. To that, L.E.S.M.A. in effect entered a disclaimer in 1932, but this sloughing away of the limbless disabled only modifies without essentially weakening the contrast with the United States, with France and with pre-Hitler Germany.

Given the total membership, the 'density' and the degree of 'concentration', the zeal of both leadership and rank and file has obvious importance. A small society like BLESMA may make up in fervour what it lacks in size; by the same token, a large society like the Legion may add cubits to its stature. All associations have had their leavening of dedicated men. Some of them have been 'political personalities', assertive, pugnacious, determined, who gave to the ex-service cause what might in different circumstances have been harnessed for one of the great reform movements. Others have been votaries of a cult of the dead who have turned with a quasi-religious zeal to the service of the living, both those who survived all perils and the dependants of those who did not. For the beneficiaries of pressure in a general association are not simply or even primarily the members themselves, still less the dedicated few. In the Legion, for instance, just as 80 per cent or more of its individual case-work in pensions is for non-members, so the influence it exerts is on behalf of the whole ex-service community, non-members (including ex-members) as well as members, the widows and orphans as well as the wounded. This is the real meaning of the Legion's motto: 'Service not Self'. But what-

---

[1] Hist. B.L., p. 42.

ever the source of the zeal, the effect of having an active few with 'push and go' has been, of course, to increase the apparent numerical strength.

The term 'leavening' may be given a geographical as well as an organizational meaning—the dispersion of organized ex-servicemen throughout the country as a whole, which may affect not only public opinion but also the calculations of the decision-makers themselves. In this context BLESMA (with only 120 or so branches) is evidently weak but the Legion, by contrast, has always been extremely strong. The 116,000 members who, theoretically, faced Bonar Law in 1922 were distributed in some 2,000 branches, which made them thin on the ground but on the ground almost everywhere. Today there are some 5,300 branches. No one supposes that these are all active or really 'alive'; on the other hand, the local service (*i.e.*, benevolent) committees (officially calculated at 5,000), the clubs and the village halls help to sustain an impression of ubiquity that few pressure groups can rival and perhaps none surpass. That impression probably enters into the consciousness of the official groups and becomes part of the premises on which decisions are taken.

Like mere numbers, mere wealth may easily be rated too highly. It can never be thought of apart from other factors or apart from a particular social context. It may be irrelevant to influence, which can come from having the 'right connexions' (the Comrades) or from the official groups' need for co-operation (the Legion). Much or most of the wealth may not be available for influence-work; thus the Legion's 'social services' took altogether something like £800,000 in 1957, or not far short of two-thirds of its income. On the other hand, it would of course be stupid to write off wealth as an asset to the exercise of influence. The fate of the Comrades after the rich had ceased to provide on a sufficient scale and of the Federation after 1919 illustrates the essential point—that wealth makes possible a viable organization. So long as BLESMA had to struggle to survive, it obviously could not impinge on the political process; it began to do so only when it had achieved, if not wealth, then financial stability in terms of its particular role and commitments. Of course, as with the Legion, most of BLESMA's income is earmarked for its 'social services', but in terms of influence that restriction is less inhibiting than it seems. A BLESMA made viable for service in the one sense is capable of being used in the other. Above all, a British Legion made the vehicle for benevolence on a grand scale is put in the position of being able to convey influence as well. The purpose of Poppy Day is certainly not to finance a pressure group; its effect, equally certainly, is to produce and sustain virtually an independent centre of political power. And the very act of disbursing the proceeds of Poppy Day helps the Legion to maintain a favourable image that in turn enhances its political influence.

Here one reaches the nub of this discussion: it is not mere numbers, nor wealth as such, that account for whatever success ex-servicemen's associations have enjoyed, but rather, as the greatest single factor, a favourable image, or prestige. It has two sides and three roots, one of which does not spread beyond official circles. There is, in the first place, prestige in the eyes of the public at large: compare the public's attitude to the T.U.C. or still more to individual trade unions in recent years, or, on the other hand, to the F.B.I., about which there is probably no public opinion at all. Prestige with the public is likely to mean prestige with official groups, if only because some of these are elective.

The most fundamental source of prestige is obviously 'services rendered'. With the exception of BLESMA,[1] such services are not credited to the very men who join and run the associations, which rather reflect the glory of soldiers, sailors and airmen generally, including, perhaps especially, those who died before their time. Across the path of the early associations lay the shadow of Delville Wood. Through the R.A.F.A. we see the boy-men laughing—and then disintegrating—in the morning sunlight. The Legion is a prism of many flashing colours: the Somme, Gallipoli, Jutland; Alamein, the Ardennes and the war at sea.

All the early associations, including the Comrades in the eyes of some unimpeachable Conservatives, were under some suspicion because of their connexions with 'the politicians'. The lessons of seventeenth-century England and of contemporary Russia had not been lost upon people generally, who regarded a political (ex-)soldiery with apprehension. Thus, 'ditching the politicians' was a source of prestige, quite certainly in the eyes of official groups but probably among the public at large too. That 'ditching' was virtually concluded in the course of founding the Legion; neither BLESMA nor R.A.F.A. showed any signs of reversing the trend. Nor, the politicians having been ditched, did any of these associations ever deal with them again in *party* terms. The Legion even slowly acquired a reputation for being not simply non-party but above-party, a higher pinnacle of achievement.

Prestige in this general sense may have consequences that reinforce it. Out of prestige came royal patronage, which, in an age of great royal popularity, in turn increased prestige. Prestige generally means a good press: with few exceptions, Fleet Street and hundreds of provincial editors and reporters have been ready to give the ex-servicemen's cause a boost, which is true also of the broadcasting and

---

[1] St. Dunstan's is not an association *of* ex-servicemen in the relevant sense.

television authorities. How far the Legion's own **P.R.** output contributed to this support by mass media, what that support achieved and what impact the Legion may have made on the public independently, no one can say, but it is reasonable to suppose that it sustained the 'image' if did not produce, immediately, a single decision.

The third source of prestige is specific to the decision-makers. In the last resort, despite disagreements, the associations have generally continued to co-operate with the authorities. The Federation and even the Comrades were willing to resort to non-co-operation, and once practised it, but their successors, especially the Legion, never followed their example. As we know from the discussion of bargaining,[1] the Legion leaders have been reluctant to make the fullest use of their bargaining asset (the authorities' need of them) by even the *threat* of non-co-operation. So, too, with the more general attempts to exert influence.

Is it certain, however, that the associations would have obtained more, over the whole period, by withdrawing co-operation if only for a time than they actually won by capitalizing their prestige? It is by no means certain. On some issues, such as the proposed merger of the Ministry of Pensions with the Ministry of National Insurance in 1953, a *real* determination to cease to co-operate in the administration of (war) pensions, locally as well as nationally, might well have saved the day. It would never, on the other hand, have brought about a doubling of the basic rate of pension. But of course on these issues prestige was barren too.

On the general issue two considerations have to be weighed. On the one hand, the unwillingness of the leaders to follow the doctors, farmers and solicitors in even a threat of non-co-operation does not prevent the bargaining asset from earning some interest of its own accord. The official groups are perfectly well aware of the usefulness of bodies such as the Legion and BLESMA, and that awareness enters into the premises of their decisions. So the objective fact of the need for co-operation does yield something even in the absence of sanctions. On the other hand, prestige may inhibit counter-pressure. There is no 'natural' opposition group to the Legion, still less to BLESMA (except perhaps, on some issues, the trade unions); nevertheless, prestige may have prevented any potential counter-group from mobilizing.

In the last resort, this is an 'if' question and unanswerable; what we know is that prestige *has been* the factor mainly relied upon by the associations for most of the period under review, though it was a prestige buttressed by an objective need for their co-operation. But two other factors have also to be mentioned. Because the leaders

[1] See chapter XIX.

were in command of the ship, they could change course and speed rapidly, unhampered in practice by the restrictions of the 'lower-deck' (or radical) theory of democracy. Secondly, cohesiveness (based on shared experiences and comradeship) has been a significant factor. Specifically in the Legion's history, the word 'unity' has had the status of a key symbol: *unity* to parallel the unity they *thought* had won the war on the Western Front . . . *unity* negotiations leading to 'the *Unity* Conference' that gave birth to the Legion. Cohesiveness has turned the Legion into a hammer for use by the governing few in their substantially successful efforts to forge decisions out of prestige.

Thus, among the associations' own qualities, characteristics and 'situation', a number of factors bear upon successful influence, but the most important single one is prestige, based fundamentally on 'services rendered'—

> 'Tis not in mortals to command success,
> But we'll do more, Sempronius; we'll deserve it.'

CONCLUSIONS

E X-SERVICEMEN'S associations in this country were products of the peculiar circumstances of our first citizens' war and of the divisions within the political culture that then appeared. The circumstances included economic elements, (*e.g.*, war pensions) but also elements of another character—a Cabinet decision, expressed in an Act of Parliament, that outraged the returned soldiers' and sailors' sense of justice. Divisions within the political culture were even more significant: the community ceased to be agreed in the values and beliefs relating to the objects and modes of government. These differences, with their concomitant emotional attitudes, tended to set the veterans apart from their fellows. Isolated in this sense, they formed societies of their own, which had no previous history but like Athene sprang fully armed from the head of Zeus—a sign of the cultural conflict.

The circumstances and the political culture not only produced the associations but also shaped their aims. The economic factors and the outraged sense of justice provided much of the substance of ex-servicemen's demands, but the divisions in the culture gave rise to aims of another kind—those, 'external' to the associations as such, that reflected the general social and political conflicts. In the degree that organized ex-servicemen took up positions for or against the socio-economic order, they were advancing beyond the pale of interest-group politics into the battlefield of party politics. Accordingly it is no surprise that among the methods employed to achieve aims was alignment with political parties. In the sense that these ex-servicemen were not simply exerting influence within a given socio-economic framework but even challenging it, the movement was becoming extremist.

The country was saved from the danger of (ex-)soldiers as such in politics by a closing of the gap in the political culture. Even during the war, some official (*i.e.*, Cabinet) decisions helped the process of reaching a new consensus, but it may be that the nature of the new weapons, the character of the soldiers and veterans and the quality of their experiences were, indirectly and cumulatively, of greater importance. For these were the factors that shaped the role of ex-servicemen's associations as important agents of cultural change in this period. They articulated the demands not only of their members but also of the many veterans who did not join, or who joined but left as soon as their specific grievances were settled. They constituted an entirely new grouping in the political life of the country; it was vital that their demands should be made known systematically to the decision-makers.

The closing of the gap in the culture affected both aims and methods. The 'domestic' aims (and so the necessary decisions) ceased to be so urgent; fewer 'first-order' decisions were required. 'External' aims lost their *raison d'être*; alignment with a political party whatever degree of justification it might have had. The joining together of the major societies in 1921 to form the British Legion marks the 'neutralization' of the movement. One association committed to transforming the social framework went its own way into oblivion; later a Communist body shot into the air like a rocket on 5th November (or 4th July) and as quickly disappeared. The founding of the Legion meant that the danger of an extremist movement had passed.

Thereafter the Legion, joined by the R.A.F. Association and BLESMA, could settle down to being an interest group proper, exerting influence to achieve its objectives within an accepted social system. In content, the objectives gradually changed in the inter-war years to take account of the economic collapse in 1920 and the falling price-level (and hence rise in the real value of pensions) that followed. Employment policy became the dominant theme.

In methods, for reasons partly of royal pressure but fundamentally of the changed determinants of strategy, ex-servicemen gradually withdrew from the *electoral* process as well as from the other relatively direct attempts to influence the Cabinet. What determines the strategy of influence? Strategy reflects the structure of official power; the articulation of unofficial groups, including the petitioning group itself; the circumstances and the political culture (or sub-culture) which shape the claims that groups make and accordingly the decisions they require. During and immediately after the First World War, these factors made for a series of relatively direct approaches to the Cabinet, but as the years advanced a strategy of indirect approach became more appropriate.

This new strategy entailed an attempt to exert influence indirectly both within the complex of official groups (*e.g.*, via the Ministry rather than by seeking out the Prime Minister himself), and as between official groups and unofficial groups (a greater stress on public relations methods in the hope of creating a climate favourable to certain decisions). No association can say what the public relations method achieved, but only a very bold or even foolhardy association would have deliberately turned its back on it. After the 1939–45 War, some reversal to a direct strategy was observable on BLESMA's part, but on the whole the trend towards indirectness was sustained.

How effective were these attempts at exerting influence? To answer this question, the exertions of the British Legion were examined over a period of thirty-six years, and from an admittedly crude assessment it appeared that the important successes outnumbered and outweighed the important failures, and that the Legion might well rank high in the universe of pressure groups. BLESMA was not subjected to this scrutiny, but can be judged (*e.g.*, from its age allowance campaign) an effective pressure group.

The Legion's effectiveness having been crudely assessed, interest naturally turned to the methods deemed to have been successful, and three 'influence-patterns' were identified. In searching for 'internal' factors (as distinct from methods) to account for successful influence, numerical strength was evaluated, and attention drawn not only to absolute size but also to the degree of 'concentration' achieved, to zealous leadership and support, and to dispersion 'on the ground'. The significance of wealth as a kind of matrix for pressure-group activity was then noted, but more importance was attached to the internal structure and mode of government of the associations, which make possible quick decisions of a tactical and policy kind with no danger of a reverse or lack of support by the rank and file. Cohesiveness, too, is important, but the fundamental factor was seen to be prestige, buttressed by the official groups' need of organized ex-servicemen's co-operation.

In more general terms, this inquiry throws light on the nature of cultural change and on M. René Rémond's discussion of extremist ex-servicemen's associations;[1] it also throws light on the actual working of British politics, conceived of as a policy-making process, and so has implications for the study of politics and for the role of pressure groups in communities of the liberal-democratic kind.

The process of cultural change is an immensely complicated subject, but judging from our experience in the First World War, new private associations may be among the more important innovating agencies. If the culture is deeply divided, then the community is tending to fall apart. It will not come together again until a new consensus is reached. New associations embodying new values, beliefs and emotional attitudes seem to be important instrumentalities tending towards that new consensus, although the willingness, in the end, of the decision-makers to make the necessary accommodation is another prerequisite.

Where the cultural gap is, for whatever reason, not closed, there would one expect to find an extremist ex-servicemen's movement.

[1] See above, p. 11.

Some British veterans did tend, for a short period, towards violence, did present some challenge to the existing social order and so did tend to behave in a fashion more appropriate to a political party than to an interest group. The movement did throw up a determined left wing; extremism was in the air. All the same a new consensus was reached and the moment of danger passed. Where, however, the political culture remains divided, as in France, the ex-servicemen's movement will naturally tend to be extreme.

If these suggestions are valid, two questions arise. Why did ex-servicemen's organizations in France apparently not rival the British ones in assisting the community to reach a new consensus? A part of the answer might be found in the structure of French society: the well-known inadequacy (in numbers and 'genuineness') of its un-official group life, *i.e.*, its tendency towards atomization, may have been reflected in ex-servicemen's groups that were too weak to bear the burden of new values and beliefs, and so to act as agents of cultural change. But one suspects that the gap in the culture was already so deep that no efforts of the kind suggested could have bridged it, and, if so, ex-servicemen's associations would in any case have tended to reproduce the general conflict. In Britain in the years before the First World War, serious cultural conflict existed and was perhaps increasing, but we had no continuing history of such conflict of which the years 1789, 1830, 1848 and 1871 are but reminders of the most dramatic manifestations.

If in this country the rifts within the culture were closed, how does one explain the survival of the ex-servicemen's groups? The relevant groups did not for the most part continue separately, of course, but rather in unity, itself significant in this context. But why even a united body? The answer is twofold. Ex-servicemen have social as well as political purposes to serve; their associations are vehicles for a cult of the dead, for good fellowship and for a kind of social service as well as engines of social change and political decision. Secondly, in so far as they wish to extract decisions, the very reaching of a new consensus provided a reason for continued existence. The establishment of the Ministry of Pensions in 1916, for instance, symbolized one form of the new consensus about the objects of government. But a Ministry of Pensions requires (or at least required) a British Legion.

The process by which we as a community reach our innumerable political decisions is far more complicated than most of the standard discussions had led us to suppose. No one had imagined that policy was formulated in a vacuum: the politicians themselves, civil servants, journalists, even dons knew that it emerged from a continuous inter-play between the community's authorized decision-makers on the one hand, and certain highly articulated 'interests' on the other, the whole procedure taking place within, and circumscribed by, the broad guidance deemed to have been given by the electors 'last time' and that which they are expected to give 'next time'. But politicians generally lack time to write books; civil servants prefer not to; journalists are journalists partly because, although better writers than most dons, they lack the stamina that is too often the academic substitute for literary skill. The dons themselves, until recently, had their eyes fixed on certain traditional forms (*e.g.*, Cabinet and Parliament) to the neglect of the procedures by which those forms were made to work. Those who discovered 'procedure' naturally gave their attention first to electoral choice and to the role of the political parties. The organized interests, if they appeared at all, came on as 'bit players', vaguely Mephistophelian as in Ramsay Muir, or, as even in Sir Ivor Jennings, fleeting, grey shapes disappearing into the prompt corner almost as the curtain rises.

Of course, the scene is already changing: Professors Beer, Eckstein, W. J. M. Mackenzie, S. E. Finer and H. H. Wilson as well as Doctors Stewart, Potter and Hunt have passed this way. But it cannot be said that their work has yet transformed the conventional picture of the British political system. What we now need in the standard books (if necessary, new standard books) is some acknowledgement of the role of pressure groups in policy-making, so that the present lop-sided emphasis on official groups and their election is corrected. Meanwhile, we stand in urgent need of many more detailed studies of specific associations, seen 'in depth' from the 'inside' and against the background of the political culture and historical circumstances; we also need, in due season, some broader studies that will bring into focus the activities and contribution to policy-making of politicians and civil servants, electors and parties, as well as of pressure groups. It is time, in short, to remove our blinkers and to try to see our political procedures in the round.

The existence and operations of pressure groups may be justified on theoretical grounds: a fundamental right to petition the government, or, in another formulation, the freedoms of speech, association and assembly. What this inquiry provides is an unanswerable justification for these particular pressure groups in these particular historical circumstances. Justice may never be done, but without these ex-servicemen's associations there would have been no approximation to it. In 1916–17 nobody cared much for the veterans, so they began to take care of themselves. Any community worth living in must make it possible for men and women to take care of themselves in this way. From the standpoint of the community as a whole, too, the veterans, by in fact helping to achieve a new consensus, made their contribution to solving a basic problem in any political system—that of reconciling change with stability.

Justification, however, should not mean automatic approval. It is important not to go to the extreme of either accepting pressure groups on their own terms or assuming that their activities are immune from criticism or free from danger. Because the effect of P.R. is, in this instance, unknown, it does not follow that the community need never consider its regulation. The resources allocated to it in this field alone make it a legitimate subject for further investigation both among pressure groups and in the wider context of P.R. and advertising proper.

It is again a matter for further inquiry whether the activities of all the great pressure groups together entail a risk of 'pluralistic stagnation', in which the capacity of the official groups to act is hedged about by the power of the main unofficial groups. Official groups have no special wisdom denied to private groups, but they do embody some overall consensus, and they do have to take decisions for us all according to some conception, however dim, however 'rationalized', of the public interest. Were official groups always as ready to speak frankly and to resist what they took to be excessive demands as they have shown themselves to be in their dealings with ex-servicemen, there would be no cause for disquiet. Certainly there are cultural factors, (*e.g.*, social deference) and political factors (the two-party system) that make strong leadership possible and likely (in the long run), so that the stagnation thesis is not plausible. It should nevertheless be made the subject of inquiry, especially in relation to the great economic interest groups, which may well exercise more veto power than do ex-servicemen's associations. The economic interests, too, are always with us in strength, whereas old soldiers' associations must weaken as the years go by even if they do not quite fade away.

The concentration of power within associations may also be a source of danger. By the ex-servicemen's leaders it has been rarely abused, but on occasion it has enabled them to initiate a policy without reference, except retrospectively, to the general body of members. The Legion leaders' visit to Germany in 1935 (arranged before Conference met) may be cited as an example; they met Hitler and visited the Dachau concentration camp, where they had the wool drawn over their eyes by the Nazis, who had taken the precaution of substituting pink-cheeked S.S. men for the real prisoners. No wonder the gaolers were willing to open the cells of even the 'prisoners' in solitary confinement! That, and the general policy of friendship with German ex-servicemen, may have done no real damage: the Legion leaders were fooled on that occasion but not the Government (nor

King George V). Nevertheless, it gives point to the well-known questions: how representative are the pressure-group leaders? Do they speak chiefly for themselves?

Judging by this inquiry, one would answer that the voice of the associations is the voice of the active few. Does this matter? It would be sentimentality to suppose that policies emanating from the rank and file would have been consistently wiser than those the leaders actually adopted, but that is not the issue. The concentration of power within private associations in fact raises many issues, of which only its implications for the 'public interest' can be touched upon here. The threat to the public interest from this source is less obvious than it is often taken to be. Since no one can define the 'public interest' in terms of the substance of decisions, one may be driven to saying that the fundamental public interest is to secure orderly change. But this desideratum pressure groups help to achieve, and the more effectively because they are oligarchically controlled.

Yet, whatever the theoretical difficulties, one has to recognize in practice that 'overmighty subjects' (or oligarchs), especially in the economic pressure groups, may make demands on official groups that people generally would regard as excessive and in some vague sense contrary to the public interest. How, then, shall we escape the perils and dangers of this night? *Escape* we cannot in a permanent sense, for the risks are inherent in a pluralistic society. I myself would do everything possible to strengthen the non-elective official groups, *i.e.*, rely for our defence chiefly on the (career) civil servants as the ones most capable of taking a large view of our long-term interests as a people with something still to contribute to the world. On the other hand, I would construct some central system of registration for all groups that set out to exercise political influence, and appoint a registrar endowed with real powers of inspection and supervision. The right of pressure groups to shape policy must be itself defended, but it is a right that ought to be exercised on terms and by methods that are familiar to all. Open pressure politics openly conducted—that is the ideal, and some success would attend even the inevitable failure to achieve it.

A NOTE ON SOURCES

NO general bibliography will be offered here. The study itself is based on unpublished material of my own gathering, but since, in a sense, it is more important to know where a writer acquired his concepts than where he discovered his information, I have thought it worth while to list the authors, apart from obvious classics (chiefly the Italian school), to whom I am *conscious* of being indebted.

General derivations

This study clearly belongs to a tradition that is concerned with what Albion Small called the 'real analysis of social processes'. This I absorbed from three American sociologists: Edward C. Hayes (10 A.J.S. 1905); Edward Ross (9 A.J.S. 1903 and *Foundations of Sociology*, 1905); Albion Small (10 A.J.S. 1904 and *General Sociology*, 1905).

For me American sociology represented by these three students was then joined to Austrian sociology in the person of Louis (Ludwig) Gumplowicz (*Sociologie et Politique*, Paris, 1898), who, with his notion of society as the interplay between groups, combined with the others to prepare the way (in my mind) for Arthur Bentley (*The Process of Government*, 1908). Something of Bentley's influence is discernible in these pages, both directly, as in the three case studies, and indirectly, *i.e.*, through Charles B. Hagan (in Richard W. Taylor, *ed.*, *Life, Language and Law: Essays in Honour of Arthur F. Bentley*, 1957), Taylor's own article (5 West P.Q. 1952), and David Truman (*The Governmental Process*, 3rd ed. 1955). Truman, however, has had some influence on me in his own right. But in this context I owe very much more to Earl Latham (*The Group Basis of Politics*, ch. 1, and 46 A.P.S.R. 1952), having even borrowed some of his terminology (*e.g.*, 'official group').

If Albion Small led on to Arthur Bentley, Edward Ross is linked (in fact as well as in my reading) with George E. G. Catlin (21 A.P.S.R. 1927), whose (at that time) daring assertion that political science is not 'the study only of governments and the stage properties of law and administration' (p. 255) came to me at least as a revelation. Catlin's approach was reinforced for me by Charles E. Merriam (*Public and Private Government*, 1944), Richard C. Snyder, H. W. Bruck and Burton Sapin (*Decision-making as an Approach to the Study of International Politics*, 1954), and Roy C. Macridis (*The Study of Comparative Government*, 1955).

After Catlin I see in retrospect a number of writers 'converging': Peter H. Odegard (*Pressure Politics*, 1928); William Bennett Munro (*The Invisible Government*, 1928); Pendleton Herring (*Group Representation before Congress*, 1929, *Public Administration and the Public Interest*, 1936, *The Politics of Democracy*, 1940); Charles Beard and John D. Lewis (26 A.P.S.R. 1932); Lane W. Lancaster (13 *Social Forces* Dec. 1934);

A Note on Sources

Oliver Garceau (*The Political Life of the American Medical Association*, 1941, and American Academy of Political and Social Science, *Annals*, Sept. 1958); Mary E. Dillon (36 A.P.S.R. 1942); Avery Leiserson (*Administrative Regulation*, 1942 and 11 J.P. 1949); E. E. Schattschneider (*Party Government* 1942); Belle Zeller (42 A.P.S.R. 1948); V. O. Key, Jr. (5 J.P. 1943 and *Politics, Parties and Pressure Groups*, 2nd ed. 1947); Stephen K. Bailey (*Congress Makes a Law*, 1950); George C. Homans (*The Human Group*, 1951); Seymour M. Lipset (in Morroe Berger, Theodore Abel and Charles H. Page, *Freedom and Control in Modern Society*, 1954); Bertrand de Jouvenal (5 *Revue Française de Science Politique* 1955); N. C. Hunt (12 *Occidente* 1956); Gunnar Heckscher (*The Study of Comparative Government and Politics*, 1957); Gabriel A. Almond (*rapporteur*) (52 A.P.S.R. 1958); and Henry W. Ehrmann and Samuel J. Eldersveld (in Henry W. Ehrmann, *ed.*, *Interest Groups on Four Continents*, 1958).

In that 'converging' list all but three are Americans, but there is a native influence too: the English pluralists, who flourished in the years before the First World War only to be then virtually destroyed, as some contemporary remarked, by the Defence of the Realm Acts. This tradition has its immediate origin, of course, in F. W. Maitland's translation of Gierke (*Political Theories of the Middle Age*, 1900, introduction), but my sources were rather Figgis, Orage, S. G. Hobson and Cole.

That Bentley left himself open to criticism was (in effect) brought home to me by someone writing before he had even published his celebrated book: George E. Vincent (10 A.J.S. 1904, 150–51). Later came R. M. MacIver (*The Web of Government*, 1948) but the main corrective came from Harvard rather than Columbia, notably in the writings of Samuel H. Beer (26 P.Q. 1955; 50 A.P.S.R. 1956; 51 A.P.S.R. 1957; *Patterns of Government*, 1958, Part One; Academy of Political and Social Science, *Annals*, Sept. 1958, of which a revised version may be read in William N. Chambers and Robert H. Salisbury, *ed.*, *Democracy in the Mid-Twentieth Century*, 1960). Beer's work, of course, constitutes more than a corrective and has been for me, in its own terms, the greatest single inspiration. I am also much indebted to Harry Eckstein (26 P.Q. 1955; *Patterns of Government*, Part Two; and *Pressure Group Politics*, 1960). It was through Beer and his colleagues that the concept of a 'political culture' reached me, but I must acknowledge its ultimate source: Gabriel Almond (18 J.P. 1956).

Specific Sources

Comrades: Annual Reports, 1918–20; the *Comrades' Journal*; the Constitutions; miscellaneous leaflets and documents; interviews.

Federation: Minutes of N.E.C., General Purposes and Finance Committee meetings; Annual Reports, 1919–20; the *Bulletin*; miscellaneous leaflets and Conference documents; the Constitutions; interviews.

Association: *The Bayonet*; Conference Reports; Blackburn Press, especially *Northern Daily Telegraph*; Town Clerk, Blackburn; Constitution; interviews.

N.U.X.: *The New World*; interviews.

Officers' Association: Annual Reports; interviews.

Early associations generally: *The Ex-Service Man*; local weekly news-papers, as recorded in footnotes; the Ashley Papers.

The Legion: Minutes of National Executive Council and Finance Committee meetings; volumes of circulars to branches; volume on Constitution and Bye-Laws; Verbatim Reports of Annual Conferences; Annual Reports; the *Journal*; the Lister-Griffin correspondence; the Haig-Crosfield correspondence; interviews with leaders and others, past and present; letters from Sir Frederick Lister to writer.

BLESMA: Annual Reports; *Blesmag*; Headquarters' files; interviews.

R.A.F. Association: Annual Reports.

Generally: *The Times*.

Appendices

Appendix 1

THE BRITISH LEGION AND THE
GENERAL ELECTION, 1923

(i) Special Circular, 21st November

The attention of all Area Conferences, Area Councils, County Councils, and Branches, as well as of all individual members of the Legion, is drawn to the Constitution of the Legion in reference to the Legion's policy with regard to the forthcoming General Election.

It is particularly important that it should be made perfectly clear to everyone concerned that the Legion is in no way whatever associated with any particular political party, or with any party political organization. For this reason the Legion at the forthcoming General Election will not be supporting any particular party, although members in their INDIVIDUAL capacity and WITHOUT committing their Branch may be doing so. An individual shall not speak on a political platform in the name of the Legion.

Enclosed with this Circular is a copy of the general questionnaire prepared by the National Executive Council to be put by all Branches before any candidate seeking Parliamentary election. Special steps should be taken by Branches to see that each candidate receives a copy of the questionnaire. All candidates should be specially requested to give their replies in writing. *Upon receipt of the reply to this questionnaire*, such reply should be duly published to all members of the Branch who will then be entirely free to decide for themselves how they propose to vote. *It is essential that after the Election the original replies, signed by the successful candidates themselves, should be forwarded to these Headquarters with the least possible delay.*

It is within the power of a local Branch of the Legion, after having considered at a General Meeting of the Branch the replies received from *all* the candidates for Election in the Constituency (special care being taken to ensure that all replies are considered), to decide to take action if they so desire in support of, or in opposition to, any particular candidate, but this should NOT be done unless one or more of the candidates is distinctly unfavourable. It must be distinctly understood that such action should only be taken under very exceptional circumstances, and that in no case whatever must it be understood to commit in any way any other Branch or part of the Legion or the Legion as a whole.

The National Executive Council have definitely ruled that no Branch of the Legion may take any action whatever with reference to the forthcoming General Election outside its own Constituency. Any action of any description including the addressing of questions to candidates must be confined entirely to the Constituency in which the particular Branch is situated.

(ii) Questionnaire to candidates, 21st November

1. Would you support the policy of the Legion that, in Government and Municipal employment and in all schemes for employment financed or controlled by the National or Local Authorities, or guaranteed under the Trades Facilities Act, ex-servicemen should be given preference?

2. Are you in favour of setting up a National Employment Committee to advise upon and recommend to the Government Employment Schemes of Public utility? This Committee to be non-party in composition, representative in character, and having purely advisory powers.

3. In order to finance immediately such schemes as are suitable, are you in favour of floating a National Work Loan to be publicly subscribed, since the efforts to absorb the 900,000 unemployed ex-servicemen by provision out of current revenue have proved unsuccessful?

4. In view of the findings of the Select Committee of the House of Commons on the voluntary scheme to secure employment for disabled men are you prepared to support legislation introducing a compulsory scheme for the allocation on a scientific basis of disabled men to industry?

5. Are you in favour of the Legion's policy that the position of ex-service smallholders throughout this country should be reviewed with a view to proper and expert assistance and advice being given to groups of smallholders with a view to improving their present position?

6. Are you in sympathy with the League of Nations and will you support all steps taken in the direction of securing permanent peace?

7. Do you support the Legion's policy that November 11th should be instituted as a National Day of Commemoration and will you resist any attempts to minimize the solemn observances of the day?

8. In order to check the high death-rate among tubercular ex-servicemen, who, having been temporarily cured in sanatoria, relapse owing to their return to prejudicial surroundings, will you support the establishment of Village Settlements for tubercular ex-servicemen on the lines of the Inter-Departmental Committee's Report of 1919?

9. Will you support the continuance of a separate Ministry of Pensions, there being still 699,000 disabled men, 164,000 widows, and 1,547,000 other dependants in receipt of pensions and allowances?

10. Are you in favour of the rates of pensions being permanently fixed, and will you strenuously oppose any attempt to reduce the present standard rate of pensions?

11. Are you in favour of the seven-year limit in connexion with widows' pensions and in favour of the right being given to a widow to put forward a claim to pension whenever her husband's death may occur, and to receive such pension if the death is due to or aggravated by War Service?

12. Will you support the Legion's claim for an inquiry into the method of assessment of Final Awards of Pensions in view of the fact that 230,000 disabled men have been wiped off the pensions list through the operation of the Final Awards Regulations since January 1st 1922, and are thus precluded from claiming further pension even if their condition has become worse?

13. Are you in favour of the post-war disabled man and the widow of the post-war sailor, soldier, or airman having the right of appeal to the Lord Chancellor's Pensions Appeals Tribunal on the question of pension in the same way as the Great War disabled man or widow has the right of appeal?

14. Are you satisfied that a pension of 10s. 6d. per week is adequate for the widow of a soldier who has died of a disability due to service since September 30th 1921? Will you press for this amount to be increased?

15. If elected will you co-operate with the local Branch of the British Legion in redressing injustices to ex-servicemen, widows, and dependants and raise in Parliament any reasonable questions proposed by them?

(iii) The Prime Minister's (Baldwin's) reply to the questionnaire

1. I am in favour of a reasonable preference to ex-servicemen and this is already the accepted policy of the Government.

2. There is already a special Committee of the Cabinet dealing with all aspects of the Unemployment problem. Through this Committee the Government receive expert advice and are in constant touch with the Cabinet and the Treasury. The Government are convinced that the establishment of another Committee would only lead to delay in dealing with schemes.

3. The Government are advised that an attempt to float such a Loan would adversely affect the unemployed. In this connexion I would draw attention to the following extract from the reply of the Prime Minister dated 17th November 1923, to the British Legion manifesto:

'I do not think it can be disputed that the raising of so large a sum (£200,000,000) would at once bring to a standstill the loan operations of Local Authorities, of the Trade Facilities Committee, and of the Dominions for Empire Development, and it would thus stultify most of the arrangements which are now in progress for the relief of unemployment.'

4. I am in favour of every encouragement being given to voluntary effort to provide employment for disabled men and I should deprecate any resort to compulsion unless and until it has been shown that voluntary efforts have failed to achieve their object. Accordingly, I am fully in sympathy with the following extract from the Interim Report of the King's Roll National Council, a Body of which Earl Haig is Chairman and which includes among other prominent members of the Legion Major-General Sir John Davidson, Major Cohen, M.P., Mr. Pielou, and Captain Appleby:

'The Council have formed the conclusion that the system of decentralized voluntary effort is right. Provided therefore that the winter does not bring another severe slump in trade, we believe that with the continued assistance of the local Committees and the Press, and the maintenance, at least, of the present support given by the public, it should be possible to make, by existing means, coupled with the recommendations we have submitted, a substantial improvement in the position, without recourse to alternative methods of compulsion.'

5. Yes. I am heartily in favour of every possible help being given to ex-service smallholders by way of expert advice and assistance, particularly

by giving special instructions to the County Agricultural and Horticultural organizers and instructors in England and Wales and to corresponding officials in Scotland, to place their services at the disposal of ex-service smallholders, and by all other available means such as the provision of demonstration plots, etc.

6. Yes. I am in full sympathy with the League and will cordially support its efforts to secure permanent peace.

7. I am in favour of the continued observance of Armistice Day as a National Day of Commemoration and I will oppose any attempts to minimize the solemn observance of the day.

8. I desire that everything possible should be done for ex-servicemen suffering from tuberculosis. But at present it has not been established that the placing of such men permanently in settlements of the kind referred to is the best solution of the difficulty. The Government have agreed to make a grant to provide additional cottages for tubercular ex-servicemen at each of the two existing village settlements, and this experiment will be carefully and sympathetically watched.

9. Yes, so long as the number of beneficiaries remains at anything like the present figure. The interests of pensioners must determine the matter.

10. I am in favour of securing permanently established rates of war pension and should be opposed to any attempt, under present conditions, to reduce the pension rates of disabled men.

11. I am in favour of the widow of any disabled man whose death is due in a material degree to the effects of War Service, being entitled to put forward a claim to pension whenever the death occurs.

12. Every disabled man who receives a Final Award from the Ministry of Pensions, is, I understand, safeguarded by a Right of Appeal to an Independent Appeal Tribunal. It would be a serious matter to upset the Final Awards already made, and would not be in the interests of disabled men. If, however, any change in method is clearly shown to be necessary the Government would, no doubt, be prepared to give the matter careful consideration.

13. In my opinion the existing rights of Post-War Pensioners are sufficiently safeguarded. Soldiers' pensions are awarded by the Commissioners of Chelsea Hospital, a predominantly military body which is not subject to the control of the War Office in its administration of the pension regulations, and I doubt whether it is desirable to provide for the indefinite continuance of the expensive system of Pensions Appeals Tribunals by giving the tribunals jurisdiction over Post-War pensions.

14. The 10s. 6d. rate is the rate of pension of a young and childless widow able to earn her living. This is double the rate given before the War to the widows of men in the Army and Navy. Allowances are also paid to widows with children, and to those unable to earn a living.

Appendix 2

THE BRITISH LEGION AND THE
GENERAL ELECTION, 1929

(i) Special Circular, 22nd April

The National Executive Council desires to draw the attention of Area Councils, County or District Committees, and Branches to the position of the British Legion in regard to the forthcoming General Election.

It is important that no Councils, Committees, Branches or individual members of the Legion should take any action which could in any way infringe the principle that the Legion is completely independent of Party Politics and is unconnected either directly or indirectly with any Political Party or Organization.

It is appreciated that in their individual capacity many members of the Legion will be taking an active part in the General Election. In order, however, that such action shall not be misconstrued, the following points should be borne in mind:

(a) Persons holding official positions with the Legion should not allow this to be advertised in connexion with political propaganda or meetings.

(b) Members making political speeches should not introduce the name of the Legion either directly or indirectly.

The attention of Branches is particularly directed to the revised policy pamphlet enclosed herewith and Branches are requested to send a copy to each of the candidates in their constituency asking them to be good enough to acknowledge receipt and to state their views thereon.

In cases where two or more Legion Branches exist in one constituency, it is desirable, if practicable, to co-operate. This is preferable to each Branch writing to candidates separately.

In addition, every effort should be made to bring the contents of the Policy pamphlet to the notice of the general public.

The interests of the Legion and, therefore, the interests of the ex-service community, will, in the opinion of the National Executive Council, be best served by Branches recognizing that the duty of the Legion ends when it has placed before its members, the public and the candidates, its policy upon certain matters and when the views of the candidates on this policy have been communicated to members. The Legion in no way interferes with the political liberty or right of an individual member to support such candidtae as he or she may choose, but it does most emphatically impress upon every Branch, that it would be entirely wrong to take any action in its corporate capacity as a Branch as a result of the replies received from any one or other candidate.

Appendix 2

(ii) Specimen letter to candidates

Dear Sir,

On behalf of the ———— Branch of the British Legion, I have much pleasure in sending you herewith a copy of 'Outlines of Legion Policy' which I am to request you to be good enough to find time to read through.

If after perusal you will kindly favour me with your views thereon and inform me of the extent to which you, if returned to Parliament at the forthcoming Election, will be prepared to support the proposals therein outlined, I shall be happy to place the information before the members of my Branch.

Appendix 3

THE BRITISH LEGION AND THE
GENERAL ELECTION, 1950

(*i*) *Special circular No. 2, January*

The attention of Branches is directed to the terms of the Memorandum overleaf, indicating the conduct which should be pursued by Branches in connexion with the General Election. It will be appreciated how important it is that it should be made clear to everyone that the Legion, as the Legion, is not in any way concerned with the Parties with which candidates are associated in the forthcoming General Election.

In accordance with the decision of the 1949 Annual Conference, Branches are urged to approach their respective candidates for their answers to the attached questionnaire.

When all candidates have been approached and their answers received, the replies should be forwarded to Headquarters in the stamped addressed envelope enclosed.

(*ii*) *The Memorandum*

1. A reference to Clause 4 of the Charter will show in clear and detailed terms the objects for which the Legion exists, while Rule 1 clearly defines the principles which guide it in the achievement of those objects.

2. Briefly stated, the objects of the Legion include:

(a) In respect of those who have served in the Armed Forces of the Crown, and their dependents, to maintain that their interests in re-settlement, employment, pensions, compensation and all social services are a national responsibility.

(b) In respect of the National interests, to foster the comradeship of those who have served as a contribution to social order, goodwill and national unity.

3. In pursuance of these objects the action to be taken by the Legion should be:

(a) To approach the Government and Local Authorities in order to see that existing legislation or regulations are interpreted and administered in the most favourable way in dealing with individual cases.

(b) To take appropriate action as indicated below where in our opinion legislation or regulations are not meeting the position:

(i) By approaching the Government in regard to amending existing legislation or directing Local Authorities.

(ii) By approaching Government Departments and Local Authorities with regard to the amendment of regulations and/or the application of such regulations;

(iii) By approaching members of all parties in the House of Commons on both (i) and (ii);

(iv) At elections, placing the policy of the Legion before candidates;

(v) Arranging that Members of Parliament who are ex-servicemen shall join the House of Commons Branch of the British Legion and make themselves familiar with the Legion policy.

4. It is most undesirable that the Legion should nominate candidates at elections whether Parliamentary or Local Government and equally it is not the function of the Legion to give directions as to how a voter should exercise his vote. MOREOVER, RULE 4 (A) OF THE CHARTER PROHIBITS THE USE OF ANY PART OF THE FUNDS OF THE LEGION FOR, OR FOR ASSISTANCE IN, ELECTIONEERING EXPENSES.

5. If the Legion were to run candidates, it would in effect be entering party politics, because such candidates would inevitably be opposed by candidates bearing the label of one or other of the recognized political parties. They would have to be fostered by an organization and that organization would be a new party which would require funds.

6. If there is any attempt to form an ex-service party, even in Local Government, the Legion should stand aloof, leaving its members free to join that or any other party.

(iii) The Questionnaire

1. GENERAL

Do you agree as a general principle that those who served in the Armed Forces in War have a right to special consideration on their return to civil life?

2. PENSIONS

(a) Are you in favour of an Inquiry into War Pensions and Allowances?

(b) Will you support a Select Committee for this purpose?

(c) If the answer to (b) is 'No', what form of independent inquiry would you support?

3. EMPLOYMENT

Are you in favour of the Government giving special consideration to ex-service men and women in regard to employment and in the case of redundancy in Government Departments and factories, will you support the claim that the period spent in the Armed Forces should count as equivalent to service in such employment?

4. HOUSING

Do you support the Legion in its claim that special consideration should be given to ex-servicemen and women in the allocation of the tenancy of houses by Local Authorities?

Appendix 4

LETTERS AND CIRCULARS TO M.P.s:
THE BRITISH LEGION

(A) *The Employment of Disabled Men, 1924*

(*i*) *Special circular to branches, 1st July, with specimen letter to M.P.s*

As is well known throughout the Legion, the second reading of the Bill for the Employment of Disabled Men was passed on 23rd May. The immediate question now arising is whether the Government will grant the necessary facilities for the progress of the Bill.

At a recent meeting of the National Executive Council it was decided to urge all Branches to petition the leader of the House of Commons, the Right Hon. John Robert Clynes, J.P., M.P., to so arrange the business of the House as will allow the Government to grant facilities for the Legion's Bill. In this connexion a stamped envelope addressed to the Leader of the House of Commons is enclosed, and appended herewith is a specimen letter which every Branch of the Legion should address to Mr. Clynes and post not later than Monday, 7th July.

I am desired on behalf of the ———— Branch of the British Legion to communicate with you with regard to a Bill on the Employment of Disabled Men which passed its second reading in the House of Commons on 23rd May.

This Bill, as you are no doubt already aware, has the full support and approval of the whole of the British Legion, and it is the earnest desire of the ex-servicemen of this district that it shall at the earliest possible moment become law.

The ———— Branch of the British Legion recognizes that it is a matter entirely in the hands of the Government as to whether or not the time of the House of Commons shall be so arranged as will allow of the necessary facilities being granted whereby the Bill may become law.

I am therefore writing on behalf of the ex-servicemen of this district to urge that the necessary steps may be taken to ensure that time shall be given for the further discussion of the Bill, and it is the sincere hope of my members that you, as Leader of the House of Commons, may see your way clear to grant the necessary facilities for this measure, which means such a great deal to the future of our disabled comrades.

(*ii*) *H.Q. circular to M.P.s, 10th December*

At the request of Mr. Douglas Pielou, M.P., and on the instructions of the National Executive Council of the British Legion, I have pleasure in enclosing herewith a copy of a Bill drafted by the British Legion, entitled

'Employment of Disabled Ex-Service Men', together with a Summary of the same.

You are probably already aware that Mr. Pielou introduced this Bill on 23rd May last, and in a very full house it received its Second reading without a division.

It is the desire of my Council that the Bill should again be introduced, and I am writing to ask whether you would be good enough, if successful in the Ballot for Private Members' Bills, to choose this Bill as the one to be introduced by you.

The British Legion feels very strongly that the only permanent solution to the problem of the industrial future of the disabled ex-serviceman is to be found in the adoption of legislation such as is suggested by this Bill, and on behalf of my Council I sincerely hope that you will be able to assist and support us in this matter.

> I am, dear Sir,
> Yours faithfully,
>> (Sgd) E. C. Heath,
>> Colonel, General Secretary.

(B) *Merger of Ministry of Pensions with Ministry of National Insurance, 1953*
(i) Chairman (S. H. Hampson) to M.P.s, 18th June

The British Legion in National Conference on 25 May, passed nem con., this resolution:

'That this Conference views with concern the proposed merger of the Ministry of Pensions and the Ministry of National Insurance and urges the Council to do all in its power to prevent the merging of the Ministry of Pensions and the Ministry of National Insurance.'

You may be desirous of knowing the major reasons why the British Legion took this decision. The Legion regards the proposed merger—or as I prefer to term it, the downgrading of those things for which the Ministry of Pensions now stands and, above all, of the national responsibility to the war disabled and war widows—as violating a principle which is one of the fundamental bases of the Legion. That principle is that not only shall there be preference for ex-servicemen and women, and particularly for those disabled in war, and war widows and orphans, but that such preference shall also be manifest. The establishment of a Ministry of Pensions in 1917, we contend, supported the first point and made possible the second.

Now, when there are approximately a million war pensioners and the annual expenditure of the Ministry is £84,000,000 compared with the 750,000 pensioners and £39,000,000 expenditure in 1939, it is suggested that the Ministry is redundant. The Legion, with an impressive unanimity, condemns this proposed reduction in the status of the war pensioners as not only inimical to their direct interests, but also indicative of the withdrawal of the special place that they have occupied in national policy since 1917.

In the compass of a letter of reasonable length, it is clearly impossible to traverse the eight and a half closely printed octavo pages of the White Paper. The Legion has subjected it to close examination and contends that it does not deal with the principle involved in the merger, but treats the Ministry of Pensions purely as an administrative machine. I may, perhaps, without undue trespass on your time, be allowed to give four tightly summarized major objections by the Legion, from the others, to the administrative proposals set out in the White Paper:

1. Its failure to recognize the special conditions attaching to war pensions, conditions which relate to none of the far more numerous pensions now administered by the Ministry of National Insurance.
2. The division of the functions of the Ministry of Pensions between two Ministries—Insurance and Health—to the detriment of the pensioner and implying the need for the education, a longish process, of the two new operators.
3. The nebulous and unsatisfactory arrangements for the hospitalization of war disabled pensioners, which arrangements, if they do not destroy their present rights, at least leave only the façade of those rights intact.
4. The very tentative financial advantage claimed by the authors of the White Paper for this far-reaching innovation. It is stated under the heading of 'Economies to be effected' that 'the immediate savings will not be large' (note: No figure is indicated) but within 'the next two or three years' savings in administrative costs should be 'of the order of £500,000 a year'.

The Legion draws attention to the vagueness of these two figures, which I am sure will not have escaped you, and suggests that even if this saving were achieved, as prophesied, it would be out of all proportion to the cost involved to the pensioner and to those who work on his behalf. The Legion is, of course, enthusiastically in favour of the elimination of waste in national administration, but it can never regard as a true economy a saving in £.s.d. achieved as the result of worsening the already, as it contends, unsatisfactory situation of so many war pensioners.

I have set out shortly the major reason, and a few of the supporting arguments on administrative grounds, why the Legion views with so much concern the proposed merger of the Ministries, and resolutely maintains that the continuance of the Ministry of Pensions is essential.

Moreover the proposal comes at a time when our major claim in relation to war pensions, with which Ministers and Parliament are familiar, has not been met.

I am instructed to ask for your support for the Legion's views and for your opposition to the motion implementing the White Paper if such a motion be presented, but in the meantime the Legion has requested the Government to withdraw the White Paper.

(ii) Chairman to selected M.P.s, 29th June

I have noted with interest that you have signed a Motion calling on the Government at an early date 'to take a further step beyond that taken in 1952 to accord to disabled ex-officers and men and their widows that priority of relief to which their sacrifices entitle them'.

May I in this connexion emphasize the importance of the decision that will be taken following the debate on the Government's draft order for the amalgamation of the Ministry of Pensions with the Ministries of National Insurance and Health, which decision, I understand, will be made next Tuesday, 30th June. The position of the British Legion, on behalf of which I write, is that such [a] merger would be a grave obstacle to the achievement of the purpose envisaged by your Motion.

I have taken the liberty of enclosing a very short statement of the Legion's case on this matter. I hope that this note in conjunction with the letter that I recently addressed to you will enable you to take the line that opposition to the merger motion is essential.

My Lord,

I am informed that the Motion approving the Government's proposals for the merger of the Ministry of Pensions with the Ministries of National Insurance and Health appears on the Order Paper for your House on Thursday, 2nd July.

I beg to inform you that Lord Carew, who is a member of the National Executive Council of the British Legion, will, in the course of his speech, be presenting the Legion's case against the proposed merger. I take the liberty of enclosing a short note on that case which is a condensed version of the letter that I had the pleasure of addressing to you last week.

I am in the name of the British Legion to invite your support of the Legion's opposition by voting against the Motion.

Appendix 5

LETTER FROM MINISTER OF PENSIONS (RT. HON. J. A. BOYD-CARPENTER) TO CHAIRMAN OF BLESMA ALL-PARTY PARLIAMENTARY COMMITTEE (SIR ROBERT CARY, Bt.), 4th MAY, 1956

Shortly before Christmas you brought a deputation to see my predecessor on behalf of the All-Party Committee which is concerned with the claim put forward by BLESMA for the limbless pensioners of the 1914–18 War. Later you brought a deputation to see me.

As you know, I have been going into this question and I have of course discussed it with my colleagues.

The BLESMA representations raise very difficult issues. The problem, as I know with your own experience of these matters you will fully appreciate, is this. War Pensions are, and always have been since 1917, assessed on the basis of the loss of function resulting from the injury on the basis of a comparison with a normal person of the same age and sex. This principle has been generally accepted, and has of course been applied to disabilities of all kinds. So it seems to me clearly impossible to depart from it in the case of one particular kind of injury without being unfair to other perhaps even more serious cases. In other words, I do not see how we could apply a different principle in the case of the limbless from that which we have applied and are continuing to apply to, for example, the blind and the paraplegics. The same human and sympathetic feelings which we all feel for the limbless we must obviously feel equally for these other cases, and I am sure you will agree that fairness between man and man is essential in any war-pensions scheme.

I understand that at the discussion with my predecessor you asked that the claim should be given special consideration by the Government on humane grounds and without reference to the Hancock and Rock Carling Reports. I hope that we shall always deal with all the disabled humanely and sensibly. But if we are also to deal with them fairly I think we must deal with them all on the same principle, and the principle of basing assessments to the best of our ability on 'the gap' is, I am sure, the fairest and indeed the most humane way of dealing with cases of war disabilities.

The practical point, therefore, which faces us is whether 'the gap' does widen with age. The Hancock Committee, as you will appreciate, came to the conclusion that it did not do so, at any rate to any general or measurable extent. The Rock Carling Committee, for whom extensive clinical

281

work has been done, came to the clear conclusion that amputation cases were not associated to any significant extent with a higher mortality rate or with the initiation or aggravation of cardio-vascular disorders.

None the less any increasing relative disability which can be shown to have developed as a consequence of the war injury is recognized. The schedule of assessments for amputations relates only to uncomplicated cases without any special features, and the 1914 War Limbless in common with other 1914 War pensioners have had their pension assessments increased in later life, whenever it has been found that the war disablement itself has grown permanently and materially worse or that there is some added disability directly connected with it. Increases in the scheduled assessments for example can be and have been given when the condition of the stump prevents the man from wearing an artificial limb normally, or where consequential disability arises such as arthritis of the hand, wrist or arm from pressure of walking stick, flat-foot or osteo-arthritis of the sound leg, or obesity due to immobility resulting from the loss of a limb. It may interest you to know that in the year 1955, increases were made in the assessments of three hundred and twenty limbless war pensioners.

This does not, of course, go as far as your general proposition that even where the disability itself remains unchanged and is not associated with any specific condition of aggravation the relative position of a limbless man deteriorates with age in comparison with an uninjured man of the same age.

You will appreciate from what I have said above that it would be difficult for the Government to accept such a proposition or to give practical effect to it unless there were some real evidence or consensus of expert opinion to modify previous authoritative findings to the contrary. I am, however, more than willing to arrange for authoritative investigation, independent of my Ministry, of any such evidence as may be adduced. Indeed, to this end I have myself been and am in touch with certain of the eminent medical gentlemen who have been reported as giving some support to the BLESMA claim.

Appendix 6

APPEALING TO PUBLIC OPINION:
BRITISH LEGION, 1953

OUT OF SIGHT—OUT OF MIND?

Out of sight, out of mind applies to the disabilities of Britain's 687,000 war pensioners, so far as the majority of us are concerned. They cannot push their own case to the top of—and over—the Chancellor's priority queue. Yet if the voice of the general public can amplify the voice of the British Legion, the war pensioners' and the war widows' case will be heard.

You would help if you knew the facts. You may know already that the basic rate for 100 per cent disablement is 55s. a week. Yet 483,000 war pensioners receive only 22s. basic rate pension a week or less. 42,450 of the remainder have extra disability allowances given at the discretion of the Ministry of Pensions.

If you lost a leg in battle you might get 33s. a week.

If you were blinded in one eye you would get 17s. 6d.

War pensioners who cannot work average £6. 5s. 0d. a week—while the average male wage packet in Britain is £8. 13s. 7d.

Shattering, isn't it? Hardly encouraging to the morale of the serviceman of today. And this does not reflect on any particular political party but on all of us as a nation!

Is there any simple way to give war pensioners justice?

We suggest you compare living costs for today and just before the war, when the full pension was 40s. The official price index of consumer goods and services shows that 40s. in 1938 provided the equivalent of 92s. in 1952. That seems overwhelming backing for the British Legion's claim that 90s. should be the basic rate, with comparable increases for the lesser disabled.

Not enough perhaps, but a fair target to aim for. The average increase for all war pensioners would be about 8s. a week.

Do you doubt that war victims should be first in the queue for the Chancellor's benefits? They have *not* been. Both post-war Governments have taken the view that what little they could share out should go automatically to the industrially disabled as well and as much as to the war disabled. (Remember that in many civilian occupations contributory pensions schemes operate, while the serving man has no such opportunity).

If the nation cannot yet afford a 90s. pensions for both these groups, then the war victims, including the widows of the men who fell, should have priority. Money cannot compensate for the saddest of all bereavements but we must prevent the constant difficulties many war widows undergo. Many get less as a pension by right than they can get by application to the National Assistance Board.

There is a long queue of claimants for the Chancellor's attention before next Budget Day. Let it be known that the casualties and bereaved of Britain's war are *your* priority.

What you can do to help:

1. Let your Member of Parliament know this is a matter for his urgent attention.

2. Make this case known in any voluntary organization you belong to— such as a trade union, a chamber of commerce, a rotary group, etc.

3. Support your local British Legion in its efforts to arouse public feeling on this issue.

4. If you require further information ask the British Legion locally or write to General Secretary, British Legion, Pall Mall, London, S.W. 1.

YOU
are public opinion

All at Westminster
will respond
to it.

INDEX OF NAMES

INDEX OF SUBJECTS